909

D0906373

Child Poverty
and
Inequality

Child Poverty and Inequality

Securing a Better Future for America's Children

DUNCAN LINDSEY

OXFORD
UNIVERSITY PRESS
2009

OXFORD
UNIVERSITY PRESS

Oxford University Press, Inc., publishes works that further
Oxford University's objective of excellence
in research, scholarship, and education.

Oxford New York
Auckland Cape Town Dar es Salaam Hong Kong Karachi
Kuala Lumpur Madrid Melbourne Mexico City Nairobi
New Delhi Shanghai Taipei Toronto

With offices in
Argentina Austria Brazil Chile Czech Republic France Greece
Guatemala Hungary Italy Japan Poland Portugal Singapore
South Korea Switzerland Thailand Turkey Ukraine Vietnam

Copyright © 2009 by Oxford University Press, Inc.

Published by Oxford University Press, Inc.
198 Madison Avenue, New York, New York 10016

www.oup.com

Oxford is a registered trademark of Oxford University Press

Library of Congress Cataloging-in-Publication Data
Lindsey, Duncan.
Child poverty and inequality : securing a better future for America's
children / Duncan Lindsey.
p. cm.
Includes bibliographical references and index.
ISBN 978-0-19-530544-9 (cloth)
1. Children—United States—Social conditions—21st century.
2. Children—United States—Economic conditions—21st century. 3. Child
welfare—United States. 4. Poverty—United States. 5. Saving and
investment—United States. I. Title.
HQ792.U5L57 2009
305.230973—dc22
2006026273

9 8 7 6 5 4 3 2 1

Printed in the United States of America
on acid-free paper

For Sierra and Ethan

Preface: The Future
of Children

Children are the future. We rebuild our nation anew with each new generation. Children represent the growth and vitality of our nation. In this book, my concern is what we provide our children to build their future. P. D. James begins her novel, *The Children of Men*:

> Early this morning, 1 January 2021, three minutes after midnight, the last human being to be born on earth was killed in a pub brawl in a suburb of Buenos Aires, aged twenty-five years, two months and twelve days.

Twenty-five years earlier, women were no longer fertile. They were no longer able to become pregnant and give birth to children. The consequence of this plague slowly reveals itself. Life as we know it—life among human beings—is coming to an end. When children no longer arrive, we learn that our future fades. P. D. James is able to portray a world without children after 25 years of no new births. It is a world without future. There is no reason to worry about the impact of our actions on the future of the planet. Neither will we know the future, nor will our children. The world—at least for human beings—is coming to an end.

Our future is renewed each year with the birth of a new cohort of youth. They inherit a world we contribute to and create. The United States has historically been a land of opportunity for young people. We have provided opportunities to children to participate in the wealth that is the fruit of our democratic political institutions combined with a free market economy. Our citizens have been rewarded with prosperity and personal satisfaction. The greatness of the United States has been its inclusion of the middle class in the nation's economic prosperity. Each new generation has had hope and opportunity before them. In recent years, however, there has been a troubling change. A wide-ranging shift in public policy has favored those with assets and wealth and led to a substantial increase in the prosperity of the top-income and wealth holders. The middle class has failed to participate in the economic growth and prosperity to the same degree it did in earlier decades. Those at the bottom have faired even worse.

Children from middle class and low-income families have been particularly hard hit by these trends. Their opportunities have been declining. As a result, we are rebuilding and replenishing our society, but the children who are the future of the nation are inheriting a land of receding opportunity. In the childless world created by P. D. James, we learn that with no children to care for and no future to care about, those who remain are completely self-absorbed, pampering themselves, exploiting immigrants, and turning control of political affairs over to a dictatorship that guarantees their safety. But life is without meaning, purpose, and joy, not just for the exploited but for all inhabitants. It is not until we restore the opportunities and hope of birth and children that we see new life and a future for the world. Such is the lesson from P. D. James.

Inequality and declining opportunity is not our destiny. In earlier decades, the nation embraced the participation of all income groups into economic prosperity and opportunity. We can restore the foundation and commitment to opportunity for all groups. This is the vision and direction of the discussion here. It begins with the children. The children are our future.

Acknowledgments

Conversations among colleagues, friends, and family are the wellspring of my work. In the preparation of this book, I have had the great fortune of many conversations with those who share my concern with the future of children. We live in a troubling time where progress toward equality of opportunity has eroded and too many children are denied hope and a future.

As I have been writing this book, I have shared it with the students in my courses at UCLA. I begin by thanking them and specifically recognizing Kush Cooper, Kelly Hoehn, Darcy Merrit, Sacha Mareka Klein, Ellen Polamero, Gina Albert, Brenda Batarse, Amy Billings, Reiko Kimiko Boyd, Jessica Denise Brown, Doris Chau, Wai Lam Chu, Maggie Cenovio, Erica Corley, Rocio De La Torre, Megan Doyle, Kathleen Edwards, Lauren Finkel, Juan Gomez, Jacqueline Gonzalez, Mariela Gonzalez, Shaghayegh Guerami-Dahi, Luz Guevara, Tara Henry, Kelly Suzanne Hoehn, Mahsa Hojat, Whitney Holum, Linh My Huynh, Gagandeep Kaur, Grace Lee, Paul Loya, Carolee Matias, Raven Letrice Maxie, Fernando Mallory, Rebecca Mcguire, Abigail Mecham, Jason Nitz, Jessica Okhovat, Dena Orkin, Elizabeth Phan, Spencer Daniel Presler, Monica Ravizza, Chelsey Rice, Kylene Richards, Carmen Romero, Sahar Sepidehdam, James David Simon, Sepideh Shahri, Cheryl Singzon, Wendy Skillern, Paul Stevens, Shana Ann Stewart, Ronen Stromberg, Raha Tabankia, Dustin Tillman, Diem Tran, Nicole Vazquez, MaryAnn Wee, and Tiffany Williams.

I have also shared the emerging book in various forms with several colleagues, including David Stoesz, Neil Gilbert, Jill Duerr Berrick, Leroy Pelton, Tom McDonald, Eileen Gambrill, Diane DiAnda, Alfreda Iglehart, Ailee Moon, Rosina Becerra, Robert Goldstein, Kelly Hernandez, Laura

Abrams, William Epstein, Andrew Bridge, Michele Hawkins, Wes Hawkins, Aron Shlonsky, Bruce Jansson, Michelle Johnson, Bridget Friesthler, Howard Karger, Dan Doyle, Renji Mathew, Ginny Lo, Paul Nicholson, Sharon and Esawey Amasha, Ellen Todras, and Mark Needleman.

I have had the great fortune of working with individuals and organizations working to make a difference for the future of children, including Eli Broad and Edythe Broad of the Broad Foundation, and Jane and Michael Eisner of the Eisner Family Foundation, and Neal Halfon and Todd Franke of the Center for Healthier Children, Families and Communities. The national effort for a child savings account has been led by Robert Friedman, Andrea Levere, and Carl Rist of the Committee for Economic Development (CFED); Michael Sherraden, Deb Adams, and Margaret Clancy of the Center for Social Development; Frank DeGiovanni and Kilolo Kijakazi of the Ford Foundation; Benita Melton of the Charles Stewart Mott Foundation; Lisa Mensah of the Aspen Institute; Ray Boshara and Reid Cramer of the New America Foundation; Eugene Steuerle of the Urban Institute; Rick Williams of the Charles and Helen Schwab Foundation, and later with Realize Consulting Group; Irene Skricki of the Annie E. Casey Foundation; Andres Dominquez of the Edwin Marion Kauffman Foundation; Ellen Tower of Citibank; Leslie Meek of the Citigroup Foundation; Darlene Hall of the Evelyn and Walter Haas, Jr. Fund; Gray Stangler of the Jim Casey Youth Opportunities Initiative; Helen Dorado Alessi of the Edwin Gould Foundation for Children; April Hawkins of the Metlife Foundation; Eric Sloan of the Richard and Rhoda Goldman Fund; and the numerous others working to make a difference for children. I am also grateful to members of the SEED Research Advisory Council, including Lawrence Aber, Larry Davis, William Gale, Tom McDonald, Robert Plotnick, and Christine Robinson and the SEED policy leadership of Fred T. Goldberg, Jr. and Melvin Oliver.

Among the most important creative work being done to improve the economic futures of children is the research and experimentation being conducted by the SEED Community Partners, including Linda Thompson and Chris Krehmeyer of Beyond Housing, Phil Arendall and Francine McGriff of Boys and Girls Clubs of Delaware, Gina Martinez of Cherokee Nation, Melissa Garcia of Foundation Communities, Liza Gallardo of Fundacion Chana y Samuel Levis, Serina Moya and Caressa Singleton of Harlem Children's Zone, Gabe Mello and Christy Saxton of Juma Ventures, Philippe Marquis of Mile High United Way, Susan Mosqueda and Don Jones of OLHSA, Adrea Padron and Dennis Mann of People for People, Nancy Wilson of Sargent Shriver National Center on Poverty Law, and Mindy Maupin, and Angela Duran, and Ramona McKinney of Southern

Good Faith Fund. The work of these organizations is at the forefront of fundamental social policy reform.

I am particularly grateful to Michael Sherraden, Bob Friedman, Andrea Levere, and Ray Boshara for involving me in their work toward achieving a child savings program at the state and national levels. I have told close friends over the years that I will have a chance to go to heaven if we ever achieve a national policy of savings for all children similar to what we provide for seniors with Social Security. No one has worked harder and or been more successful in this enterprise than these champions of all children.

This book has benefited from the careful reading and suggestions of my twin brother Buck Lindsey and my son Ethan Lindsey. My wife, Debbie, has been at the center of this study and my life. Our daughter, Sierra, has been one of the most important sources of my interest and concern with these issues. Her compassion and commitment to making this a better world is infectious. I especially recognize the contribution of my mother to my work in this field. It all began with her. My family has sustained me through the years and been instrumental in developing my views. I thank Aaron and Midore McDaniel, John and Rene McDaniel, Paul McDaniel, Jerry McDaniel, Anne Marie McDaniel, Rebecca McDaniel, Sean Lindsey, Garrett Lindsey, Jenny Lindsey, Marcy and Paul Cauthorn, Dan, Kirsten, Lucas, Aidan, and Arthur Kaufman, and Saimon Kos.

I extend a special thanks to Maura Roessner for planting the idea for this book and supporting the work over its extended development. It would be hard to imagine having a better editor. I am also grateful for the support, care and advice of Mallory Jensen.

I have benefited from the editorial assistance of Deirdre Day-MacLeod and Alan Forray. Deirdre's contribution to the study has been significant. She has been instrumental in making this a readable and engaging story. Alan has helped with organizing several of the chapters into a coherent story. I want to express my great appreciation for their help.

I want to close with a memorial to Betty McDaniel and Howard Wade. I dedicated my last book *The Welfare of Children* to Betty. More than anyone she has inspired my work in this field. More than anyone, Howard contributed to the development and writing of that book. I miss both of these loved ones so much. Betty and Howard's voice and influence are found through out this study. I so wish I could give them a copy.

Contents

Child Poverty
and
Inequality

Introduction

Children enter the world full of promise matched only by the dreams and aspirations of their parents. They embark on life's journey with relatively equal potential regardless of race, ethnicity, sex, or economic background. DNA and RNA code will govern their physical development. Their economic and social development will be primarily influenced by the opportunities their parents, community, and society provide. Collectively, we are responsible for making sure the road ahead is safe and filled with opportunity. African-American and Hispanic infants enter with similar genetic potential as White and Asian infants, but in a matter of a few years the outcomes for these children will be very different. Why? That is the central question that drives this inquiry.

The seeds for the very different childhoods and life trajectories for African-American and Hispanic youth compared to White and Asian youth are not found in the delivery room, but in the experience of poverty and inequality that awaits many of them when they leave the hospital and begin life in America. Children who are poor often embark on a life of poverty. It is very hard to break the cycle of child poverty. In a previous time education was the springboard to entering the economic mainstream. However, education is no longer as effective in creating opportunity. Schools in the United States have come to reflect the economic status of their communities.[1] Schools in poor communities have fewer resources and often the least effective teachers. Children leave school with their relative status little changed from when they entered. The expanding opportunities for personal betterment and entering the middle class that existed in earlier times have receded.

After World War II, the United States began an "era of the middle class," where virtually all segments of American society participated in the growing wealth of the country. During the 25-year period from 1950 to

3

1975, the inflation adjusted median income in the United States doubled.[2] All groups, including the poor and low income and working class families experienced substantial income gains. However, since 1980 the "era of the middle class" has come to an end, and we have entered what can best be described as the "era of the wealthy class." During the 25-year period after 1980, the country has experienced the same phenomenal growth as it experienced during the prior 25-year period. The personal computer, wireless phone and handheld devices, the Internet, and other technologies have transformed the nation and the world. During the era of the wealthy class, the incomes and wealth of the top 1 percent and the top 10 percent have more than doubled, whereas the income and wealth of the middle class have stagnated and the economic situation of the poor has declined.[3] The doubling of wealth at the top has been at the expense of middle class participation in the new economic growth.

Our individual economic futures begin in childhood. Today, the economic future of children is tied more closely to the income and wealth of their parents than ever before. Children from low-income and poor communities have very limited opportunities. They begin life with little true hope of escaping the economic grind that takes their mother away from them for long hours.[4] They too often fail to receive the care and attention children need in their earliest years.

In America today, there are essentially two worlds of childhood.[5] White and Asian families represent more than 75 percent of the population in the United States. Their children represent more than 60 percent of the children. White and Asian children growing up in two-parent families have a poverty rate of less than 5 percent.[6] Most of these children live in families that are doing well. In contrast, the poverty rate for African-American and Latino children ranges between 35 and 40 percent. The majority of African-American children are born to single parents (more than two-thirds), and their child poverty rate is close to 60 percent.

Children who begin lives in poverty are at a substantial disadvantage.[7] They will not have the developmental enrichment opportunities that most children experience. They will likely experience substandard child care while their parent is working at a low wage job. They may lack health insurance. They will experience hunger and the pain of poverty for long periods during critical development in early childhood.

Child poverty and growing inequality are intertwined and contribute to each other. In this book, I examine these developments. I argue that we cannot solve these problems separately. If we want to reduce the growing inequality then we will need to reduce child poverty, which is where the inequality most often begins and is sustained.

Chapter 1 examines the current situation of child poverty in the United States. Two major factors define child poverty—single parenthood and race and ethnicity. In this chapter I examine the "color of child poverty" in the United States. The United Nations recently reported that the United States had the highest child poverty rate among more than 30 industrialized nations studied.[8] This is difficult to believe, given the fact that the United States is the wealthiest nation in the world.[9] How could the wealthiest nation in the world have the highest child poverty rate? The answer, of course, is that the United States has what can best be described as two worlds of childhood. The highest rate of poverty is found among African-American and Latino children—several times higher than found among White and Asian children. The poverty these children endure is often debilitating. The restrictions of opportunity that begin in the earliest years are carried into adolescence and young adulthood. As a consequence, the opportunity of getting a college education is out of reach for most children raised in the other world of poverty. The likelihood of getting a four-year college degree is less than 1 in 15 for children coming from poor families.[10] Chapter 1 explores the very different opportunity structures that exist in the two different worlds of childhood. I also examine the role of standardized testing in restricting the opportunities of poor and low-income children.

Chapter 2 examines the growing inequality in the United States. According to the Internal Revenue Service, in 2005 the top 1 percent of income earners received more than twice as much income as everyone in the bottom 50 percent combined.[11] Two decades earlier, the bottom 50 percent earned twice as much income as the top 1 percent. In this chapter, I examine the origins of the growing inequality in the United States. The half century after World War II can essentially be divided into two periods. The first period I call the "era of the middle class." This was the time when the American middle class emerged in full force. During this period, for the first time in history, a majority of Americans graduated from high school. College and university enrollments tripled. Televisions, refrigerators, and automobiles became standard commodities found in most homes. Home ownership increased from 40 to 60 percent—the highest rate of home ownership in the world.[12] The real (inflation adjusted) incomes of the average family doubled. Prosperity was experienced by all groups—from the wealthy, who saw their income double, to the poor who saw their ranks decline substantially.

The era of the middle class began to close in 1970 and essentially came to an end by 1980. In 1980, Ronald Reagan became the president of the United States and ushered in a new "era of the wealthy class." President

Reagan removed what he saw as the impediments to building wealth. Taxes on the highest income earners were reduced from 70 to 50 percent in his first term. In his second term, Reagan reduced the rates on the highest income earners to 25 percent. The result has been an extended period of prosperity for the wealthiest families in America. The number of millionaires and billionaires—controlling for inflation—more than doubled during the period.[13] The amount of privately held wealth more than doubled during this same period. The incomes of the wealthiest 10 percent more than doubled.[14] But the increase in wealth and income was not experienced by all. During this same period, the income of the median family essentially stagnated. If some families earned more, it was primarily because there was a substantial increase in the number of families with two full-time workers.[15] During the "era of the wealthy class" tax rates were cut substantially for the wealthiest families, whereas the taxes for middle income families rose.[16] The capital gains tax cut and the dividend tax cut directed more than 80 percent of its benefits to the wealthiest 10 percent. The major federal tax borne by the middle class has been the employment tax, including Social Security and Medicare, and it has increased substantially during this same period. As a result, the wealthiest families have been able to save more and accumulate more wealth and further improve their relative wealth and prosperity. In contrast, the middle class and the poor have seen their portion of the nation's income and wealth decline. The result has been the most dramatic increase in inequality in the nation's history. The middle class has found itself over this period less able to save and invest. The result has been a decline in the nation's saving rate. The only families that have had the ability to save have been the high income and wealthy.

As there has been a substantial improvement for the wealthy, there has not been a concurrent decline in poverty. During the period after World War II, two groups accounted for most of the poverty in the United States: children and seniors. The foundation for ending poverty for seniors was put in place with the Social Security Act passed in 1935 as the nation came out of the Great Depression. By the early 1950s, the majority of seniors became eligible for Social Security benefits. From a poverty rate for seniors well above 30 percent in 1959, there has been a steady decline over the years to less than 10 percent today.[17] Although there is a difference in senior poverty rates by race and ethnicity, it is not nearly as great as the difference for children. During the period, when the senior poverty rate was cut to almost one-third of what it once was, the poverty rate for children has essentially remained the same. However, in recent years the poverty rate for children has begun to increase.[18] Why has the nation been so successful in reducing poverty among seniors but ineffective in reducing child poverty?

In Chapter 3, I examine the impact of Social Security on ending poverty among seniors. The Social Security Act also included what we commonly refer to as the welfare program (originally called Aid to Families with Dependent Children, AFDC and now, after welfare reform, referred to as Temporary Assistance to Needy Families, TANF). Social Security was built on a "social savings" model and required seniors to set aside money for their retirement. As a result, all seniors have a floor of income support that assures them, even if they have no other source of income when they retire, that they will not live in poverty.

In contrast to the Social Security program, welfare was built on a "means-tested" approach designed to target income assistance to the most needy. Single mothers and their children who could prove that they lacked the means to provide for themselves were provided cash assistance through the welfare program. In contrast to Social Security that has popular support, over the years the public has grown weary and skeptical of welfare. Many have come to view welfare as encouraging dependency and out-of-wedlock births. Conservative critics of the program have published studies and made arguments that support the public's widespread skepticism. Chapter 4 begins the discussion of welfare reform.

Chapter 4 examines the impact of welfare reform on child poverty. In response to public disenchantment with welfare, the program was fundamentally altered in 1996 with the passage of welfare reform. Supporters of welfare reform suggested that it would lead to improved lives for those impacted by the welfare program.[19] In the first several years of welfare reform, the country was in the midst of a period of historic economic growth and prosperity. Many of the single mothers removed from the welfare rolls found jobs in the expanding economy. The early results of the reform were a small increase in employment for welfare mothers and a substantial drop in the number of children receiving welfare benefits. The number of children receiving welfare declined from about 9 million in 1996, just before the enactment of welfare reform, to about 3 million today.[20] Looking at these numbers and the early studies of welfare reform would suggest that welfare reform has been successful in reducing child poverty. But this is not the case. In Chapter 4, I examine the impact of welfare reform a dozen years after its enactment. What we find are more children in poverty, more children receiving food stamps, more children receiving federally subsidized free lunches (even controlling for population changes) than prior to welfare reform. Although the architects of welfare reform have argued that it has been successful, particularly in reducing child poverty, the empirical data in this chapter suggest just the opposite—child poverty and the economic situation of poor children has grown worse.

Although welfare reform has failed to make a difference in reducing child poverty, it is not likely to be restored. In fact, the welfare program was fundamentally flawed. In Chapter 5, I examine the limitations and flaws of the welfare program and suggest different approaches to solving child poverty that have been used in most of the other industrialized nations of Europe, Australia, and elsewhere.[21] The two central approaches to reducing child poverty that have been used in most other industrialized nations are effective child support collection and a progressive children's allowance. The United States has among the worst record in the world in terms of assuring child support collection. This problem is particularly important for poor and low-income children. If the United States were to adopt child support collection approaches used in Europe, Australia, New Zealand and elsewhere, it could cut child poverty rates in half. Furthermore, if the United States were to adopt a progressive children's allowance as is found in most other countries, it could further substantially cut child poverty.[22]

The advantage of the approaches to ending child poverty presented in Chapter 5 is that, like Social Security, they are universal and not means-tested. Recipients do not have to be poor. The major limitation with welfare was that it was limited to the poor. Whenever a welfare mother earned enough money to exit poverty, she would lose her welfare benefits. This "claw back" effect of means-tested welfare provided, in a perverse manner, an incentive to remain poor. Furthermore, it created a high "effective tax rate" for welfare mothers who worked. As they worked, they would lose benefits while also paying employment tax. Studies by the Urban Institute and others pointed out the welfare mothers paid among the highest effective tax rates in the country.[23]

The universal programs examined in Chapter 5 would substantially end the poverty of single mothers and poor children in the United States. These approaches would allow child poverty to decline in a fashion similar to the declines in poverty rates for seniors. This reduced child poverty would have widespread effects in terms of reducing child abuse, improving educational opportunities for all children, reducing crime and the need for welfare.

During the last quarter of a century, there has been a substantial increase in the prosperity of the wealthiest families in the United States.[24] The fortunes of the top 1 percent and the top 10 percent have increased dramatically. However, the same benefits have not been shared by the middle class and the poor. The children of the middle class and the poor need to learn about the importance of saving and investing if they are to have hope of improving their economic situation.[25] In the last several decades, there has been a substantial increase in inequality largely because ownership of the assets and capital of the nation have become increasingly concentrated at the top. Those with assets and capital are able to save and invest. They are able to multiply their fortunes with careful investment and savings. Even more important, tax policies during the last several decades have allowed those with capital to keep more of the income and wealth generated by their assets. This has led to greater national wealth. In Chapter 6, I argue that we need to embrace the mechanism that makes wealth possible—capitalism—and the opportunity and prosperity it provides. More importantly, we need to insure that all children have an opportunity to participate in wealth ownership, which is the heart of capitalism. We need to embrace an "assets-based" approach to ending child poverty. Central to this approach is providing all children the resources and opportunity to accumulate wealth. The main program that would allow this is a progressive child savings account.

Beginning in 2002, all children born in Great Britain have had a child savings account opened in their name.[26] The government seeds these child savings accounts and provides extra benefits for low-income and poor children. The idea is to provide all children with an asset base when they reach the age of majority and are ready to leave home and venture forth in the free enterprise market economy. Having a child savings account will provide them with money for college, for a down payment on a house and with a "grub stake" of seed capital for building their own savings account.

For most of the children from upper and high income families, this resource is already in place. In fact, the government provides a 529 savings account that allows parents to put money aside for their children tax free. It is estimated that more than 70 billion dollars are in these accounts currently and that by 2010 more than 225 billion dollars will be in these accounts.[27] Unfortunately, middle class and poor children rarely have 529 private child savings accounts. Virtually all of the accounts are held by children of upper-income and wealthy families. The funds in these accounts, because of tax sheltering, are almost matched by the government. In other words, were it not for the tax savings features of these accounts, the funds would have about half their value at maturity.

Whereas all children in Great Britain have a child savings account, children from middle class and poor families in the United States are essentially excluded from participation The roughly 10 percent of children who have these tax favored 529 savings accounts in the United States are from the top-income families that have the wealth needed to take advantage of them. To remedy this inequity, I propose a child savings account for *all* children in the United States. As in Great Britain, when the child is born, we should open an account in his or her name and deposit a seed amount that can grow and be added to over 18 years of childhood. When the child comes of age, we can make the funds in their capital account available to them for restricted purposes including education, apprenticeship training, a down payment on a house, or starting a business. During the 18 years the account is growing, we should encourage the children to learn about saving and investing. We should provide opportunities for financial education during their school years (6–18 years old). We should encourage the children to save, work part-time, and invest their savings in their child savings account. We want to encourage young people to learn the importance of saving and investing and managing their money wisely.

I believe a child savings account program has great potential for both reducing inequality and child poverty. The genius of the American free enterprise market economy—capitalism—is found in the wise and careful financial decisions of individuals. We want to make sure all young people have the resources, education and opportunity to participate in the wealth of the nation.

In the closing chapter of the book, I argue that government policies and programs substantially shape the world we live in. Our social and economic world is largely of our own making. In the last several decades, I believe our nation has taken a turn away from the philosophy of a Jeffersonian democracy that proposed that all in the nation should participate in wealth and prosperity. This view that prevailed during the founding of the country has seemed to recede. We are moving toward a nation of haves and have-nots. Too many children are left out of the opportunities that the nation provides. As a result, we are leaving our children a less free, less democratic, and less equal country than we inherited. We need to change direction. We need to change policies so that the world we leave our children provides greater freedom and opportunity.

1

❧

The Color of Child
Poverty

Twenty-two percent of children in the United States today are living in poverty according to the United Nations.[1]

For most of us, this statistic seems simply preposterous. At no point in our daily lives do we encounter child poverty rates of that magnitude. Out of every five children we meet, it is just not the case that one of them is living in poverty.

But in its latest report on the state of the world's children in the developed world, the United Nations does indeed find that although the United States ranks as the richest country in the world, it simultaneously has the highest percentage of its children living in poverty.

We are accustomed to the idea of poverty in poor countries, with their many slums filled with suffering children where mothers clutch their starving babies as they beg on street corners, but we seem to believe poverty has been banished from America.

In many ways, those of us who are White are correct in believing that the United Nations is not talking about us. If the United Nations had confined its study to examining the status of America's White population (75% of all persons in the United States), then its conclusions would have been altogether different. White children make up 60 percent of the nation's child population. If the United Nation's study had been limited to just these children, then the United States would have scored one of the world's lowest child poverty rates. However, in order to come to such a conclusion, the United Nation's study would have had to exclude the more than 35 percent of the nation's child population who are Black and Hispanic. In short, the United Nations would have had to consider the United States as two separate and unequal nations who simply share the same national identity and government. We may live in the same land but we do not share equally in the nation's prosperity.

For children there is, of course, a second nation here—the one comprising primarily Black and Hispanic children. Their economic circumstances and opportunities are extremely different. More than a dozen years after welfare reform was supposed to have reduced poverty rates for these groups, we find poverty levels for the youngest children at levels not seen anywhere in the developed world. Although the rate of child poverty dropped after welfare reform, it did so while the economy was experiencing rapid expansion. In recent years, the rate of child poverty, especially for Black and Hispanic children, has reversed course and is now higher than before welfare reform.

In non-White America, children attend schools where there are fewer books and where classes are too often held in dilapidated buildings; children are not certain that they will have dinner tonight or breakfast tomorrow.

These children have parents, or usually only one parent, who works at a diner or factory, as a maid or, ironically, a child care provider.

> An estimated 2.3 million Americans are paid to care for young children in child care centers or organized play groups, or as nannies. They feed the children, change their diapers, sing songs to them, read to them, and tend to their bruises (physical scrapes as well as occasional hurt feelings). The median wage of child care workers is $6.60 an hour, usually without benefits.
>
> Robert Reich, The Great Divide[3]

Should a hurricane, earthquake, or terrorist attack occur, these are the children who cannot evacuate. These are the ones who live on the edge, uncertain all the time about what the future holds. In fact, there is very little in this other nation that is reliable, not food for certain, and not even basic opportunities. With infant mortality rates that rival those in the third world countries and a far greater chance of disease and violence, these children see a world where little is guaranteed.

These children rarely receive preventative health care. The doctors these children see work only in emergency rooms. There are televisions but not owner occupied homes—they live in rental housing. In 2004, 55.3 percent of Black children and 52.2 percent of Hispanic children lived in rental housing.[4]

However, if we return to White Americans, just 18.3 percent of these children live in rented homes. Their private or at least well-funded public schools have new buildings and even newer books. Their parents send them off to school after eating a full breakfast. In the parallel universe where White Americans live, the poverty rate is less than 10 percent.[5] In 2005, according to the Census Bureau, White children living in two-parent families have a poverty rate of 4.5 percent—meaning, of course, that more than 95 percent of White children in this country are not considered poor (see Table 1.1).[6]

Across the divide in non-White America, 37.8 percent of Black children under 5 live in poverty,[7] whereas Hispanic children of the same age experience poverty at the rate of 31 percent. Asian children, the one minority exception, along with their White counterparts, reported a child poverty rate of less than 10 percent (see Table 1.2).

The dividing line between these two countries turns out not to be one of color only but also of gender. The other determining factor in predicting the likelihood of poverty for children is family composition—mainly living in a single-parent households headed by a women.

As seen in Table 1.1, about one-half of White children under 5 who live in mother-only families fall below the poverty line, whereas more than 58 percent of Black and Hispanic children in the same situation suffer from poverty. Although it is true that White and Asian children in mother-only

Table 1.1 Poverty Rates for Children by Family Type (2005)

| | Children Under 18 (%) | | Children Under 5 (%) | |
	Two Parents	Mother Only	Two Parents	Mother Only
White	4.5	33.0	5.5	48.7
Black	12.5	50.1	11.1	58.1
Hispanic	20.1	50.1	22.7	59.0
Asian	9.3	25.6	8.7	n/a*

Source: Census Bureau (2006). Online at: http://pubdb3.census.gov/macro/032005/pov/new03_100.htm
* Sample size too small to estimate. n/a indicates not available.

Table 1.2 Poverty Rates for Children Under 5 (2005)

	Children Under 5 (%)
White	11.9
Black	37.8
Hispanic	31.4
Asian	8.9

Source: Census Bureau (2006). Online at: http://pubdb3. census.gov/macro/032006/pov/new03_100_04.htm

Table 1.3 Annual Family Income (2004)

	Under US$30,000 (%)	Over US$50,000 (%)	Over US$75,000 (%)	Child Population	% of Children
White	19.6	62.2	40.1	43,262,000	61
Asian	18.4	61.7	39.7	2,752,000	4
Black	52.3	27.0	13.8	11,424,000	16
Hispanic	47.0	29.0	14.1	13,752,000	19

Source: Census Bureau (2005).

families fare better than their Black and Hispanic counterparts, clearly the family structure is the major determinant of poverty.

Just 35 percent of Black children live in two-parent families compared to about 75 percent of White children.

Witness the American poverty line at its most extreme: two-thirds of Black children are raised by a single mother and they have a greater than 50 percent chance of living in poverty. Now, three-quarters of White children live in two-parent families. They have less than a 5 percent chance of living in poverty. Black children in America, especially when they are under 5, grow up in very different economic circumstances than their White counterparts.

The data in Table 1.3 provide a more detailed view of the differences in family incomes for Black and Hispanic children compared to White and Asian children. Less than one fifth of White and Asian children live in families with income less than US$30,000 a year, compared to about half of Black and Hispanic children. In contrast, White and Asian children are more than 2.5 times as likely to live in a household with annual family income greater than US$75,000 than Black and Hispanic children.

The Differences Between the Two Worlds of Childhood

So why then do these two Americas continue to exist side by side? What is it that allows for one America to be so blessed and wealthy and its cousin to be so poor and suffer so?

Let us be honest with ourselves, the very real specter of racism cannot be ignored. Race undoubtedly is one of the strongest correlations between children above and below the poverty line.

But then again, neither can the preexistence of poverty be ignored—for it is true that being poor sets one up to remain poor. Regardless of their

Table 1.4 Median Family Income by Family Structure and
Race/Ethnicity (2004)

	Married Couple (in US$)	Mother Only (in US$)
White	70,948	28,543
Black	57,498	22,004
Hispanic	43,361	21,275
Asian	75,811	39,828

Source: Census Bureau (2005). Online at: http://pubdb3.census.gov/macro/032005/faminc/

race, 50 percent of single mothers live below the poverty line. In 2004, the
median income of female-headed families was substantially less than one-
half of married couples (see Table 1.4). The single mother and her children
comprise the most vulnerable group in the United States.

Single Mothers Are Poor for Various Reasons

The mere fact of supporting children on one income, in a time when most
families have found that two incomes are necessary, immediately puts
single mothers at a disadvantage. In addition, parenthood is a unique condition requiring a great deal of emotional and physical resources that extends
beyond its more easily quantifiable financial demands. Raising children
is a labor-intensive activity—with very heavy demands on mother's time;
thus two parents are much better able to cope with the demands and to
handle the burdens. The traditional two-parent structure, which for most
of the twentieth century prevailed, has however increasingly become less
prevalent throughout the world regardless of race and class.[8]

Even given access to adequate, reliable and inexpensive day care, single
mothers will still find themselves at a disadvantage in the labor market—for
most single mothers do not have access to quality day care.[9] These mothers do
not have flexible work schedules and often have to miss work in order to meet
the demands of motherhood. Typically lacking a college degree, the poor single mother is competing for minimum wage jobs—jobs that will never, even
if the women were capable of working 50 hours a week, every week of the
year, match the costs of feeding, housing and caring for their children.[10]

More than two million Americans work in nursing homes—bathing and feeding
frail elderly people, cleaning their bedsores, lifting them out of bed and into wheel-
chairs, and changing their diapers. They earn, on average, between $7 and $8 an
hour. Some 700,000 people work as home health care aides, attending to the elderly,

sick, or disabled at home. Their pay averages between $8 and $10 an hour—less than $20,000 a year. Another 1.3 million Americans work in hospitals as orderlies and attendants, at about the same rate. Adjusted for inflation, most of them also are earning less than they did 15 years ago.

Robert Reich, The Great Divide[11]

The often depressing existential nature of the kinds of jobs available to single women in America is captured in Barbara Ehrenreich's exploration of the life of the working poor, *Nickel and Dimed*.[12] These women find themselves in low-wage jobs that demand long hours and hard work. Whether serving up eggs and pancakes as a waitress at a 24-hour coffee shop, or making beds and cleaning toilets at a budget hotel, or ringing up sales at a Wal-Mart, women are strictly supervised and under constant threat of losing their job if they do not meet the expectations of low-paid supervisors. These service jobs pay low hourly wages and provide few benefits.[13] In recent years, with the erosion of labor unions, most of these workers are at the mercy of the good intentions of their employer who is competing with others to lower the cost of wages and benefits so that they can compete with superstores, companies in bankruptcy that have cancelled their union contracts, and companies willing to outsource work overseas.

Although other developed countries have safeguards in place—for instance, day care at night for women who have to work evening shifts, safe state-run day care, guaranteed health care for children—the United States has pursued a path of continually eroding support for single parents over the past 20 years.[14] In many European countries, day care is far more than the glorified babysitting that many of the preschool children from poor families in the United States are subject to.[15] There is no television blaring in the corner, no chaotic and unsupervised clutter of experiences. Europe's preschool centers are called *academies* and their focus is on *school readiness* as they prepare their small charges for success down the line.

Welfare reform was primarily targeted at single mothers, and despite the rhetoric and initial claims otherwise, it has not alleviated their situation. Employment rates for single mothers rose throughout the nineties; however, as the economy softened, it seems as if these women were the first to lose their marginal or low-paying positions. According to the Center on Budget and Policy Priorities, the employment rate among single mothers fell from 73 percent in 2000 to 69.8 percent in 2003, a comparatively larger decline than among the general population.[16] For never-married mothers the decline was even greater. The greatest losses occurred to Black single mothers whose employment rate declined 4 percentage points overall and 2.3 among the never married. The decline in employment overall was 2.1 (from 64.4

Table 1.5 Distribution of Real Income for Households With Children

	2000 (in US$)	2005 (in US$)	2000–2005 (in US$)
Quintile			
Lowest	18,800	16,800	−10.8
Second	39,400	37,500	−4.8
Middle	59,100	57,200	−3.3
Fourth	83,700	83,900	0.3
Highest	176,300	175,800	−0.3

Source: Congressional Budget Office based on the U.S. Census Bureau's Current Population Surveys from 2000 to 2006.[17]

Note: Income in 2005 dollars.

to 62.3). As seen in Table 1.5, the economic situation of households with children has declined in recent years, but the decline has been most severe for low-income households.

What is the situation for children in the households presented in Table 1.5? Clearly, for the 20 percent of children in households with an average income of US$16,800 a year in 2005 it is one of deep poverty. We have then a segment of the population unable, even if they work full-time, to reach above the poverty line for themselves and their families. These are women who must find ways to get to work whether via public transportation or in cars they can barely afford. They must find ways to juggle the costs of their children's food and clothing, as well as the electric and gas bills. When they come home exhausted and wrung out, are they likely to have the energy or the time to sit down and read books with their kids? Will they engage in vocabulary-rich conversations about current events? Will there be money left over for books, computer learning programs, and lessons?

Although many children gain from Internet access, DVDs, and a host of other modern inventions that enrich and inform when used well, the children of the single mother are too often left behind. These children will enter kindergarten not able to recognize the alphabet, let alone manipulate a computer mouse or tell you the name of the U.S. president. The children of a single parent will suffer innumerable wounds beyond what can be calculated financially.

Being in the position of raising children alone puts a mother at a great disadvantage. Single mothers are therefore a "problem." In the African-American community, this problem is even more pronounced.[18] Given that growing up in a single-parent family increases the chances of being in poverty to a fifty-fifty chance, being born African American raises the odds of being born to a single parent. After all, 70 percent of African-American children are born to single mothers.

Paths Out of Poverty

In America, opportunity has traditionally been signified by access to higher education. However, even from the start, the academic performance of children born into poverty is compromised—although how exactly the varying factors of single parents, who have little time or energy to engage their children, interact with the general impoverishment in the home environment, inadequate schools, poor health care, and just plain not having enough money is not easy to decipher.

As we have seen, poverty and single parenthood are intimately intertwined. \Returning to our two Americas, children from single-parent families struggle in school far more than their peers who have the benefit of two parents. It may not be simply that having one parent causes these problems, since poverty itself can cause many of the same problems; poverty can cause a marriage to break up as well as result from a broken marriage. Children in single parent families are twice as likely to drop out of high school, 2.5 times as likely to become teen mothers…as children who grow up with both parents."[19]

Children from single-parent families have lower grade point averages, diminished aspirations, and are more likely to be truant. McLanahan and Sandefur's study of the effects of family disruption on children found that having one parent had less effect on Black children.[20] McLanahan and Sandefur observed, "Thus, for the average white child, family disruption appears to eliminate much of the advantage associated with being white."[21] However, it seems that it is the diminishment of resources whether it is in terms of "quality time" or financial deprivation or both that have the greatest impact on very young children.

Origins of Disadvantage

Children are a major responsibility. They require food, clothing, and shelter. They require love and attention. Child rearing is a labor-intensive activity that is critical to proper child development and the nurturance of effective citizens. Unlike women who share household and child rearing chores with a spouse or have the resources to hire help, most single mothers are denied the opportunity to provide the early nurturing and personal attention that is so important in the earliest years.[22] The financial costs of day care are one thing, but the costs in human terms are much more difficult to count. But they can be measured when the children enter school. They enter kindergarten far behind their well-off counterparts and do not have a chance to catch up.

As seen in Figure 1.1, Black and Hispanic children in Los Angeles County (with 700,000 students) enter school substantially behind their White and

Asian counterparts.[23] These children never catch up. Throughout the twelve years in school they remain substantially behind. The central question is why these children start so far behind. This is where the disadvantage these children face first shows up. From this point of entry in school these children start way behind and are unlikely to catch up.

What is the explanation for why they start so far behind? Charles Murray and Richard Herrnstein declare "Among the experts, it is by now beyond much technical dispute that there is such a thing as a general factor of cognitive ability on which human beings differ and that this general factor is measured reasonably well by a variety of standardized tests, best of all by IQ tests designed for that purpose."[24] In their book, *The Bell Curve*, they argue that Whites are substantially more intelligent than Blacks and that it is this genetic difference in intelligence that explains the difference seen above.

The view put forth by Herrnstein and Murray has been repudiated by academic and scientific reviews. Yet they argue it is the futile effort to change these "facts" that makes the problem worse. The poverty of White people (Caucasians) in the former Soviet states is recognized by these same analysts as result of the limits on opportunity imposed by restrictive social and economic systems. Many in these socialist economies are very intelligent but they are bridled by failed economic policies. Likewise, many in the United States find their opportunities limited by social and economic policies that limit their opportunities. Probably the greatest harm to the

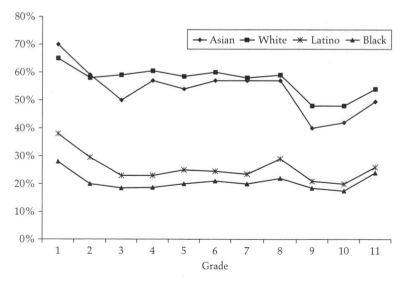

Figure 1.1 Reading Scores on the Stanford 9 (LAUSD)

Data Source: Meersman, 1999, note 21.

opportunities for these children in single-parent families and children of color is done in the earliest years of their life. These children suffer as much from those who fail to believe in them as by the barriers imposed on them by the brutal reality of daily poverty.[25]

What makes child poverty and inequality so difficult and intractable to political solution in America is that it is so tightly intertwined with race and ethnicity. As we have seen in the beginning of this chapter, child poverty is primarily concentrated among children of color—Black and Brown children. The view that these children have limited intellectual capacity perpetuates the view that nothing can be done. The result is that too often, very little is done to improve the opportunities and life chances of these young people. The sense for the majority that this is not "our" problem because it is so highly concentrated among minorities increases the cynicism and despair that perpetuates the problem and makes it even more difficult to solve. It is difficult to discern the role and influence of racism in perpetuating child poverty. Race and racism is a difficult subject to talk about. But there is little question that we need to examine and challenge the barriers imposed by racism to finding solutions.[26]

Restricting the Economic and Social Opportunities of Children

Other explanations for the disadvantage of Black and Hispanic children are more complicated. One of the most important series of studies to explore the early learning environment of children was conducted by Betty Hart and Todd Risley.[27] Perplexed by the limited impact of their efforts to provide remedial education to children in preschool programs, Hart and Risley sought to find out what was happening to children from welfare families who entered school so far behind in terms of language development.

Visiting the homes of these children they noted that there were few newspapers and magazines. These children do not see their parents reading books or experience the pleasures of having books read to them. Even the conversations in these early learning environments are too often brief and fail to nourish.

Millions of Words

For more than two years, Hart and Risley studied the home environments of children from a variety of backgrounds.[28] They recorded the interactions of the children with their parents, including how the parents dealt with questions from their children. They found that, on average, parents from welfare families spoke 176 words every hour to their children (see Table 1.6). This compared with 487 words every hour that affluent parents spoke to their children and 301 words for working-class parents. In their book, *Meaningful Differences*, they assert that these differences are meaningful because the manner and extent to which parents interact with their children impact their vocabulary development and literacy levels.[29]

At a very early age, children learn vocabulary that they can then use to communicate. Later, after they learn a sufficient number of words, they can begin to string together words into sentences and develop their cognitive abilities. The recent research on brain development in the earliest years has stressed the importance of nurturing cognitive development in the earliest years because it has such a profound effect on development in later years.

Betty Hart and Todd Risley write, "There was a difference of almost 300 words spoken per hour between professional and welfare parents. As a result, by age 3, the professional families' children actually had a larger recorded vocabulary than the welfare families' parents."[30] In one year, children from wealthy families had access to around 11 million words, children from the working class encountered 6 million, and children on welfare only had the opportunity to learn 3 million words. Vocabulary growth not only determines IQ scores but also a child's relationship with his or her environment; "Vocabulary defines and labels a child's experience in terms of the family culture. Language reflects the parent's view of what children should notice and think about the world, family, and self."[31]

Once the child is ready to start school, he or she has fallen behind more affluent children and the distance does not diminish.[32] From the start, poor children have the disadvantage of limited access to education. Whereas their wealthier counterparts frequently interact with their mother at an early age, the poor children are often left in front of a television set or to fend for themselves while in the care of others. From pre-K through elementary school, the gap between the impoverished and the more fortunate yawns increasingly wide.

Table 1.6 Number of Words Heard From the Time Child Was 10 Months Old to 3 Years of Age for Different Families

Family	Words per Hour	Total Words in a Year
Children in professional families	487	11 million
Children in working class families	301	6 million
Children in families on welfare	176	3 million

In *The Shame of the Nation*, Jonathon Kozol describes an educational system that is as segregated by race (as well as class) as it was in 1960.[33] Even though it has been shown that economic diversity benefits all students and despite Brown vs. the Board of Education, the Civil Rights Project at Harvard University reports that "American public schools are now 12 years into the process of resegregation. The desegregation of Black students, which increased continuously from the 1950s to the late 1980s, has now receded to levels not seen in three decades...during the 1990s, the proportion of Black students in majority white schools has decreased...to a level lower than in any year since 1968....Almost three fourths of Black and Latino students attend schools that are predominately minority."[34] The schools these students attend are both separate and unequal.[35]

A student in a minority New York City school would have received an US$8000 a year education, whereas another in a suburban community nearby would have the benefit of US$12,000 a year, and in one of the cities wealthiest suburbs not only did students benefit from US$18,000 worth of learning but their teachers were also paid nearly US$30,000 more than their urban peers.[36] Local public schools receive most of their funding from local taxes. As a result, children from wealthier communities will attend better-funded schools. Over the years states have, to varying degrees, tried to mitigate the influence of these differences but the gap remains.[37]

In addition, in wealthier school districts the Parent Teachers Association (PTA) has taken a role in fundraising so that private money supplies even more resources: art, music, and such "extras" that the poor schools could not provide were supplied through the financial support of richer parents.

We can see this discrepancy in California's high schools (Table 1.7).[38]

Seven hundred and seventy-one of the 1233 graduates at the states five top schools were admitted to the state's University of California campuses.

Of the more than 1000 high school graduates attending the bottom public high schools, 4 were admitted to the University of California.

Four.

Why such a discrepancy?

Despite studies proving that quality pre-K benefits children intellectually, few children have access to such programs. Kozol observes that by the time standardized testing takes center stage (in most schools third grade), "Children who have been in programs like the 'Baby Ivies' since the age of two have been given seven years of education...nearly twice as much as the children who have been denied these opportunities; yet are required to take, and will be measured and in many cases penalized severely by, the same examinations."[40]

Table 1.7 Admission to the University of California From the Top Public and Private High Schools and the Bottom Public High Schools[39]

High School	Graduates	Graduates Admitted to UC	Percentage Admitted
Top Public			
Whitney High	171	141	82.5
California Academy	118	81	68.6
Piedmont High	198	126	63.6
San Marino	295	171	58.0
Davis Senior High	451	252	55.9
Top Private			
Lick-Wilmerding	92	79	85.9
College Preparatory	75	63	84.0
Head-Royce	80	67	83.8
San Francisco Univ. High	96	78	81.3
Harvard-Westlake	262	190	72.5
Bottom Public			
Washington High	255	0	0.0
Centennial High	227	1	0.4
Mesa Verde	196	1	0.5
Escondido Charter	186	1	0.5
Rosamond High	140	1	0.7

Then as public schools struggle to keep up with the mandates of standardized testing, focusing upon preparing students for certain kinds of thinking, it is almost as if a national tracking system has fallen into place with one set of children headed toward college and the other toward minimum wage and the same deprivation they already know too well.

Kozol suggests the role of the school has been converted into preparing poor children to serve as a new generation of low-wage service workers and limiting their access to routes out of the inner city: schools manufacture "preferences" for students and do "this to the direct exclusion of those options other children rightly take as their entitlement."[41] Career paths are shaped in elementary school where other options—such as college—are rarely presented.

The SAT and Access to College

Each year some 2.5 million high school students match wits with the Scholastic Aptitude Tests. The results go a long way to determining who gets into the most selective colleges. The tests are the subject of a growing debate. Do they really discover the best and the brightest? Or do they chiefly identify the richest and the most expensively educated?

James Fallows, How Fair Are the College Boards[42]

Today, the childhood experiences for Black and Hispanic children are worlds apart from their wealthy White and Asian counterparts. They are often raised by a single mother trying to earn a living so that she can feed, clothe, and shelter her children. The mother encounters a labor market that is not sympathetic to the needs of her family. She is unlikely to get much help from the government—the recent effort has been to wean her off dependence on the state. Her children will be the main victims of her inability to overcome the barriers the single mother faces in the current economy. Her children will likely miss out on the intensive personal interaction with a parent. Carrying the burden of full-time work and responsibility for all household chores—meal preparation, cleaning, shopping—she is unlikely to have the time to focus on engaging, talking, and reading to her children. As a result, the children will fall behind in the development of the vocabulary and language skills that are so critical to cognitive growth. The children will be ill prepared to enter school and when they enter they will likely test well behind their better-off kindergarten classmates.

These disadvantaged students are likely to start behind and stay behind. They will attend disadvantaged schools and rather than helping them catch up are more likely to contribute to them falling even further behind. If the children try hard and do their best in school, they are still likely to encounter major barriers to success. At the end of the high school experience, as they prepare to enter college they will face the final coup de grace—the SAT.

The SAT is, in part, a sort of diagnostic assessment of the deficit the children suffer during their earliest years before they enter school.[43] In this sense, it measures the long-term developmental deficit these children acquired in their preschool years and were never able to make up. Without question, this is an important deficit that impedes their learning. But it is not clear whether this deficit is central to determining success in college, particularly if the student's record of performance during the 12 years in school as measured by their grade point average (GPA) (and courses completed) is taken into account. To the degree the SAT is a measure of the vocabulary deficit acquired in early childhood, using the SAT puts poor children and children of color at a distinct disadvantage that they can almost never overcome.

What begins in the earliest years and carries over to the start of kindergarten and is sustained through grade school and high school reaches its apex when the Black and Hispanic children try to attend the best public and private universities. For the Black or Hispanic young person who is able to defy the odds and graduate from high school, they encounter the ultimate barrier—the SAT. No other obstacle is more of a direct barrier to the futures of young Black and Hispanic high school graduates than this allegedly objective test.

Originated by Francis Galton and Edward Thorndike, the mental test movement came out of work in eugenics: the science of how certain human qualities are hereditary.[44] Eugenics proponents view humans as limited by the indisputable determinants of their genes. They point to a child's height as a hereditary trait. Children of tall fathers tend, on average, to be taller than children of short fathers. The early genetic research of Francis Galton and others in the nineteenth century and Arthur Jenkins and Charles Murray in the present day, believed in intelligence as "by far the most important human trait."[45] They also believed intelligence, as a genetically determined trait, was connected to racial characteristics.

According to Sylvia Spengler, a geneticist at U.C. Berkeley and a part of the human genome project, genetic experts all over the world view Herrnstein and Murray's *The Bell Curve* as having no standing in physiological or genetic science.[46] She points out that the DNA sequence that controls racial characteristics such as skin color are independent of the DNA sequence that affects intelligence. Arguing that skin color is connected with intelligence has about as much basis as suggesting a link between height and intelligence.

During World War I, Robert Yerkes, a leading member of the IQ testing movement, persuaded the U.S. Army to let him test all recruits for intelligence. This test—the Army Alpha—was the first mass administered IQ test. One of Yerkes' assistants was a young psychologist named Carl Brigham, who taught at Princeton. The army wanted Yerkes to design a test that could be administered en masse rather than only to individuals. For many years, the army maintained this interest in testing.[47]

In 1922 Walter Lippmann, one of the most distinguished intellectuals of the day wrote:

One only has to read around in the literature of the subject ... to see how easily the intelligence test can be turned into an engine of cruelty, how ... it could turn into a method of stamping a permanent sense of inferiority upon the soul of a child.[48]

Nevertheless, Brigham's modified version of Army Alpha (precursor of the SAT) was first administered experimentally to a few thousand college applicants in 1926.

In 1933, James Bryant Conant, the President of Harvard, employed the test so that he could find gifted boys from outside of the typical boarding schools attended by the Eastern elite.[49] Henry Chauncey, an assistant dean at Harvard, set about finding a means to evaluate applicants on the basis of their abilities without regard to their upbringing or the quality of their education. Brigham's test seemed to fit the bill and by 1938, Chauncey had convinced all of the member schools of the College Board, 40 or 50 prestigious private colleges in the Northeast, into using the SAT for scholarship applicants. In 1942, the College Board required all college applicants to take the SAT.[50] In brief, the SAT was originally used by elite colleges to foster admission based on merit and to reduce the advantage of pedigree. The irony is that over the years this same test has now come to have the opposite effect. Instead of assuring access to disadvantaged students, the test has become the dominant barrier to higher education for poor children and Black and Hispanic children in particular.[51]

If the SAT were an accurate predictor of performance in college, then perhaps requiring it for admission decision-making would be understandable. However, there has been limited predictive value found for what is essentially a test of vocabulary and language development rather than student performance in college. Since so much depends upon decoding a set of questions on the basis of knowledge that is not innate but learned, children whose early years have been enriched by substantial parental interaction are far more likely to know the difference between *enumerate* and *enunciate* for instance. Children raised by mothers with demanding work schedules and heavy housekeeping demands will be unable to devote the hours needed during their children's early years. Years later, when their children take the SAT, the early disadvantage will be magnified and lead to SAT test scores that will essentially block access to the best colleges and universities.

At its inception the acronym, SAT, stood for Scholastic Aptitude Test.[52] However, the notion that aptitude could be measured by some type of vocabulary and linguistic test instrument was repudiated both by the original authors of the SAT and cognitive development researchers. Consequently and somewhat ironically, the name of the test is now simply the SAT and the letters have come to signify nothing.

Why is it so widely used? The experience of California is illustrative. As the number of applicants to the University of California began to greatly exceed the number of openings, the University needed a simple method to make an objective decision. The decision to admit is a high stakes decision that greatly concerns parents and legislators. The SAT provides a simple and seemingly objective method to base admissions on. The University of

California originally adopted the exam even though it was clear that the test did not substantially improve its ability to predict how well a student would do in college.[53] Even if it was not a good indicator of intelligence, if at least the test was a good predictor of college performance it might be justifiable. But it is not.

The empirical studies have demonstrated that after taking into account a student's high school GPA, the SAT adds very little to predicting college success. It is a better indicator of parental income and race and ethnicity than it is a predictor of future college performance.

In fact, college admissions offices could just as accurately use a measure of parental income to estimate an applicant's college performance as to use the SAT. Although using the SAT does not seem as unfair as granting admission on the basis of parental income, it does result in barring the poor, including Blacks and Hispanics. Gerda Steele of the NAACP writes that standardized tests "are used in ways that keep certain segments of the population from realizing their aspirations. Most of all they limit access of Blacks and other minorities to higher education."[54]

The University of California was not the first to require the SAT. But once it had adopted the test for their applicants in 1968, the SAT had become firmly ensconced as the most objective approach to making admission decisions based on "merit."[55] Between 1950 and 1970, enrollment at institutions of higher education in the United States tripled. Most of the growth was concentrated in public colleges and universities. A standardized achievement test was promoted during this period as a simple solution to making competitive admission decisions. But what was the alternative? Most colleges combined the SAT with the GPA to make admissions decisions and this approach has continued as the dominant approach up to the current period.

The available evidence suggests that once a student's GPA is known, adding information from the SAT makes a negligible addition to improving the prediction of performance. The University of California studied a sample of 77,983 admitted students over a several year period (1996 to 1999) and found that once the student's GPA is known, the SAT contributes less than 2 or 3 percent to the prediction equation.[56] In short, it is of very little use in predicting success at college. Its primary value is simplifying the admission decision for colleges and universities. For instance, in 2008 UCLA received more than 54,000 applications but was able to enroll only 4,800. How can the university decide who to admit? When the admissions office is able to use SAT scores, then its work is made easier. But the main support for the SAT does not come from the admissions office. It derives its support from upper-income families whose children benefit from the test by putting the working class and poor children at substantial disadvantage.

Table 1.8 SAT I Mean Scores by Race/Ethnicity for
UC Fall 2000 Applicant Pool[59]

	Average SAT I Verbal + Math
White	1228
Black	1050
Chicano/Latino	1061
Asian	1217

UC, University of California.

Table 1.9 Racial/Ethnic Composition of the Top 10 Percent of
SAT Takers and 18-Year-Olds in California, Fall 2000

	SAT I Verbal + Math (%)	18-Year-Olds (%)
White	47.7	40
Black	0.8	7
Chicano/Latino	2.9	41
Asian	48.6	12

Source: University of California, Office of the President (2003); State of California,
Department of Finance (2008).[60]

Those who benefit from the test are unlikely to be persuaded that the test is unfair. They provide the political clout needed to insure that the test, which would have otherwise been abandoned, survives and continues to be given great importance.

The minimal benefit of the SAT in predicting performance in college—almost negligible—has to be weighed against its potential bias in excluding or including various groups.[57] The differences between average SAT test scores for Black and Hispanic children versus White and Asian students is over 150 points (see Table 1.8).[58] The SAT tests put Black and Hispanic students at a disadvantage in the college admission process that is very difficult to overcome. Thus, Black and Hispanic students who perform equally well in high school, in terms of their earned GPA, are essentially sent to the end of the admissions line after taking the SAT tests.

When the SAT is used for competitive college admission decision making, it leads to a virtual exclusion of Black and Hispanic students. As seen in Table 1.9, among the top 10 percent of SAT test takers in California, Black and Hispanic students represented less than 4 percent of this group even though they constituted almost half of the states children.

Clyde Kennard—The Struggle for Access

After returning as a decorated Korean War veteran, Clyde Kennard returned to his family's small chicken farm in rural Forrest County.[61] In 1959 he decided to apply to the University of Southern Mississippi in nearby Hattiesburg. No Black had ever applied to the University before. Once White leaders learned of Clyde's plans, they took great pains to persuade him to change his mind and apply to the traditionally all Black university. Clyde Kennard, however, was determined to attend the local campus. As he submitted his application he met with University President McCain who attempted to dissuade Clyde. As he drove away from McCain's office, Clyde was arrested and accused of "speeding and driving with alcohol in his car." The president of the university learned of what happened and complained that Clyde was framed. Shortly after he submitted his college application, the local farm cooperative foreclosed on his chicken farm. His insurance company cancelled his insurance. The local Sovereignty Committee attempted to secure his bank records, and he was arrested and charged with a theft from the local farming Cooperative. He was sentenced to prison for seven years. After several years in prison Clyde died of cancer which was exacerbated by the poor medical treatment he received. Clyde had done nothing but try to go to college.

Income, Wealth, and the SAT

Not only does the SAT restrict access for Black and Hispanic children, it is a major barrier for children from poor and low-income families. As seen in Figure 1.2, there is a systematic advantage for students from high-income families on the SAT.

SAT Prep Courses

A more egalitarian college admissions system would run counter to the interests of upper-middle-class parents, who wield great influence in the politics of higher education.

Ross Douthat, College admissions 2005[62]

The growth of expensive SAT preparatory programs such as Kaplan and the Princeton Review makes it clear that students can boost their scores. The test is not the pure and unbiased measure that it was intended to be. With increased competition for the most selective colleges and universities, the SAT's importance has grown. Because the SAT has become

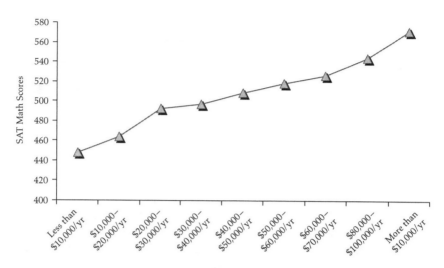

Figure 1.2 SAT Math Scores and Family Income

crucial in evaluating intelligence, many people incorrectly assume their scores are real and accurate measures of innate intelligence. Even as the test prep business booms, people view SAT scores as evidence of the natural brainpower.

Even though Brigham, the father of the SAT, eventually disowned his off-spring, the SAT test has become a dreaded but inevitable part of the life of every college-bound student. "But through it all, the SAT's underlying social function—as a sorting device for entry into or, more likely, maintenance of American elitehood—has remained ingeniously intact, a firmly rooted icon of American notions about meritocracy."[63] Despite all the evidence that the SAT is a better measure of social position than anything else: "A test-taker whose parents did not complete high school can expect to score 171 points below the SAT average, College Board figures show. On the other hand, high school grad-uates whose moms and dads have graduate degrees can expect to outperform the SAT average by 106 points" (Sacks). The SAT remains the penultimate obstacle for this nation's poor who are able to survive to high school graduation.

In California and most other states today, Blacks are not denied admissions to the state's best universities based on race. In fact, in California state law (Proposition 209) specifically prevents the University from considering race for admission decisions. However, in California and most other states the major public universities depend upon the SAT to determine who is eligible and as a result millions of Black and Hispanic applicants are denied entry. The doorway entrance is no longer blocked by a bigoted political official. The new SAT barrier is more subtle and elusive but equally restrictive.

As seen in Table 1.10, Black children are substantially underrepresented at the state's top public university in almost every state. In these same states, Black children are substantially overrepresented in the state's welfare program, the state's juvenile detention facilities, and the state's foster care system. The level of overrepresentation of Black children in the state's involuntary and restrictive programs—juvenile detention and foster care—should raise alarm bells. The overrepresentation of Black children in the

Table 1.10 Percentage of Black Children Admitted to the Top State University, on Welfare, in Juvenile Detention and Foster Care by State*

	Population	At Top State University	Welfare	Juvenile Detention	Foster Care	Number of Black Children
New York	18	5	42	60	45	834,839
Florida	21	8	55	49	45	751,146
Georgia	34	7	81	64	58	739,709
Texas	12	3	30	35	29	729,958
California	7	3	23	25	33	656,738
Illinois	19	7	74	57	74	600,408
North Carolina	26	11	66	58	49	514,580
Louisiana	40	9	87	77	62	484,260
Michigan	17	8	55	43	40	449,068
Maryland	32	12	78	67	78	432,619
Ohio	14	8	56	42	41	410,144
Virginia	23	9	69	58	51	401,539
Pennsylvania	13	4	55	50	52	371,122
South Carolina	36	17	76	65	61	367,509
Alabama	32	14	78	58	55	357,248
Mississippi	45	13	87	59	57	346,509
New Jersey	16	8	61	65	63	325,659
Tennessee	21	7	66	48	38	295,088
Missouri	14	6	54	38	42	204,160
Indiana	10	4	52	34	41	162,163
Arkansas	21	6	67	53	39	140,156
Nevada	24	2	26	24	22	121,296
Wisconsin	8	2	50	58	54	113,607

*States with more than 100,000 Black children in residence. All figures are for 2000. *Population* represents percentage of state child population in the particular program or institution that is Black. *At top State University* represents percentage of undergraduates at state's top university (in *US News* ranking) who are Black. *Welfare* represents percentage of state's welfare population under 19 that is Black. *Juvenile Detention* represents percentage of children in state's juvenile residential facilities who are Black. *Foster Care* represents the percentage of children in state's foster care system, who are Black. The final column is the number of Black children in the state.

means-tested welfare program should also raise concerns about the economic plight of Black children in America. Finally, the high school dropout rate for Black youth portends a bleak future life trajectory.

We have devoted a lot of time in this chapter to discussion of the SAT. The reason is that this test is one of the most important impediments to the entry of children of color into the mainstream. No other barrier does more to deny children of color the vital opportunity of a competitive college education than this test. If, in fact, there were empirical evidence to suggest that the SAT has substantial predictive value of success in college beyond the earned GPA, it might make sense to require it. In the absence of such evidence,—which when one considers the amount of time and money invested in the SATs by students and the importance of the test in determining the future—colleges and universities should consider dropping the test or, at the very least, making submission of the SAT test scores optional, at least until evidence that the test does not discriminate against Black and Hispanic students is demonstrated.

In December 2005, I purchased the SAT Interactive Handheld Tutor from a half-page advertisement in the *Wall Street Journal*.[64] The electronic device was slightly larger than Apple's iPhone and cost about US$200. It allows the user to practice taking SAT tests and continually assess progress. Any faith I had about the ability or precision of the SAT to measure intelligence was substantially diminished after spending hours with this device.

The SAT is not an objective measure. It is not like measuring height or income (although, as seen in Figure 1.2, it is a good indirect measure of income). The SAT essentially punishes children from "impoverished" early learning environments. The SAT measures cognitive and intellectual development that is beyond the control of the child. This is the main reason that the SAT is so unfair. It tells children and youth from impoverished environments that no matter how well they perform in school, as assessed by their grades, there remains a barrier that they have little prospect of overcoming—and that is the SAT.

The main support for the SAT comes from those it advantages. Those who benefit from the exam can be expected to strongly defend it, even though there is no greater barrier to admission to America's competitive colleges and universities for African-American and Hispanic youth.

Closing

Four decades ago, under the presidencies of John Kennedy and Lyndon Johnson, the nation tackled the problem of child poverty. But those efforts have long since faded. In the last half century, essentially nothing of significance has been done to address the problem of child poverty and, in particular, the problem of children of color who make up the majority of children living in poverty.

What is needed, and what we examine in the following chapters, are social policies and approaches that would reduce child poverty. Children who grow up in poverty can hardly be held responsible for remedying their situation. A good and just society would make efforts to ensure authentic opportunities for all children, regardless of color.

The most severe blemish on the character of American society is our treatment of poor children and children of color. We breed anger and cynicism when we allow the unfair and restrictive situations children of color too often experience. The soul of the nation is damaged when it fails to address the bleak circumstances and even bleaker futures that await our youngest and most vulnerable citizens.

Why has there been a decline in the life prospects that await almost one-third of the nation's children—who are predominately Black, Hispanic and poor? In the next chapter, we examine the declining opportunity in America that has resulted from policies that have shifted the tax burden increasingly from capital to labor. During the first several decades after World War II, the nation expanded opportunity growing the middle class and providing for participation of all income groups in the growing economy. But this broad participation has morphed into a system that has accelerated inequality. Since the triumph of conservatism and the presidency of Ronald Reagan the country has transitioned from the "era of the middle class" to an "era of the wealthy class." Understanding the consequences of this transformation is central to understanding the declining opportunity for children of the poor, working, and middle classes.

2

Growing Inequality: From the "Era of the Middle Class" to the "Era of the Wealthy Class"

> In 2005, the top 4 percent of tax filers reported more income than the bottom two-thirds.
>
> Internal Revenue Service

> "The test of our progress," said Franklin Roosevelt, "is not whether we add more to the abundance of those who have too much; it is whether we provide enough for those who have too little." It is by that great test that we must measure our progress in the years ahead.
>
> John F. Kennedy, 1960 [1]

One of America's great achievements has been the development of a broad middle class that has allowed the majority of citizens in our free enterprise democracy to participate in the fruits of the nation's economic abundance. Most Americans refer to themselves as middle class. In a 1992 CBS poll, 75 percent of those surveyed called themselves middle class. And so the idea of the middle class as well as its reality are central to an understanding of America itself and particularly, America's treatment of those who fall within and outside the definition—those who live in the hinterland between the middle class and poverty.

A society can be judged by the degree to which it serves the majority of its members. We do not gauge the wealth of America solely by the achievements of the very rich. These achievements are important, but the central measure of how well our society is performing is how well the broad majority in the middle are doing. America saw the emergence of an affluent middle class after World War II. The growth of the middle class was largely propelled by the public policies and programs that encouraged home ownership and higher education. The major public program in this regard was the GI Bill. It provided substantial funds for returning veterans to pursue a college education.[2] In addition, the GI Bill provided for low-cost loans and assistance in purchasing a first home.

The emergence of the affluent middle class coincided with and contributed to spectacular economic growth. After World War II, the United States was the economic engine of the world. Its factories accounted for 52 percent of the world's industrial output. The middle class saw their income double during the 25-year period after World War II. At no other time in history had the economic fortunes of the broad middle class experienced such growth and good fortune.

What facilitated and sustained the emergence of the affluent middle class were economic policies that encouraged the middle class to work hard, save, and invest. The rise in home ownership during this period was spectacular, and the investment in education during this period was high.

Not only was the quarter century after World War II a time of prosperity for the middle class, it was also a time of economic advancement for the poor. The nation was moving quickly to end poverty. Toward the end of the second decade, President Johnson declared war on the remnants of poverty and set about to develop government programs to end poverty.

Unfortunately, just as the metaphorical War on Poverty was beginning, President Johnson became embroiled in a real war in Vietnam. This war was televised and provided daily glimpses onto the battlefield where American soldiers and Vietnamese citizens were being killed. The horror and pain of that war and the divided view of Americans toward it sidetracked the other war on poverty.

The decades of optimism and hope largely came to an end with the debate and conflict over the Vietnam War. During the seventies America backed away from the excesses of the sixties. However, the decade of the eighties represented a new direction for the country that no longer focused on fighting poverty but turned its eyes on unleashing the capitalist economic

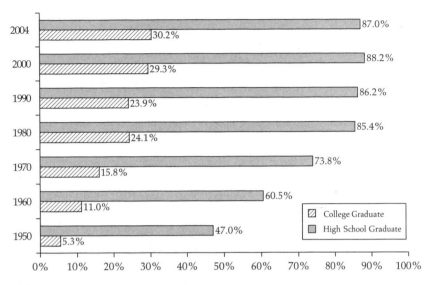

Figure 2.1 High School and College Graduates Among 25- to 34-Year-Olds in the United States

equality, a prevailing optimism, and sense of social responsibility continued into the sixties. As America entered the sixties the election of a young president endowed with a vast store of charisma gave the impression of a youthful dynamism in government. Kennedy seemed to believe that government, in concert with the actions of the electorate, could actually create a better world that would end poverty, particularly among Black children.[3]

Extending Opportunity to All: The Civil Rights Movement

I am not satisfied until every American enjoys his full constitutional rights. If a Negro baby is born, and this is also true for Puerto Rican and Mexicans in some of our cities, he has about 1/2 as much chance to get through high school as a white baby. He has about 1/3 as much chance to get through college as a white student. He has about 1/3 as much chance to be a professional man. About 1/2 as much chance to own a house. He has about 4 times as much chance that he will be out of work in his life as the white baby. I think we can do better. I don't want the talents of any American to go to waste.

John F. Kennedy, Presidential Debate

Once Lee Harvey Oswald's bullet cut short the life of the young president, his legacy of reform was handed off to a powerful legislative leader from

Texas, Lyndon Baines Johnson. Johnson's vision was one of a government working to solve social problems.[4] Whereas, Kennedy had promised a "New Frontier," Johnson proposed a "Great Society." Both presidents shared a commitment to civil rights. President Johnson orchestrated the enactment of the Civil Rights Act and sought to end destitution in America. In March 1964, with the declaration of a War on Poverty, he set into motion the programs of his Great Society. Within the next year, Johnson signed into law the Equal Opportunity Act, the Elementary and Secondary Education Act, the Medicare Act, the Voting Rights Act, plus programs such as Head Start and Legal Aid.

The Civil Rights movement emerged in the middle of the 1950s. Rosa Parks refused to give up her seat to a White man and move to the back of the bus. She was arrested, and her arrest led the Montgomery Improvement Association to begin a boycott of the bus company. Out of this protest emerged a powerful champion for civil rights—Dr. Martin Luther King. The new television media brought images of the mistreatment of Blacks into homes across the nation. Later in 1960, students organized a sit-in at the Woolworth lunch counter in Greensboro, North Carolina. Freedom rides on interstate buses were organized. The civil rights movement fundamentally changed the way Blacks were treated in the South and throughout America. In 1964, 23 percent of Blacks were registered to vote. The Voting Rights Act was passed in August of 1965. By 1969, 61 percent of voting age Blacks were registered to vote.

Along with his leadership on civil rights, President Johnson also embarked on a War on Poverty. However, as his major assault on poverty was getting underway, a literal war half a world away began to engage his attention and the result was that his War on Poverty faded into the background.

As a result of the bitter feelings that the war in Vietnam inspired, it was foreign policy that occupied the minds of voters in 1968. Richard Nixon, a Republican, was elected to the White House in 1968 on the campaign promise that he had a secret way to end the war.[5] Nixon, who had served as vice president during the economic boom of the fifties, may not have actually ended the war in Vietnam, but there is no doubt that he did end the War on Poverty programs and began to dismantle Johnson's Great Society agenda. Throughout the seventies, the federal government shifted away from Democratic leadership and policies to Republican management and stewardship. The public also grew increasingly disillusioned by some of the excesses of the sixties—the counter culture movement. The extreme versions of the antiwar movement, radical politics of groups such as the Black Panthers, and a sense the loosened mores of "Hippies" who accepted illegal drugs and casual sex seemed out of step with and potentially dangerous to middle class values.

It is fair to say that the Nixon era did not produce fundamental change in the economic landscape of America. Nixon often adopted policies antithetical to traditional conservative economists.[6] He proposed a negative income tax that would have assured a minimum income to every citizen in the United States. This approach, although viable then, would today be considered beyond the pale of reasonable public policy regardless of its merits.

Nixon's presidency ended abruptly when operatives of the Republican Party bungled a break-in into the national headquarters of the Democratic Party. Efforts to conceal the connection between the White House, the Watergate burglars, and the subsequent covering up of their illegal actions led to an unraveling of Nixon's administration. The impeachment proceedings and his eventual resignation obscured almost everything else about Nixon's presidency.

Although it is difficult to pinpoint precisely the exact moment when the fortunes of the affluent middle class began to recede, many will argue that the descent began during the administration of Nixon's successor, Gerald Ford. Shortly after being sworn in during the summer of 1974, Ford proposed tax cuts for the wealthy, limited social spending and high defense expenditures and increased taxes upon imported oil.[7] The Democratic Congress opposed many elements of Ford's programs, but the President repeatedly employed the power of the veto.

Gerald Ford lost the election bid in 1976 to Jimmy Carter, the Democratic former Governor of Georgia.[8] Thus, the fall of Nixon was complete. This moment has been widely interpreted as the beginning of the ascendancy of modern Republican Conservatism. Carter's victory occurred while America brimmed with patriotic pride as it celebrated the bicentennial anniversary of the signing of the Declaration of Independence. Carter hearkened back to Harry Truman, appearing as a man of the people, an image he took pains to reinforce. His earthy public image contrasted with the pomp usually associated with the presidency. Informal in dress and speech, he often spoke informally at his frequent press conferences. Carter's ambitious programs for social, administrative, and economic reform met with significant opposition within the Congress, despite Democratic majorities in both the House and the Senate. By 1978 Carter's initial popularity had dissipated in the face of his inability to convert his ideas into legislative realities, and his management of the economy was arousing widespread concern. The inflation rate had been climbing each year since he had taken office: rising from 6 percent in 1976 to more than 13.5 percent by 1980. The prime interest rate for banks reached a high of 21.5 percent; unemployment reached 7.1 percent in 1980.[9]

The campaign theme of Ronald Reagan, "Are you better off now than you were four years ago?" resonated with broad public discontent.

Ronald Reagan popularized the so-called misery index that had been developed by economist Robert Garro. This measure simply added the inflation and unemployment rates to indicate they had reached historic peaks during Carter's administration.

In addition, Carter's foreign policy suffered as the Soviet Union invaded Afghanistan. But the coup de grâce came with the taking of American hostages by radical fundamentalist revolutionaries in Iran. The ticking of the hostage clock distracted from the major successes of the Camp David Accords that brought peace between Israel and Egypt.

By the presidential election of 1980, the American people had lost confidence in President Carter and he was soundly defeated by the Republican nominee, Ronald Reagan.[10]

The Triumph of Conservatism and the Era of the Wealthy Class

With Gerald Ford's loss to Jimmy Carter in the Presidential campaign of 1976, the Conservative wing of the GOP decided that they had had enough of the moderates within their party. Harboring a discontentment with government hearkening back to the 1930s, they had long regarded the policies of the moderates as a compromise of party principles and even betrayal.[11] Not unlike the Roosevelt Democrats who had forsaken America's blue-blooded upper class in favor of common people, the moderates were viewed as snakes in the bosom. The downward distribution of wealth arising from public policies set in place in the thirties had irked and enraged Conservatives for nearly 50 years. Dwight Eisenhower, who presided over the greatest expansion of the middle class in American history, had done nothing to assuage them; nor did Richard Nixon who had done little to reverse the trend placate them.[12]

Upon Ford's defeat, the Conservatives turned to the man who had been their first choice in 1976, Ronald Wilson Reagan. The former actor turned politician successfully served as governor of California, expressing a philosophy of government between 1976 and 1980 that made him the clear choice for a majority of Republicans. With Carter floundering in the maelstrom of the Iran Hostage Crisis, the American people turned away from the unfulfilled promise of enlightened government to the uncomplicated and easily understood pledge of smaller, less intrusive government. The New Right, as Barbara Ehrenreich has pointed out, promoted itself as "the ally of the 'little guy,' the Middle American, even the blue-collar worker, against the cynical manipulations of the 'liberal establishment.' "[13]

"Government is not the solution to the problem," Reagan said in his first inaugural address, "Government is the problem." At the end of the Carter administration and the decade of the seventies, America entered a new era of the wealthy. The country was embarking on a major economic transformation from a nation with a broad middle class and wide economic participation to a land of a powerful ownership class that had concentrated wealth at the top. The middle class increasingly finds itself on the outside looking in at the continued economic growth and the owners who prosper from the growth of the American economy. In the earlier era of the middle class, the broad population benefited from the growth of the American economy. The middle class saw its fortunes coincide with the growing prosperity of the nation. However, tax policies and increasing federal debt have resulted in a cutting of the tether that bound the middle class to the nation's economic prosperity.

At the dawn of the 1980s, the self-styled cowboy nicknamed Dutch won soundly enough to act decisively—he had a mandate to bring about major change in America.[14] The new president moved swiftly and decisively to enact the fundamental changes in tax policy that would shape the economic future of the nation for decades. President Reagan developed bold new tax policies for the nation, and challenged the trade unions, which he saw as an impediment to his economic reforms. In September 1981, when the nation's air traffic controllers (who were federal employees) went on strike, Reagan fired every one of them—all 11,359. Despite the enormous safety risk this posed to the traveling public, the Conservative Republicans rallied around the new president, praising him for his bold and decisive action. They were particularly pleased that Reagan stood up to the union and, in the final analysis, ruptured the spirit of the union movement in America.

Tax Policies

In the vast arena of tax policy, the centerpiece of the Reagan administration was supply-side economics. This economic theory stresses the idea that supply creates its own demand and that the incentive to individual investors matters more to the economy than equitable distribution of wealth. Reagan believed that the wealthy were being taxed too much and that this was harming their ability to accumulate wealth. He believed it was the fortunes of the wealthy which fueled economic growth and prosperity for all. Accordingly, barriers to the building of wealth and the amassing of great fortunes had to be removed, particularly with respect to taxes.

The Laffer Curve

The center piece of Reaganomics was the reduction of the tax burden on the wealthy. Cutting the top marginal tax rates had long been a goal of Conservatives, and President Reagan was squarely behind this objective.[15] Under his Economic Recovery Tax Act (1981), the top personal tax bracket would drop from 70 percent to 50 percent. The capital gains tax was decreased from 28 to 20 percent. Reagan also cut spending on domestic programs by over US$140 billion, continuing the dismantling of the Great Society and War on Poverty programs. Reagan declared, "We conducted a war on poverty, and poverty won." At the same time, President Reagan embarked on major new spending for the military, increasing defense spending by US$181 billion.

The main thrust of Reagan's legislative effort was to reform the tax code. In this effort, he drew upon the work of Dr. Arthur Laffer. The Laffer Curve, which was supposedly first sketched on a cocktail napkin at a Washington restaurant, suggests that although increasing taxes will increase tax revenues, as tax rates continue to rise, there will come a point where the burden is so onerous that it outweighs the benefits of work. This lack of incentive leads to a fall in income overall and therefore a fall in tax revenue. The logical endpoint in Laffer's view is that once tax rates reach 100 percent no one will bother to work at all as tax revenue plummets to nothing and the government goes broke. Conversely, according to Laffer's theory, if taxes were to be decreased, tax revenues will eventually rise, inspired by the desire to bring home a greater share of their paychecks, and people work harder to earn more.[16] As tax rates are lowered, individuals produce more, and thus generate greater economic activity. In the final analysis, tax cuts rather counter intuitively lead to even greater total revenue collected. Even though the tax rate is lower, the base the tax is applied to will be so much larger that the net result will be more revenue collected. Eventually, the government collects, the theory suggests, more revenue with a lower rate applied to a larger base.

Laffer's curve fails, however, in one major respect. It neglects to consider the impact of tax policy on the equitable distribution of income and wealth in society. Tax policies are largely responsible for the long-term shape of the distribution of wealth and income. A progressive tax policy assures the equitable distribution of income and wealth (it moves the area under the curve, indicating accumulated wealth, in Figure 2.2 up vertically). A neutral tax policy is, in effect, a regressive tax policy because of the inherent nature of the private enterprise economy to accelerate the shift of wealth toward the top end.[17]

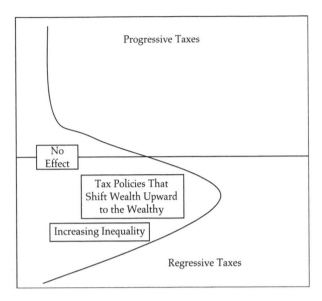

Figure 2.2 Regressive Taxes—Impact of Tax Policies on the Distribution of Wealth: Regressive Taxes Shift Wealth Upward Above the Median

Collecting Revenue

The distribution of wealth and income shift in ever increasing proportion to those who have saved or invested and accumulated wealth, even though the accumulation of capital is, as, Adam Smith pointed out, to the advantage of everyone.[18] The capital the wealthy accumulate is invested and reinvested in the plants and machinery necessary to drive the economy. However, the economy relies on wise and careful investment of wealth, so the individuals who put their precious capital at risk are disproportionately rewarded as their capital grows both returning their investment through earnings and dividends. Their continued success leads to an even greater acceleration of advantage.

Monopoly Effect

There is also the fact that wealth, like debt, is self-replicating. Compound interest turns wealth into more wealth and debt into more debt. Other things being equal, those with interest bearing savings accounts will end up richer after the year, and those who must pay interest on credit card or consumer household debt will end up poorer.

Ray Boshara, The $6,000 Solution[19]

It is important to save and invest. Money accumulated through savings and investment becomes working capital. While it is invested or saved, it can earn more money and grow. Money that is safely and wisely invested can grow substantially faster than inflation, and thus, it grows ever larger. Once a substantial capital base is assembled, it can be used to both produce income and to grow the capital. Individuals with substantial capital usually concentrate on growing the size of their accumulated capital. The more capital an individual has, the greater their ability to accumulate more; the more they accumulate, the faster their share of the wealth grows. However, as their wealth grows, so does the amount of tax they have to pay. Before the major tax reforms were proposed and signed into law by President Reagan, the wealthy were subject to a progressive tax system that meant they paid a higher rate of tax on their accumulating wealth. The effect of the progressive tax system was not only to make sure that those who were able to pay the most paid the most, but to dampen the accelerating advantage that accrues to wealthy owners of large (capital) fortunes. By essentially removing the progressive tax system, President Reagan shifted the tax burden off the wealthy. But if the wealthy did not pay as much tax as before, how is the difference made up? The explanation offered by President Reagan was the Laffer Curve. That is, as the wealthy paid lower taxes—substantially lower taxes—they would save and invest more, and thus the size of their wealth would increase and provide an even larger tax base which, when taxed at a lower rate, would still provide as much money for the government.

Of course, if the accelerating advantage that accrues to the accumulation of wealth were allowed to continue unregulated, eventually a highly skewed distribution of wealth would occur.[20] A few would be in possession of a larger portion of the wealth, whereas most would have very little. Just as in the game of *Monopoly,* even though all players start with the same amount of money, eventually one player takes advantage of his accumulated real estate wealth and gradually garners a greater and greater share of the game's resources. The game ends when no one else has any money left and everything is in the hands of one person.

Tax Policy and the Middle Class

Every time people try to punish the rich, the rich don't simply comply, they react. They have the money, power and intent to change things. They do not just sit there and voluntarily pay more taxes. They search for ways to minimize their tax burden. They hire smart attorneys and accountants, and persuade politicians to change laws or create legal loopholes. They have the resources to effect change. . . . The poor and

the middle class do not have the same resources. They sit there and let the government's needles enter their arm and allow the blood donation to begin.

Robert T. Kiyosaki, *Rich Dad, Poor Dad*[21]

The effects of the tax policy under Ronald Reagan have had a profound
impact on the middle class. Reagan, it seems clear from hindsight, operated upon the premise that what was good for the wealthy was good for
everyone. In fact, it has become increasingly obvious that the economy
relies on a robust and prosperous middle class. Tax policy needs to be developed to insure that the average person can benefit from overall economic
and productivity growth and thereby look forward to an improved situation.
Reagan's tax policy resulted in essentially restricting the accumulation of
wealth to the top wealth holders and resulted in the greatest imbalances and
disparities in the distribution of wealth and income that Americans have
ever witnessed. This imbalance has gradually eroded the middle class.

In 2004, the top 10 percent of families owned more than 71 percent of the
privately held wealth in America, whereas the bottom 40 percent of families
had virtually nothing, the middle 60 percent of families (or what is often
defined as the middle class) owned less than one-fifth of all the wealth.

In 1986, with the help of liberal democrats Richard Gephardt and Bill
Bradley, Reagan passed the Tax Reform Act of 1986, which for the first time
in history lowered the top tax rates and increased the lowest rate. The top
tax rate went from 50 percent to 28 percent, whereas the bottom rate was
increased to 15 percent from 11 percent.

The shape of the distribution of wealth depicted in Table 2.1 is dynamic
and changing. Over the last two decades, wealth has been channeled to the
top. In 1979, the top 1 percent owned 20.5 percent of the nation's private

Table 2.1 Distribution of Wealth in the
United States, 1998 and 2004

	1998[22] (%)	2004[23] (%)
Top 1 percent	33	34
Next 4 percent		25
Next 5 percent		12
Next 10 percent		13
Next 19 percent	50	
Top 20 percent	83	84.7
Bottom 80 percent	18	15.3
Bottom 60 percent		3.7

Data Source: Domhoff, 2006, Rose (2007).

Note: Column totals do not equal 100 because of rounding.

wealth, but by 2004 they increased their share to 34 percent.[24] In 1995, 95 percent of the top 1 percent of households were White, whereas 1 percent of this group was African American.[25] The family median net worth for Whites in 2004 was US$140,700, whereas family median net worth for Latino households was US$18,600 and US$20,600 for Blacks.[26]

The poor have seen their economic circumstances decline, but since they had so little to lose, their losses, although personally devastating, are insignificant to the larger picture. The tax policies justified by the Laffer Curve improved the advantage of the wealthy at the expense of the middle class. There has been little empirical evidence that the middle class saw any economic benefit as a result of "Laffer-justified" tax cuts which went primarily to the wealthy. Rather, the economic situation of the middle class has remained stagnant even though there are more two-income families and the overall economy continues to grow. The only families to experience substantial improvement during the eighties and nineties were families with substantial wealth. The result was that by 2004, as seen in Figure 2.3, the top 20 percent of households owned 84.7 percent of all the privately owned wealth.

Reagan's Economic Recovery Tax Act reduced the top individual tax rate from 70 percent to 50 percent. After his election to a second term, Reagan signed the Tax Reform Act of 1986, which reduced the top marginal tax rate from 50 percent to 28 percent. Although the income tax rates were being dramatically cut for the highest-income individuals (see Table 2.2), the employment tax (including Social Security tax and Medicare tax), which falls heaviest on the middle class, more than doubled since 1980. Everyone who works pays the employment tax (which is 12.4%). The Social Security tax is capped at US$102,000 in 2008. Thus, all earnings above US$102,000 in 2008 are free of the 12.4% employment tax. Removing the cap on employment tax would have had a direct benefit

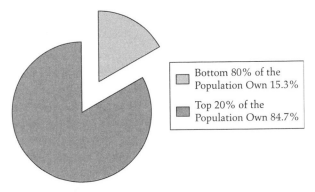

Bottom 80% of the
Population Own 15.3%

Top 20% of the
Population Own 84.7%

Figure 2.3 Distribution of Wealth in the United States, 1998 and 2004

Table 2.2 Changes in Tax Policy Since 1980

Tax		Change
Impact on Wealthy		
Income tax	Cut on top rate primarily benefits wealthy	Top rate reduced from 70% to 28%
Estate tax	Cuts here benefits wealthy	Substantially reduced with proposed elimination
Dividend tax	Cuts here benefits wealthy	Substantially reduced
Capital gains tax	Cuts here benefits wealthy	Substantially reduced
How were theses tax cuts paid for?		
Impact on the Middle Class and Poor		
Medicare tax	Cuts here benefit middle class and poor	Taxes increased
Employment tax	Cuts here benefit middle class and poor	Taxes increased
Excise tax	Cuts here benefit middle class and poor	Taxes increased
Earned income tax credit	This tax credit primarily benefits working poor	New tax credit

for the middle- and low-income earners, by allowing a much lower employment tax rate. Ironically, it is the Social Security tax, which derived from the Social Security Act developed and signed into law by Franklin Delano Roosevelt as progressive legislation to end poverty, that has become over time the major tax paid by the poor and the middle class and, in a very real sense, the tax bludgeon on their economic opportunities. The "cap" on the Social Security tax essentially exempted the wealthy from paying for a proportional share of the nation's major social transfer program.

Employment taxes are paid by all but fall most heavily on the middle class because the cap on payments only benefits those with high income. In 1960, employment taxes were roughly one-fourth of individual income taxes. By 2005, employment taxes were equal to more than 70 percent of individual income taxes.[27] As seen in Table 2.3, employment taxes represent the major tax burden for low and middle income families. In 2005, 60 percent of all income tax filers reported income below US$50,000. For this group, employment taxes were about 2.5 times larger than their income tax liability. For those reporting income less than US$100,000 a year, the amount of employment tax paid was greater than the amount of income tax. In contrast, for the highest income group, the amount of employment tax paid represented about 15 percent of their overall income tax liability.

Table 2.3 Employment Tax and Individual Income Tax (2005)

	Under US$50,000	US$50,000–75,000	US$75,000–100,000	US$100,000–200,000	US$200,000+
Income*	1,797,097,083,000	1,119,634,632,000	905,336,768,000	1,429,575,727,000	2,112,995,921,000
Income tax	105,786,470,000	99,360,874,000	92,573,567,000	200,393,602,000	491,076,838,000
Effective income tax rate (%)	5.9	8.9	10.2	14.0	23.2
Employment tax	258,163,775,560	150,136,834,928	132,161,185,820	156,625,980,065	74,158,947,903
Effective employment tax rate (%)	14.4	13.4	14.6	10.8	3.5
Number of filers	112,894,109	29,550,574	18,795,652	19,991,679	6,633,282
Percentage of filers	60.1	15.7	10.0	10.6	3.5

Source: Internal Revenue Service, 2007. Employment taxes extrapolated from reported data.[28] Joint return is treated as two filers.

*Adjusted gross income.

Note: The bottom 60 percent of taxpayers paid an effective employment tax rate more than four times higher than the top 3.5 percent.

As mentioned earlier, although individual income tax rates, dividend tax rates, and capital gains tax rates have been reduced during the last three decades, employment tax rates have been increased. For middle-income families, the employment tax has become their greatest tax burden. For the bottom half of tax filers, employment tax accounts for about 2.5 times the tax burden of individual income taxes. For high-income earners, employment tax represents only a small fraction (0.15) of their tax burden relative to individual income taxes. In fact, the highest-income earners pay employment taxes at a rate less than one-fourth of what the lowest-income earners pay. This is a result, of course, of the cap on employment taxes that provides substantial relief to the top 6 percent of income earners in the United States who have income above the cap.

Shifting the Tax Burden From the Wealthy to the Middle Class

In 1960, total individual income taxes were US$45 billion, whereas the total employment taxes collected were US$11.2 billion (see Table 2.4). By 2005, total individual income taxes were US$989 billion, and the total employment taxes collected were US$771 billion. In 1960, for every dollar collected in employment tax, four dollars was collected in individual income tax. By 2005, employment taxes had dramatically increased relative to income tax. In 2005, for every dollar collected in employment tax, 1 dollar and 28 cents was collected in individual income tax. This represented a fundamental shift of the tax burden onto employment tax. In fact, the surplus employment tax was not "placed in a locked box" to protect Social Security income for future generations. Rather, it provided much of the borrowed funding needed to cover the ballooning federal debt.

Over the last several decades, the top capital gains tax rate has been reduced from 38 percent in 1978 to 15 percent in 2008. The reduction in the capital gains tax rate has provided substantial benefit to those with high

Table 2.4 Top Tax Rates

	Employment Tax Rate (%)	Individual Income Tax Rate (%)
1960	6.0	91
1970	9.6	73
1980	12.3	70
1990	15.3	28

Table 2.5 Income From Capital Gains and Percentage Received by Income Group

	Income from Capital Gains	Percentage of Total Capital Gains Income Received	Percentage of Filers
Under US$50,000	22,111,031,000	4	60.1
US$50,000–75,000	13,874,190,000	2	15.7
US$75,000–100,000	16,600,952,000	3	10
US$100,000–200,000	57,479,241,000	9	10.6
US$200,000+	515,640,106,000	82	3.5

Source: Internal Revenue Service, 2007.

income. As seen in Table 2.5, the capital gains tax cut has concentrated the great benefits from recent tax cuts to those with the highest income.

More than 80 percent of capital gains income went to the top income group, those with income greater than US$200,000 a year (Table 2.5). The capital gains tax rate provides those with the highest income the most favorable tax treatment. In 2005, the highest-income groups paid most of the individual income tax. Those with income above US$200,000 a year represented 3.5 percent of all income reporters. Yet as seen in Table 2.5, this small group paid almost half of all individual income taxes (49.6 percent). The top 3.5 percent pay almost half the taxes because they receive such a large share of the income. The average net income tax liability for this group was 23.2 percent. In contrast, the bottom 60 percent of those reporting income received less than US$50,000 a year. The average net individual income tax liability for this group was 5.9 percent in 2005.

When employment taxes are considered the tax story is very different. The bottom 60 percent pay an effective employment tax rate of 14.4 percent. The top 3.5 percent of tax filers with annual earnings above US$200,000 a year paid an effective employment tax rate of 3.5 percent (Table 2.6). Employment taxes represented more than 71 percent of the tax liability of the bottom 60 percent of tax filers, but only 15 percent of the total tax liability of top income earners.

The reduction in the individual income tax rate for middle-income families has had a relatively minor impact on their overall tax liability because their main tax liability is the employment tax. In contrast, the reduction in the top capital gains tax rate primarily benefited the top income earners.[30] The top 3.5 percent of tax payers received more than 80 percent of capital gains income and thus received more than 80 percent of the benefit of the capital gains reduction.

Table 2.6 Source of Income and Effective Tax Rates for High- and Middle-Income Groups, 2005

	Top 3.5% of Taxpayers (US$200,000 or More)	Bottom 60% of Taxpayers (Under US$50,000)
Total income (US$)	2,112,995,921,000	1,797,097,083,000
Sources of income		
Salaries and wages (US$)	919,655,038,000	1,541,276,272,000
Capital gains (US$)	515,640,106,000	22,111,031,000
Dividends (US$)	90,202,431,000	23,867,893,000
Effective individual income tax rate	23.2%	5.9%
Effective employment tax rate	3.5%	14.4%
Number of filers	6,633,282	112,894,109

Source: Internal Revenue Service, 2007.[29]

During the last 25 years, tax policies have allowed the top income earners to keep and invest more of their earnings and to build their asset base. In contrast, the employment tax rate has steadily climbed and reduced the ability of the middle class and the poor to save and invest. As a result, the asset base of top income earners has steadily increased and allowed this group to accumulate both a greater share of the nation's wealth and overall income. Just as the mortgage deduction encouraged capital accumulation among the middle class through home ownership, the substantial reductions in the capital gains and dividend income tax rates have allowed those with capital to retain more of their earnings for further investment and capital accumulation. Over time, this process has led to an increased portion of wealth and income going to the top wealth holders and a substantial increase in inequality of both wealth and income in the United States.

Advocates of tax cuts for the wealthy have been less willing to support equitable tax treatment for the middle and working class. The *Wall Street Journal* editorial page has argued that lifting the cap [on employment taxes] "would be socking it to taxpayers who already bear an outsized share of the American tax burden." The *Journal* points to a recent study of federal tax filings that show that the top quintile (top 20%) paid more than two-thirds of all federal taxes in 1999, whereas the bottom quintile paid less than 1 percent. But this editorial does not take into account the very employment tax that is at issue. It would be more balanced to suggest that the current approach provides the wealthiest families with most favorable treatment with regard to the employment tax by exempting them from liability with a cap that only the wealthiest benefit from while also providing most favorable treatment to capital gains by taxing this source of income at the lowest rate. This income source is concentrated among the top earners.

The individual working at a low-wage service job pays a much higher employment tax rate than the wealthy financier on gains from selling stock. As Warren Buffett has pointed out, his secretary pays a higher tax rate than he does even though he earns hundreds of times more.[31]

Paying for Tax Cuts

The tax cuts did not pay for themselves as the Laffer Curve argument had proposed. Instead, the federal government failed to collect enough revenue to cover its expenditures. The result has been to put the growing annual deficit into the federal debt and leave responsibility to pay this debt to future generations (see Figure 2.4). As of June 2008, the federal debt was more than US$9.5 trillion, which translates to more than US$80,000 for each taxpayer. As Thomas Palley observed, "The wealthy were given a massive tax cut that enabled them to buy the government debt needed to fund the deficit created by the tax cut.... Though not normally talked about in such terms, the Reagan-Bush budgetary and interest rate policies effectively set in place a process for recycling middle-class tax payments into the pockets of the wealthy because ownership of bonds is massively concentrated among

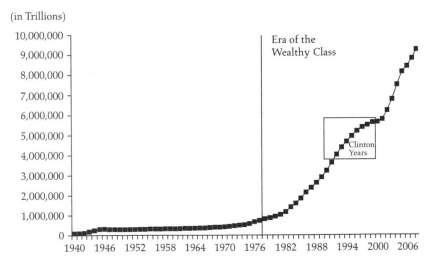

Figure 2.4 Federal Debt from 1940 to 2008

Source: U.S. Department of the Treasury, 2008.[33]

the wealthy... the top 10% [of wealthiest households] own 90.3 percent of bonds."[32]

An additional consequence of the debt is to constrain the opportunities to develop new programs to end poverty and inequality. Furthermore, this debt is viewed by some economists as constricting the seed bed for economic growth in the United States: a condition that creates an opening for the rise of economic competitors not just in Europe but also in the developing nations of India and China.

The Federal Debt

> We don't have a trillion-dollar debt because we haven't taxed enough; we have a trillion dollar debt because we spend too much.
>
> President Reagan, March 28, 1982[34]

> Tax cuts don't need to be paid for [with offsets]—they pay for themselves.
>
> Jim Nussle, Chairman, House Budget Committee[35]

The gross federal debt continued to grow throughout the Reagan presidency. The ever growing deficit and the cumulative federal debt inspired a third party candidate to run in the presidential election of 1992. Ross Perot made the swelling federal debt the center piece of his campaign. "Lift the hood," urged Perot, "and you will see that we have a serious problem."

The United States has the largest number of extremely wealthy individuals, but it also has the largest national debt in the world by several magnitudes.[36] The United States is the world's largest debtor nation. Although a substantial portion of the debt is owned by U.S. citizens, most of the debt is held by other countries. The United States is now reliant on other nations to continue buying its debt. This large debt is fundamentally a burden—a negative legacy left by those who accumulated it through deficit spending to the next generation—our children. This growing debt is expected to exceed 10 trillion dollars by the end of the George W. Bush presidency.

Redistribution of Wealth Creation: Capital Versus Labor

> Deeper forces are at work, among them the introduction of labor-saving technologies that have benefited the owners of capital at the expense of workers; the downward pressure that globalization has exerted on wages; and changes that have made the tax code less progressive and more friendly to the better-off..
>
> Ray Boshara, The $6,000 Solution[37]

The logic of the capital gains tax cut is problematic. A person who earns income from hourly wages at a low-paid service job (Wal-Mart, Motel 6, Dunkin Donuts) pays up to 30 percent of his or her earnings in federal income tax and employment tax. However, income derived from profits on the sale of stocks or other capital gains is taxed at a rate of 15 percent.[38] Thus income derived from actual labor garners less protection from taxes than capital gains. The majority of the middle class depends upon wages as their main source of income. Those with incomes of US$100,000 or less receive 4 percent of their income from capital gains and dividends, whereas those with income over 1 million receive 37.6 percent of their income from this source. Leonard Burman of the Urban Institute estimated that in 2000, more than half of all stock dividends went to the top 1 percent of families.[39]

The tax reductions achieved since the Reagan presidency did not stimulate the economic growth of the middle class. Relative to the wealthiest Americans, the middle class has lost ground. In 1980, individual income tax provided 55.4 percent of federal revenue, whereas employment taxes (Social Security and Medicare) accounted for 24.7 percent of revenue. By 2004, although income taxes from individuals had declined to 43.9 percent of total federal revenue, employment tax had increased to 41 percent.

The Reagan Legacy

During the 1980s the United States experienced a particularly massive growth and concentration of wealth. Between 1977 and 1989, the wealthiest 5% of U.S. families captured 74% of all after-tax income.

William D. Zabel[40]

The nine most frightening words in the English language are: "I'm from the government and I'm here to help."

Ronald Reagan

Many Americans view Ronald Reagan as the greatest president of the twentieth century. He won the Cold War at last defeating the Communist menace. He elevated the Conservative wing of the Republican Party to almost celestial status, and he set a course for domestic economic policy that would alter the lives of generations to come. Above all, Ronald Reagan is lauded as the Great Communicator.[41]

Reagan had an undeniable capacity for influencing, persuading, convincing, and cajoling the American public into accepting his vision of how things should be—to them he was a visionary who knew what was best and right for America. His legion of committed followers were so devoted to his expressed idealism, values, and personal moral compass that they were possessed with an almost evangelical zeal in support of his policies. None of the negative opinions from the media or academia seemed to have tarnished his pristine armor, thus his was the Teflon presidency, as most criticisms seemed to slip off. Criticism of the Reagan presidency was not only futile, but to many, downright heretical. Yet a close examination of the economic record of his presidency and the continuing effects of his policies reveal that it was a time of reversal of fortunes for the middle class and the poor.

By the end of the Reagan presidency, the richest 1 percent of America owned 35 percent of the wealth—the greatest level of inequality among all rich nations. Only in the Roaring Twenties had the United States experienced such a discrepancy in wealth. Furthermore, the richest 20 percent owned 80 percent of America—meaning, of course, that the bottom four-fifths of all Americans owned less than one-fifth. The underlying cause for the growing inequality is, however, quite simple. It takes money to make money—and those who have the money have had the power to promote tax policies and programs that favor their own interests at the expense of the interests of the rest of the nation's citizens.

At this juncture, it is important to underscore the point that the tax policies of the Reagan era have continued for years beyond Ronald Reagan's actual presidency.

In 1992, corporations formed 67 percent of all Political Action Committees (PACs), and contributed 79 percent of all donations to political parties. Studies have shown a high correlation between PAC donations and the laws that benefit the donors. Although the right to petition Congress is a constitutional one, citizens without donations are rarely granted access to their representatives, and most Americans will never attend a US$10,000 a plate dinner. It has become increasingly obvious to Americans that it is often dollars rather than votes that make the difference.

Although the first quarter of a century after World War II saw the rise of the middle class (1950 to 1975), the next three decades (1975 to 2005) saw the rise of the wealthy ownership class and the concomitant decline of the middle class.

Measuring Inequality: The Gini Coefficient

The historical shift of wealth upward during the era of the wealthy can be seen vividly in the main statistical indicator economists use to measure inequality—the Gini coefficient. The Gini coefficient is the most widely used and highly regarded measure of inequality between income groups. As can be seen in Figure 2.5, the Gini coefficient declined from the end of World War II (1947) relative to 1968. Beginning in the decade of the seventies, economic inequality began increasing and then rose sharply in the 1980s and 1990s. The Gini coefficient provides a compelling portrait of the increasing inequality created by the tax policies and programs developed and passed into law by the Reagan administration.

The consequence of inequality is that the majority of families have been left out of the great economic growth of the last several decades.

These numbers translate into a growing gap between the median and mean income. The median income is the income of the family in the middle of the income scale. Half of the population earns more and half earns less. The mean income is the sum of all family income divided by the number of families. In 1950, the difference between the mean and median family income was US$515 (inflation adjusted). In 1980 it was US$2951 but by 2001 it had increased to US$15,456. In 1950, the difference between median and mean income was 15 percent. But by 2001 it had increased to 30 percent. This represents a substantial relative decline of the middle class that corresponds to the rising inequality signaled by the Gini coefficient. The most compelling evidence, however, comes from comparing median income with disposable personal income during this period (Figure 2.6).

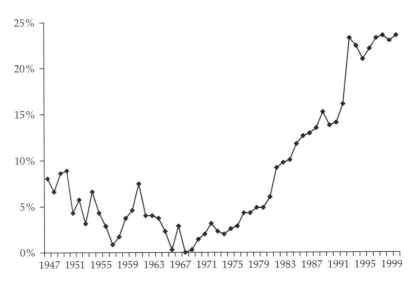

Figure 2.5 Change in Family Income Inequality, 1947 to 2000. Percentage of Change in Gini Index vs. 1968

Source: www.census.gov/hhes/income/histinc/f04.html

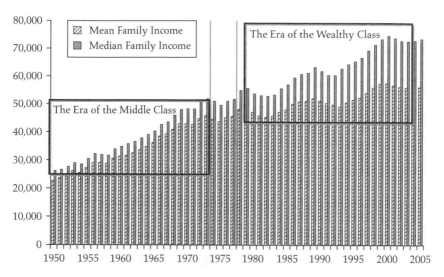

Figure 2.6 Median and Mean Family Income, 1950 to 2005

Source: U.S. Census Bureau, 2007.[42]

In the quarter century between 1954 and 1979, the median income in the United States, (adjusted for inflation) increased more than 90 percent. The growing productivity of the nation was reflected in the growth of disposable personal income. During this same period, disposable personal income (i.e., the total income left over after income taxes and social security taxes had been taken out) increased 81.9 percent on a per capita basis. The years after World War II were ones where the income of all Americans grew in proportion to that of the nation itself. Growth in disposable personal income paralleled growth in the median family income.

> Working families have seen little if any progress over the past 30 years. Adjusted for inflation, the income of the median family doubled between 1947 and 1973. But it rose only 22 percent from 1973 to 2003, and much of that gain was the result of wives' entering the paid labor force or working longer hours, not rising wages.
>
> Paul Krugman, Losing Our Country[44]

During the era of the middle class median income kept pace with disposable personal income. Although disposable personal income (on a per capita basis) increased by 81.9 percent, median income increased by 90.3 percent (Table 2.7). During the era of the wealthy class disposable personal income increased by 45.7 percent, but median income failed to keep pace and increased only by less than a third as much. Had median income kept pace with disposable personal income, as it had during the era of the middle

Table 2.7 Changes in Median Income and Personal in the Last Half Century

The Era of the Middle Class (1954 to 1979)	1954	1979	Change
Median income	26,595	50,726	90.3%
Disposable personal income per capita	12,146	22,091	81.9%
The Era of the Wealthy Class (1979 to 2006)	1979	2006	Change
Median income	50,726	58,407	15.1%
Disposable personal income per capita	22,091	32,180	45.7%
Median income if it had kept pace with Disposable Personal Income between 1979–2006		US$73,908	

Note: All figures in constant dollars (2006, inflation adjusted).[43]

class, then the median income would have been US$73,908. This represents a substantial loss for the average middle class family.

In the second 25-year period after World War II, the median income has increased substantially less—only by 15 percent. Yet just like the prior time, the overall economy has grown substantially. This was the period that witnessed the birth of the personal computer, the Internet, cell phones, wireless broadband, and Internet search engines capable of analyzing, organizing and providing instant access to literally trillions of pages of information. Science has brought a host of biotechnological breakthroughs, and such wonders as the sequencing of the human genome, cloning, and the space shuttle. During this time, disposable personal income on a per capita basis increased by 45.7 percent. However, the majority of the newly generated wealth of this extraordinarily prosperous period went to the top, to those families who controlled capital.

Participating in Economic Growth

Prosperity reached across all income groups between 1947 and 1979, as a result of the long period of sustained economic growth.[45] There was a perceptible change in the standard of living as seen in Figure 2.7.

During the era of the middle class, all income groups benefited from the growing economy. The incomes of families in the bottom income groups as well as the top saw substantial gains—with almost all groups doubling during the period. However, during the era of the wealthy class income gains were concentrated in the top groups.[46] The top 5 percent saw their

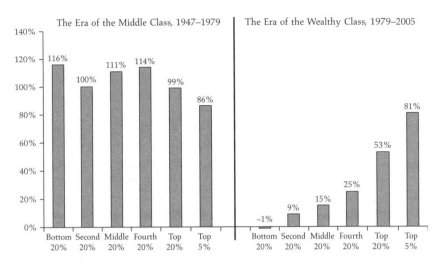

Figure 2.7 Income Gains by Income Group, 1947 to 2005

income increase by 81 percent, whereas the bottom 20 percent actually lost ground. Although there were major economic advances during the last 25 years, with the development of personal computers, cell phones, the Internet, advances in biotechnology and Internet search technology, the middle class, the working class, the blue collar workers and the poor were essentially left out. Part of the explanation is that the tax cuts and tax policy favored the owners of assets and capital. Since the middle class and the poor have such a small share of the nation's asset wealth and capital, they were unable to benefit from these policies.

As the 1980s ushered in a new economic order, it brought an end to the era of the middle class, as broad participation in economic gain ended and since then, as Robert Reich observed, most of the gain in household wealth has gone to the top. Everyone else shared a small fraction of the growth and many saw declines. This disparity showed that something was fundamentally wrong, as it is vital to reward effort in a free enterprise economy. Ackerman and Alstott observed, "Since the early 1970s the average family income has grown little, and the typical male worker has seen his real wages decline. Only the entry of vast numbers of women into the labor force has produced meager gains in median family income."[47] Any minimum gains made have been due to the increase in two-earner families. Perucci and Wysong observe that the "new reality is a society in which one-fifth of Americans are privileged, with job security, high wages and strong skills.[48] The other 80 percent belong to a 'new working class' that, despite great variability within the group, lacks the same security and high wages."

In 1969, the bottom 60 percent of income earners received more than a third (36 percent) of reported income. In 2005, this same group received less than a quarter (24.4 percent).[49] Wealth creation has been given a fabulous opportunity in the United States, and this can be seen in the significant contributions made to the Nation's wealth by a handful of individuals (Table 2.8) any one of whom has more money than is spent annually on cash assistance for the millions of poor children on welfare. The "number of households worth at least one million dollars almost doubled from the early 1980s to the late 1990s, after inflation,"[50] and with that there was a declining participation of the larger segment of the middle class in the economic gains of the eighties and nineties. All the while, there was no substantial improvement in the condition of the single mother; nor were there any substantive efforts to eradicate poverty. In 1960, the poverty line was roughly equivalent to half the median income for a family of four, but by 2001 it had declined to about 43 percent of the median family income.[51] This change reflects the substantial shift in the distribution of wealth upward. If poverty were defined in relative terms, such as one-half the median family income proposed by most economists and widely used by European economies,[52] a much greater number of persons would have been seen to have slipped into poverty than the current narrow definition of poverty, the poverty line, suggests.

The shift of income and wealth to the top wealth holders that began with the tax reform policies championed by President Reagan is illustrated by the substantial gains of the top 0.1 percent (top one-tenth of 1%) in the United States compared to the similar group in other countries. Figure 2.8 shows the growing percentage of wealth owned by the top 0.1 percent of wealth holders in the United States, France, Japan, and the United Kingdom. During

Table 2.8 The 21 Richest Persons in the United States (in Billions)

Gates, William H. III	59.0	Allen, Paul	16.8
Buffett, Warren Edward	52.0	Walton, Christy & family	16.3
Adelson, Sheldon	28.0	Walton, Jim	16.3
Ellison, Lawrence	26.0	Walton, S. Robson	16.3
Brin, Sergey	18.5	Walton, Alice	16.1
Page, Larry	18.5	Balmer, Steve	15.2
Kerkorian, Kirk	18.0	Johnson, Abigail	15.0
Dell, Michael	17.2	Icahn, Carl	14.5
Koch, Charles	17.0	Mars, Forrest	14.0
Koch, David	17.0	Mars, Jacqueline	14.0
		Taylor, Jack & family	14.0

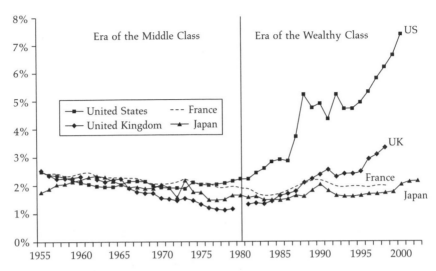

Figure 2.8 The Percentage of Wealth Owned by the 0.1 percent in the United States, France, Japan and the United Kingdom, 1955 to 2002

Data Source: Piketty and Saez, 2006; Figures 3a and 3b.

the era of the middle class the top 0.1 percent owned a smaller percentage of the nation's wealth than the bottom two-thirds. However, during the era of the wealthy class the top 0.1 percent passed the wealth holdings of the bottom two-thirds and currently holds about twice as much as this group. It was not until the era of the wealthy class that the extraordinary shift in wealth occurred. As the data in Figure 2.8 show, the greatest shift in wealth upward occurred in the United States.[54] In France and Japan, which experienced similar economic growth, the shift in wealth did not occur. However, Margaret Thatcher and the Conservatives in the United Kingdom also put in place policies at about the same time as President Reagan that began leading to a shift in wealth upward in the United Kingdom, although not nearly as much as in the United States.

The result of the tax policies ushered in under the leadership of Ronald Reagan was the creation of a new and different economic order that allowed for the accumulation and concentration of wealth. During the resulting era of the wealthy class the number of millionaires and billionaires, controlling for inflation, multiplied and led to a different country than was being created during the era of the middle class. In the earlier era of the middle class, there was widespread participation in the growing economy and resulting prosperity. In recent years, the prosperity created by the technological advances and growing economy has not resulted in widespread benefit and growth of income and wealth by the middle class. Rather, the result has been greater inequality, a concentration of wealth and a fabulous increase in the wealth and income of those in the top 0.1, 1, and 10 percent, respectively.

Closing

The social programs and tax policies prevailing during the era of the middle class—the GI Bill, the expansion of higher education, and the mortgage deduction—led to the expansion of the middle class and the doubling of median family income and the increase in income across the class spectrum from rich to poor.

All this came to a close with the triumph of Conservatism. The focus of tax policies during this period was to promote the accumulation and growth of great wealth. During this period ushered in by President Reagan, the number of millionaires and high net worth individuals grew substantially.

Today the top 1 percent own more wealth than the bottom 90 percent combined. The top 4 percent of taxpayers receive more income than the bottom two-thirds of taxpayers. During this era of the wealthy class, other income groups failed to participate in the growing economy. New wealth and income have been channeled to those who held assets and capital, primarily the rich, whereas the middle class, the working class, and the poor all seemed to lose ground. We have begun moving toward greater inequality and separation of the average family from participating in the fruits of the growing American economy than ever before in the nation's history.

After World War II, most children found greater opportunities than their parents. However, in recent years the opportunities of most children have been declining relative to their parents. Inequality has sharply increased during the last several decades leading to greater wealth for the owners of capital. Children from middle and working class families have seen their opportunities decline.

What can be done to reverse these trends and to insure opportunity for all children? After the Great Depression, the nation tackled the poverty of seniors and children. The result was the passage of the Social Security Act that provided for income support for seniors and single mothers and their children. As we shall see in the next chapter, Social Security was effective in greatly reducing poverty among seniors. However, the same program failed to improve the situation for single mothers and their children, leaving child poverty as the major unresolved social problem in America.

3

❧

Doing for Children
What We Have
Done for Seniors:
Government Efforts to
End Poverty

> While the national poverty rate for older Americans has dropped
> by two-thirds over the past three decades, the child poverty rate has
> risen by 40 percent over the same time period.
>
> Brookings Institution, 2000 [1]

Herbert Hoover was elected president in 1928, convincing the electorate that the United States had become so prosperous that an end to poverty was well within its grasp. In 1927, Americans had the highest average income in the world. The country was in the midst of a great economic expansion fueled by the emerging auto industry, oil and gas, and electrification. "We in America today are nearer to the final triumph over poverty than ever before in the history of any land. The poorhouse is vanishing from among us," Hoover said in a speech accepting the Republican nomination for president. [2]

Within 8 months of Hoover's inauguration, the stock market crashed and the Great Depression had begun. With a few short years, the Dow Jones Industrial Average would go from a high of 381 to 41. An economic collapse unlike any the country had ever experienced was underway. [3]

The Great Depression was one of the darkest periods in U.S. history. Along with plummeting financial markets, the entire U.S. economy came crashing down, as did the economies of virtually all industrialized nations.[4] Overnight, unemployment skyrocketed, hunger and homelessness were rampant, and living conditions throughout the country changed dramatically with multiple families crowding together into small houses and apartments.

Although Hoover attempted to ameliorate the devastating effects of the Great Depression by implementing the Hawley–Smoot Tariff bill and the Agricultural Marketing Act, neither relieved the anguish of the United States, and most historians believe they made matters worse. At no time in the nation's history, save the Civil War, had the country experienced such a malaise and fear of the future.

The New Deal

I see one-third of the nation ill-housed, ill-clad, ill-nourished . . . the test of our progress is not whether we add more to the abundance of those who have much; it is whether we provide enough for those who have too little.

President Franklin D. Roosevelt, *Second Inaugural Address*[5]

In 1933, after one term as president, Hoover lost a landslide election to the Democrat's candidate, Franklin Delano Roosevelt (FDR), as the nation turned to a new leader to right the ship of state. The new president moved decisively to attack the blight of the Great Depression with legislation designed to meet the immediate crisis of destitution and address the needs of the nation's unemployed. FDR established several public relief programs in the first year of his presidency, most notably the Federal Emergency Relief Administration (FERA), which made direct cash allocations available to states for immediate payments to the unemployed; the Civilian Conservation Corps (CCC), which put 300,000 young men to work in 1,200 camps planting trees, building bridges, and cleaning beaches; the Civil Works Administration (CWA), which spent almost $1 billion on public works projects, including airports and roads; and the Agricultural Adjustment Act (AAA), which attempted to raise farmer's incomes by offering cash incentives to farmers who agreed to cut production.[6]

However, it was in August 1935 that FDR instituted the most significant poverty legislation in the nation's history. With the enactment of the Social Security Act of 1935, Roosevelt set the standard for federal poverty programs, and cast upon the United States the first comprehensive social safety net.[7]

The Great Depression, and Roosevelt's New Deal, taught the nation two important lessons on dealing with economic collapse and rampant poverty:

- That self-reliance is the best approach to economic matters.
- That sometimes the individual has to rely on the State for a helping hand.

Social Security did just that, providing for the needy—seniors and single mothers and their children—at a time when they had nowhere else to turn. The Social Security Act comprised two major parts designed to protect the most vulnerable populations against poverty.[8] Over the next several decades, it became clear that the part that was the most successful was the social insurance (retirement income) for the elderly. In an age when the highest rate of poverty was among senior citizens, Social Security instituted a federal program that required citizens to save for their retirement years as soon as they began to work. Over the course of a person's work life, they would pay into the Social Security Trust Fund through automatic deductions from their pay check. The contribution would then be used to pay for a small pension at retirement (i.e., Social Security Benefits) and disability insurance in case of the individual being severely injured and unable to work. Because the program for the elderly was based on a universal social insurance model, it meant that all citizens would be included in the program and be entitled to the benefits they paid for during their working career.

However, it was not until about 15 years after the start of the Social Security Program that it began having a substantial effect on poverty reduction among the elderly.

Because it took a while for the program to accomplish its mission, the positive effects of the program were not immediate, but between 1945 and 1975 the number of recipients increased several fold[9] (see Figure 3.1). Moreover, the increase in recipients was viewed as a positive aspect of the program. The more people covered and eligible for benefits, the better.[10]

The Decline of Poverty Among Seniors

Today, the Social Security Administration regularly sends out checks of about $1,000 each to more than 34 million seniors. Without these checks, it is fair to say that almost half of all seniors in the United States would be living in poverty.

Poverty of seniors declined from 35.2 percent in 1959 to 9.4 percent in 2006. The primary reason for the decline in poverty for seniors was the impact of the Social Security program. As seen in Figure 3.2, without

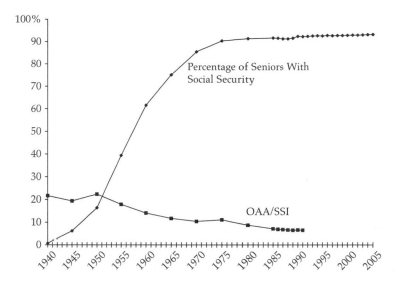

Figure 3.1 Individuals Receiving Social Security, Old Age Assistance (OAA), and Supplemental Security Income (SSI)

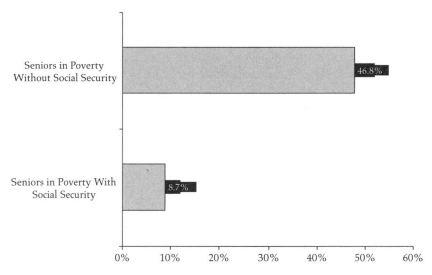

Figure 3.2 The Impact of Social Security on Poverty Among Seniors (2002)
Source: Social Security Administration, 2004.

Social Security, 46.8 percent of seniors would be living in households below the poverty line. For almost one-third of seniors, Social Security represents more than 90 percent of their income (see Figure 3.3). For almost another third, Social Security represents more than half of their income.

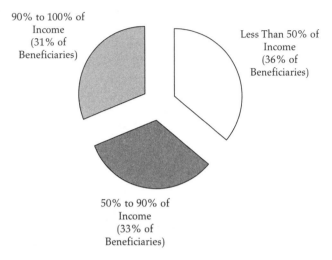

90% to 100% of
Income
(31% of
Beneficiaries)

Less Than 50% of
Income
(36% of
Beneficiaries)

50% to 90% of
Income
(33% of
Beneficiaries)

Figure 3.3　The Portion of Income Provided by Social Security
Source: Social Security Administration 2007.

Clearly, Social Security was successful in reducing poverty among seniors. In contrast, the part of the Social Security Act that was designed to combat child poverty—welfare—was not successful. Although the increased percentage of seniors receiving Social Security has been viewed favorably, increases in the number of children receiving welfare has been viewed unfavorably. The program for reducing poverty among seniors (Social Security) was quite different from the program to end poverty among children (welfare).

Poverty Among Children

The success Social Security achieved in reducing poverty among seniors was not matched in ending poverty among children. The second major part of the Social Security Act was the Aid to Dependent Children (ADC; later, AFDC) program—what we today think of as the welfare program. Welfare was a means-tested program that required proof of poverty and was intended to offer income assistance to widowed mothers with children.[11]

Welfare was the second half of the Social Security Act, designed to provide income protection for poor children and their mothers. Over the years, these programs have been changed and adapted. For the first few decades after enactment, both Social Security and welfare were widely accepted as a necessary social safety net. In the late 1950s, the federal government began an effort to define and measure poverty. Led by efforts of Molly Orshansky,

Two Major Parts of the Social Security Act

Social Security—Universal Social Savings/Insurance

- Old Age Survivors and Disability Insurance (OASDI) or what is commonly understood as Social Security.

Welfare—targeted means-tested program

- Aid to Dependent Children (ADC)—a means-tested welfare program for mothers with dependent children who were unable to provide for themselves.
- Replaced by Temporary Assistance to Needy Families (TANF) in 1996.

the Department of Agriculture developed a poverty line that took into account the number of individuals in a household and the region of the country. Essentially, the poverty line was an absolute measure based on the view that the food budget represented one-third of a family's income. Thus, poverty was defined as the amount of money required to provide a minimum food budget for a family multiplied by three. The poverty line was used by the Census Bureau to assess poverty in the United States beginning in 1959. When the measure was first applied, the largest group of persons below the poverty line was seniors, individuals 65 years or older (see Table 3.1). More than a third of seniors lived in households with income below the poverty line. However, as soon as Social Security began to provide almost full coverage to seniors, the poverty rate among seniors declined. The poverty rate among seniors now is consistently below 10 percent.

During the 1960s the welfare rolls rose to their highest level. As seen in Figure 3.4, there was a sharp rise of the welfare rolls between 1960 through 1972. This is the only 12-year period in the history of the welfare program when the number of beneficiaries more than doubled. With the election of Richard Nixon, there was a renewed concern to do something to reduce the rapidly rising welfare rolls. There was little interest in continuing the Great Society programs and its War on Poverty.

Over the years the means-tested welfare system has been viewed by some as increasing dependency for those who receive it. Since the 1950s there has been an increase in children born out of wedlock and the number and rate have continued to rise for the last 50 years. Most of the children thus born have a high likelihood of living in poverty. Therefore, some have suggested that welfare itself has been the major cause of out-of-wedlock births. For

Table 3.1 Percentage of Children and Elderly in Poverty, 1959 to 2006

	1959	1969	1979	1989	1999	2005	2006
Children	26.9	14.0	16.4	19.6	16.9	17.6	17.4
Seniors	35.2	25.3	15.2	11.4	9.7	9.7	9.4

Source: U.S. Census Bureau (various years).[12]

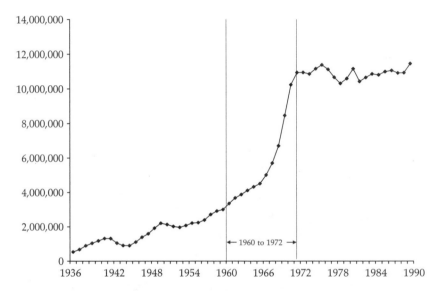

Figure 3.4 Increasing Welfare Rolls, 1960 to 1972
Source: www.acf.dhhs.gov/news/stats/3697.htm

20 years after its implementation (1936–1956), the number and percentage of children receiving welfare remained low. During the 1960s, child poverty decreased even further, although this period also saw an upsurge in children receiving welfare. There were three factors behind this.

Divorce

The birth control pill was first approved by the Federal Drug Administration (FDA) in 1960 and was adopted widely throughout the 1960s—an era characterized by the sexual revolution and an increasing awareness of women's rights.[13] There was a steady increase in the number of working mothers, even those with young children. Women who were working outside the home were still expected to shoulder the household chores, within and outside the house, leading to increased physical and psychological tension in the family to establish equitable distribution of everyday tasks. This led to an increase in the divorce rates[14] and an increasing number of children being affected by divorce, as mothers turned to welfare.

As stated earlier, the 1960s saw an increase in the number of children receiving welfare, yet there remained a significant number living in poverty. As a result, welfare rights organizations began to call for increased participation by groups that had failed to apply even when they had been eligible. This had the effect of causing many poor inner-city mothers to begin to assert their rights to welfare benefits, causing a sudden increase in the number of children on welfare during this period.

Another contributor to the increase in welfare rolls was an increased number of children born out of wedlock. Along with growth in the number of people receiving welfare, the number of welfare mothers with children born out of wedlock also increased.

From the 1950s through the 1960s, the welfare program had remained practically dormant, limited to about 2 percent of the child population (although 25% of children were living in poverty). Hence, an increase in the welfare rolls reflected the changing dynamics of society. The period following 1972 saw the welfare rolls stabilize and remain unchanged for a decade and not begin increasing again until the 1990s. As a result, a number of states, including Wisconsin, Florida, and Texas, began experimenting with benefit curbs in the 1990s. These states focused on work requirements, fixed a time limit for women receiving benefits, and placed other restrictions on obtaining welfare. All during this period, the average welfare payment consistently declined (see Table 3.2).

Table 3.2. Average Monthly Welfare (AFDC) Family Payment

	Monthly Payment for a Family (US$)
1970	753
1975	658
1980	583
1985	527
1990	516
1995	425

Source: U.S Department of Health and Human Services (2002).

Note: Weighted average for a family of four. AFDC, Aid to Dependent Children.

The Increase in Welfare Rolls

The revolution in reproductive technology (including the advent of the birth control pill), the legalization of abortion, and the growing involvement of women in the labor force, created a strained family atmosphere reflected in an increased divorce rate and a general disintegration of the traditional nuclear family. These have been the principal reasons for the dramatic increase in divorces and in welfare recipients between 1960 and 1972. One is struck by the parallel movement of divorce and the number of welfare recipients (see Figure 3.5),[15] but it is relatively independent of other changes such as the number of children born out of wedlock.

A regression analysis examining the relative impact of divorce and out-of-wedlock births between 1954 and 1992 reveals that "the increase in the number of children involved in divorce" resulted in increased welfare usage, accounting for more than 94 percent of the variation.[16] Moreover, as Patterson demonstrated in his study, the proportion of eligible families receiving welfare increased from one-third in the early 1960s to nine-tenths in 1971.[17] Divorced mothers were viewed as "deserving" welfare recipients and made full use of the program.[18]

Between 1960 and 1972, divorced women increasingly turned to welfare for income assistance. Applying a content analysis to a sample of welfare mothers from this period, Rein and Rainwater found that more than half were using

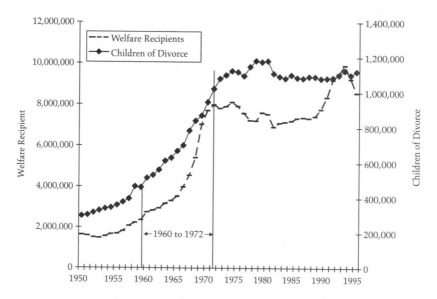

Figure 3.5 The Relation Between the Rise in Divorce and Welfare

welfare to cushion the transition following divorce.[19] Women used welfare as a backup to their economic condition for a short transition period. Thus, welfare represented for women what unemployment insurance represented for men in similar income disruptive situations. For the majority of women in their study, Rein and Rainwater found that emancipation from welfare was achieved through remarriage and only rarely through employment.[20]

The 1960s were a decade of changing social values. As seen in Figure 3.6, the period witnessed the steady increase in the percentage of mothers with young children leaving home for the paid labor force. Before the sexual revolution, unmarried young women who became pregnant would likely marry the father (the "shotgun marriage"). Between 1960 and 1972, the number of women using the birth control pill and the number of abortions increased several fold. This period was characterized by a transformation of attitudes and values about sex. Young people began to experiment with sex before marriage, a trend that has continued to the present day.[21]

Today, almost half of all girls experiment with premarital sex during their teenage years. By the time they are 15, about a quarter of girls and boys in the United States have experienced sex. By age 19, almost two-thirds of unmarried teens have had sex. By the time they turn 20, 77 percent of females and 85 percent of males are sexually active. As can be expected, this sexual activity results in a large number of teen pregnancies. In fact, the United States has one of the highest rates of teen pregnancies in the postindustrial

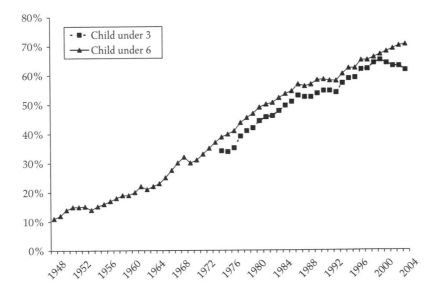

Figure 3.6 Labor Force Participation of Mothers

world.[22] In 2000, there were 479,067 births to teenagers.[23] This translates into almost 1 in 10 White teenagers and 1 in 5 African-American teenagers between the ages of 15 and 17 to become pregnant each year.[24] Compare this with the data from Canada, with a rate of fewer than 1 in 20, the Netherlands fewer than 1 in 50, and Japan fewer than 1 in 100.[25]

About 40 percent of teen pregnancies are terminated with an abortion. Fewer than 10 percent of babies born to unmarried teens are placed in adoptive homes. About half of teen pregnancies result in births. About three-quarters of these births to teens occur outside of marriage. More than 80 percent of these teens come from poor or low-income families. Akerlof has studied the increase in children born out of wedlock and suggested that it is mostly explained by the declining rate of marriages among the women who conceive outside of marriage.[26] Akerlof and his colleagues suggest that the increase in out-of-wedlock births for African-American women, for example, would have been two-fifths of what it was, had the shotgun marriage rates remained the same between 1965 and 1985.[27]

Critics of the welfare program believed that unmarried young girls found the welfare income assistance source as secure and reliable and hence did not need to get married. In the last quarter of a century, an increasing number of unmarried young women have given birth out of wedlock (see Figure 3.7). The percentage of births by unmarried mothers varies considerably by race and ethnicity. In 2006, 70.7 percent of all Black children were born to unmarried mothers. Unmarried births constituted 49.9 percent for Hispanic

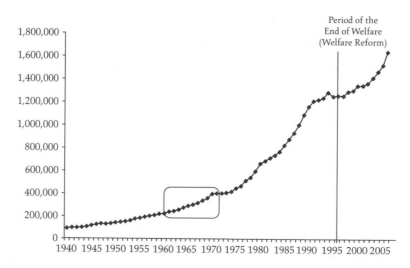

Figure 3.7 Number of Births to Unmarried Women, 1940 to 2006.

Note: The welfare rolls increased during the period in the boxed area and remained relatively flat after that.

mothers, 16.3 percent for Asian or Pacific Islander, and 26.6 percent for White mothers.[28] Of all mothers under 30 who receive welfare assistance, about 70 percent begin childbearing as teenagers, and within one year after the birth of their first child, half of all teen mothers are receiving welfare benefits.[29] Within 5 years the percentage grows to more than 75 percent.[30]

Given the paucity of government support for unwed mothers and the stigma associated with their families, children born out of wedlock are too often condemned to a life of poverty. Is this the message we intend to send? On the one hand, yes, because mothers starting a family out of wedlock are not economically self-sustaining for the most part. But, on the other hand, no, because we want to discourage young women from considering or seeking an abortion. How is this conundrum solved by the young woman who finds herself with an unplanned and perhaps unwanted pregnancy?

Welfare provides only meager assistance to the young mother and child confronted by difficult economic and personal circumstances. Today, government support is provided through the Temporary Assistance for Needy Families (TANF) program, which provides minimal assistance, averaging about one-seventh of the average family income in the United States.[31]

Yet young women continue to have babies. Reducing welfare benefits or withholding them has not been demonstrated to reduce birth rates. In fact, the poorest countries in the world have the highest birth rates.

Mixed Messages: Abortion Versus Welfare

Young women who get pregnant out of wedlock receive mixed messages.[32] Advocates for the unborn argue on moral grounds that abortion, even for unwed teenagers, is tantamount to taking of a life. The unwed mother, however, quickly learns that society, which so strongly discouraged an abortion, has little interest in supporting her and her child after her birth.[33] Even though some would like to see a child adopted and be provided with an escape from poverty, it is the least selected option.

Although more than 40 percent of unwed teens have abortions, it is, discouraged in many quarters.[34] From 1965 to 1969, there were 88,000 abortions in the United States, which increased to 561,000 between 1970 and 1974. In the next 5 years this increased to 985,000, and from 1980 to 1984, the numbers had increased to 1,271,000. Despite the availability of welfare, many young women terminated their pregnancies. During the last several decades, the percentage of pregnancies ending in abortion among unmarried women has declined (from 59% in 1980 to 41% in 1995).[35]

Baker interviewed a sample of adolescent girls across Canada and asked them how they would handle an unplanned pregnancy.[36] Almost half indicated they would keep their baby and raise it as best they could, with or without a father. About a third said they would seek an abortion. Fewer than 5 percent said they would give their babies up for adoption. Ventura and Bacharach reported that about 20 percent of White unmarried mothers released their babies for adoption before 1973.[37] Yet between 1989 and 1995, this percentage dropped to fewer than 2 percent of White unmarried women and fewer than one-half of 1 percent for African-American women relinquishing their babies for adoption.[38] This refusal to part with the baby has often been viewed as a wish to continue in a state of dependency.[39]

Right to Life or Right To Be Poor

Over the past three decades, few issues on the U.S. political landscape have garnered more attention than the matter of abortion. The fight between those who refer to themselves as pro-choice, and those who are self-described right to life, has been as volatile, contentious, and abrasive as any social issue since the Vietnam War. No public debate on any subject in recent history has been as fiercely charged and so severely discordant.

Both parties to this debate have their legions of dedicated followers and true believers; few political action movements have commanded more ardent supporters. The numbers of national, state, and organizations' PACs, lobbyists, sign carriers, web sites, professional and amateur fundraisers, community canvassers, and talk radio hosts on both sides of the issue numbers in the thousands, and the committed and unyielding supporters in each camp run into the tens of millions. There is little that the two groups are able to agree on. Unfortunately, the impoverished mothers and children of today's single-parent households live in a colorless world of shadows and darkness, where public policy seems all too stark.[40] With limited education, few job skills, and the enormous demands of a new infant, most mothers are unable to obtain and hold gainful employment. Moreover, even when they are able to secure child care and obtain employment, their income is low.[41] Given average annual incomes of less than $10,000 a year, single teen mothers confront a depressingly deep economic plight, with their children suffering as much as they do.[42] Most of the children in these families will live in poverty.[43]

Children in single-parent families have less provision and opportunity in virtually all areas of life.[44] Butler observes, "Children born to teenage mothers have been found to be at greater risk for health problems, poor cognitive functioning, and poverty."[45] They have a significantly higher likelihood of dropping out of school and will be more likely to give birth out of wedlock.[46]

The labor-intensive demands of child rearing severely limit the choices available to a young woman raising a child by herself. Not surprisingly, they soon find themselves trapped in dependency. Although welfare is difficult, degrading, and in many ways inadequate, the single mother somehow adapts to the minimal support provided.[47] In doing so, she becomes a victim of the program designed to assist her. Over time, she risks losing her pride and sense of self-worth and is viewed with disrespect by the society that is now burdened with providing for her and her children.[48] Without child care and adequate income support, she rarely has the opportunity to achieve self-sufficiency.[49] Her love and attachment to her baby seemingly traps them both in a world of economic despair.

Closing: Comparing Social Security and Welfare

Both the current Social Security program and the welfare program for single mothers were part of the original Social Security Act of 1935. Social Security was built on a model of social savings and social insurance. It established a program that required all citizens to pay into the program during their working years so that when they reached their retirement years, enough would have been paid into Social Security to pay for the monthly benefit they would receive once they retired. Thus, the monthly Social Security benefit is an earned benefit. As a result, there is no stigma associated with receiving Social Security payments. Beneficiaries view their monthly benefit as something they worked and paid for during their working years. In short, Social Security is a universal social insurance and social savings program that guarantees all working adults will have at least a small pension when they retire.

In 1959, the Census Bureau first began collecting statistics on poverty in the United States. Seniors were the largest group of poor at the time. The Census Bureau reported that 35.2 percent of seniors were living in poverty, whereas for children the rate was 27.3 percent. In 2004, the poverty rate for seniors was 9.8 percent, but it was 17.8 percent for children.

In 2006, the Social Security Administration made payments of more than $460 billion through the Old Age Survivors and Disability Insurance (OASDI) program—what we commonly refer to as Social Security.[50] The program paid benefits to more than 35 million aged beneficiaries, with an average monthly benefit of more than a $1,000. Social Security was the major source of income for two-thirds of aged beneficiaries, and it was the only source of income for one-fifth. The Social Security benefit was credited with lifting 13 million seniors above the poverty line—and effectively eliminating poverty among seniors in the United States.

In contrast to Social Security, the welfare program was not universal, but means tested and restricted to single mothers who were required to prove they lacked the necessary income to provide for themselves and their children in order to get help. Over the years, the welfare program has been criticized as encouraging dependency on the government. The program was seen as providing poor women and their children with something—welfare benefits—for doing nothing. The program stigmatized beneficiaries. Over the years, the benefits were consistently whittled down, no doubt reflecting the declining public support for the program. In essence, welfare was a means-tested handout that a reluctant public became disillusioned with. Coupled with the assertions of some conservatives that welfare was the cause of both poverty and the rising number of children born out of wedlock, efforts to end the welfare program began to gain momentum.

As we shall see in the next chapter, the disillusionment with welfare came to a head about a dozen years ago when a Democratic president who promised to "end welfare as we know it" clashed with a Republican-Controlled Congress that also wanted to change welfare but in a different direction.

4
❧

The Failure of Welfare Reform to Reduce Child Poverty

In my own travels through post welfare life, I was struck by how many working families complained about facing depleted cupboards—or just plain going hungry. ... The persistence of so much hardship poses a paradox. If incomes were rising, and poverty falling, why did so many people skip meals and fall behind on the rent?

Jason DeParle, *American Dream*[1]

In his book, *The Epic of America*, James Truslow Adams first used the term that has become so ubiquitous:[2]

The American Dream, is that dream of a land in which life should be better and richer and fuller for everyone, with opportunity for each according to ability or achievement. It is a difficult dream for the European upper classes to interpret adequately, and too many of us ourselves have grown weary and mistrustful of it. It is not a dream of motor cars and high wages merely, but a dream of social order in which each man and each woman shall be able to attain to the fullest stature of which they are innately capable, and be recognized by others for what they are, regardless of the fortuitous circumstances of birth or position.[3]

The flipside of the ideal that hard work is all it takes to achieve is the sense that those who have failed did so because they have not lived up to the promise of the dream. They are often seen as lazy, profligate, and immoral.

Although it may be possible to level charges against some of the poor and avoid blaming a systemic failing on the part of the opportunity structure in the United States itself, how can we accuse children of causing their own fate?

Throughout the last half century, debate has continued at both at federal and state levels on how to combat this scourge of child poverty. In most instances, politicians have been preoccupied with changing the nation's welfare system. In 1964, President Johnson optimistically declared a War on Poverty; two decades later President Reagan sounded the retreat announcing, "We had a war on poverty and poverty won."

The Welfare Program for Single Mothers and Their Children

The Aid to Dependent Children, or, as it was later renamed, Aid to Families with Dependent Children (AFDC) was the original safety net for the nation's most needy children. The program prevented millions of children from going without food, while allowing their mothers to provide a minimum level of care. However, AFDC failed to cure the problem of poverty itself and lift disadvantaged children out of poverty.

Because AFDC granted aid on the basis of how much need a family could demonstrate, it was virtually impossible for indigent families to escape the cycle of poverty, a fact that only served to fuel the debate in legislative halls throughout the nation.[4] On one hand were those who believed that the problem of poverty could best be solved by increasing federal welfare programs, subsidies, and initiatives. Opponents argued that welfare itself was the cause of child poverty and should be eliminated. Along with this discussion, another question surfaced that has always lain behind the debate. From the Progressive Era on, the issue of whether or not the federal government was attempting to usurp parental authority has been a constant argument.[5] This refrain inevitably lies at the heart of the welfare debate, although the question of the impact of welfare on the work habits and sexual behavior of young women has most often taken center stage.

Liberals believe that welfare should continue to provide for poor single-parent families. However, among Liberals there is some recognition that whatever value lies in compensating the poor for their condition, existing welfare laws had done nothing to break the cycle of poverty.[6] Many Liberals recognize that if a mother worked, she lost her benefits. Given that she was unlikely to find work that would pay significantly more than welfare and that she would still have to bear the increased expense and trouble of finding affordable daycare, she often had little motivation to seek employment.[7] James Q. Wilson noted

[Welfare reform] will tell young mothers to be employed, away from their children for much of each week. These children, already fatherless, will now become primarily motherless. They will be raised by somebody else. A grandmother? A neighbor? An overworked day care manager? Or they will be left alone.[8]

Conversely, Conservatives have focused upon ending the welfare program altogether. In their view, the reluctance of the poor to seek gainful employment must be solved through punitive measures, such as time limits and work requirements.[9] John Hospers observed: "There have now been over 40 years of the welfare state; people who grew up and lived in liberty and independence have died off, and been replaced by those who expect the government to support them, and militantly demand this as their right."[10]

The reforms proffered did little to help the children themselves, Conservatives argued, but rather allowed the mothers to engage in lives of profligacy and promiscuity.[11] Welfare mothers buying cigarettes and alcohol, carousing with men while their children lay at home in unchanged diapers, were a frequently deployed image. Beginning with President Reagan's welfare queen, the welfare issue was morphed from a War on Poverty and compassion for the single mom down on her luck to a campaign against a program that allowed irresponsible women to have children and become dependent on the state.[12] Clarence Page observed, "Reagan ... put a black and urban face on [poverty] from the time he campaigned against 'welfare queens' in 1980 and the stereotypes are reinforced almost daily by television images of ghetto gang wars and drug busts."[13]

Complaining that welfare only encouraged dependency by providing basic economic support while discouraging self-reliance, Charles Murray argued that welfare encouraged young poor women to have children out of wedlock and to establish families that relied on the state for income support.[14] U.S. Congressman John Mica (R-Fla.) delivered a speech on the floor of the U.S. House of Representatives in 1995.[15] With a large sign behind him that read, "Don't feed the Alligators," Representative Mica explained that game wardens erected such warnings because alligators became dependent upon handouts from well-meaning visitors and lost their will to hunt for food.[16] Mica argued that "un-natural feeding and artificial care creates dependency. When dependency sets in, these otherwise able-bodied alligators can no longer survive on their own." Even when acknowledging that humans were not alligators, Mica was of the opinion that the existing welfare system "upset the natural order." The use of animals to represent people on welfare did not end there though. Taking her cue from Mica's example, Representative Barbara Cubin (R-Wyo.) used the example of reintroducing wolves in National Parks. Wolves were placed in cages by park rangers and fed on venison and elk as a part of their rehabilitation process but when released they did not leave their cages. Calling this the Wolf Welfare Program, Cubin suggested, "Just like any animal in the species, any mammal, when you take away their freedom and their dignity and their ability, they cannot provide for themselves." As Democrats chanted "Shame, shame, shame," a tedious and vitriolic debate began anew and ended with the Republican-sponsored welfare bill. The chairman was E. Clay Shaw, Jr. (R-Fla.). His own view of welfare mothers was no less sanguine. He observed that poor teen mothers were "children you wouldn't leave your cat with on a weekend." [17]

Bill Clinton's 1992 election had inspired this new turn in the decades-long debate on Welfare Reform. Clinton promised during his campaign to bring "an end to welfare as we know it," yet he also championed the more liberal critique of welfare. He proposed reforms that would have provided income assistance to poor mothers while requiring them to work. But he would also have provided job training and child care. In addition, Clinton felt that welfare reform should provide some assurance of the availability of employment for poor mothers. But Clinton's welfare reform did not go far enough for Conservatives. They wanted to end the entitlement status, turn more control over to the states, and enforce time limits.[18]

The largest group on the welfare rolls was children—primarily children of color. Although the reform proposal represented the largest reduction in income support to poor children in history, almost none of the debate focused on these poor children but rather on their mothers. Liberals and Conservatives essentially agreed that single mothers, even those with young children, needed to be compelled to work. Dependency on the state was viewed as harmful to the mother and her children. If these mothers could be assured adequate child care and the likelihood of decent employment, Liberals felt that they could agree to the welfare reform.[19]

The Enactment of Welfare Reform

In 1994, when the Republicans gained control of the Congress, it was apparent that welfare reform would soon become a reality. Unfortunately, the public debate became increasingly strident. In the public forum, child advocates criticized the reforms backed by House Speaker Newt Gingrich (R-Ga.) as being harmful to those on welfare, especially the children, whereas Republicans held the view that welfare had made the intended beneficiaries a dependent class and harmed their capacity for self-reliance.

Both Conservatives and Liberals developed proposals for substantive welfare reform. The first major reform, proposed by a coalition of moderates in the Congress, recommended that poor single mothers be gradually transitioned from welfare to work. This early version, which was supported by the Clinton administration, provided comprehensive transition services and subsidized child care.

However, a more stringent reform package that included the Conservatives' sought after time limits and strict work requirements was proposed. The most important feature of this version of welfare reform was that it ended the entitlement status of welfare. For the first time in more than 60 years, single mothers and their children were no longer to be entitled to a minimum level of income support.

Toward the end of the debate on welfare reform, just before its passage, the opponents of the legislation at last raised the issue of children, suggesting that the bill would endanger the millions of children receiving income assistance would lose that meager assistance and would be pushed further and deeper into poverty. George Will noted

> As the welfare reform debate begins to boil, the place to begin is with an elemental fact: No child in America asked to be here. No child is going to be spiritually improved by being collateral damage in a bombardment of severities targeted at adults who may or may not deserve more severe treatment from the welfare system.[20]

Describing the new welfare bill as harmful to poor children, Senator Daniel Patrick Moynihan (D-N.Y.) predicted that "those involved (in the passage of this legislation) will take this disgrace to their graves."[21] Marian Wright Edelman, president of Children's Defense Fund, in an open letter to President Clinton, condemned the dismantling of welfare, writing

> It would be a great moral and practical wrong for you to sign any welfare "reform" bill that will push millions of already poor children and families deeper into poverty ... longer-term and perhaps irreparable damage will be inflicted on children if you permit (the destruction) of the fundamental moral principle that an American child, regardless of the state or parents the child chanced to draw, is entitled to protection of last resort by his or her national government. ... [The proposed welfare reform] ... is the domestic equivalent of bombing Vietnamese villages in order to save them. It is moral hypocrisy for our nation to slash income, health and nutrition assistance for poor children while leaving untouched hundreds of billions in corporate welfare, giving new tax breaks of over $200 billion for non-needy citizens.[22]

The Children's Defense Fund warned the program would lead to 4 to 5 million children losing their meager federal income support of about US$4.50 per day. The poorest of the poor children would have even less.

Proponents of the bill responded by arguing that the existing program had been around for more than sixty years, and had yet to show evidence of reducing poverty rates or improving the long-term conditions of children living in poverty. The liberal opposition's claims were merely the roadblock designed to preserve a failed program.

Also criticizing the Republican's reform bill, the *Washington Post* editorialized, "Now here is the part you need to know: *Mr. Clinton's own advisors have told him that it would likely consign as many as a million more children to poverty, and it would provide several billions less for childcare than his own proposal of a year ago*"[23] (italics in original).

Despite these dire predictions, Congress passed the Personal Responsibility and Work Opportunity Reconciliation Act (P.L. 104–193) in the summer of 1996. For more than three decades "welfare" had been a wedge issue dividing Democrats and Republicans. On August 22, 1996, President Clinton ended the debate and signed into law a bill that ended the entitlement to welfare and allowed states to dismantle the welfare program.

Undeterred by widespread expressions of disapproval from his own party and outrage from leading activists for children and the poor, the president decided to do as he had promised: to "end welfare as we know it." In so doing, he removed the safeguards that had entitled poor children to a national standard of income protection. Instead, block grants were awarded to the states which, although outlining certain mandates and parameters, basically allowed the individual states to develop their own welfare programs to administer as they saw fit.

Dawn of a New Era

With this passage of the Republican-sponsored welfare reform bill, public assistance to America's poorest children entered a new period in the history of domestic social policy with the role of government substantially reduced. Although it would take some years to assess the impact of the new law and the policies it embodied, initial results appeared encouraging. Welfare reform occurred as the country entered a period of great prosperity. Two years earlier, the Internet was opened up with an easy to use Web browser. A new era of technology was ushered in. Inflation was at modest levels, financial markets were enjoying an expansion and growth not seen in years, and there was a pervasive sense that U.S. business was entering a new era of innovation and entrepreneurship. Thus conditions were nearly ideal for the welfare reform legislation to flourish. And, indeed, early evidence indicated that previous welfare recipients were moving into the workplace.

Even though there are little hard data, it is reasonable to assume that economic conditions at that time may have afforded low- and no-income families new employment opportunities. At least, it is clear that the dire prognostications of the opponents of welfare reform were not being borne out. For proponents of the bill, there was an early sense of vindication. They only had to point to the dramatic decrease in the number of children on public assistance to make their case (see Figure 4.1).[24]

Yet despite the apparent good news that proponents of welfare reform trumpeted, there were a number of disquieting facts that suggested welfare reform may not have reduced child poverty. Although it is true that there are fewer children on the federal welfare rolls than in 1996, the decline of children receiving welfare did not necessarily mean these children had exited poverty. It may seem logical to assume that the movement of children off of welfare is the result of the children's improved economic conditions. Historically, the number of children receiving welfare mirrored the number of children living in poverty. However, with the implementation of the welfare reform legislation, each state developed its own approach to public assistance and thus it became difficult to accurately assess the bigger picture. To understand the impact of welfare reform required an analysis of state-level data.

Several states that have been in the forefront of welfare reforms (e.g., Wisconsin, Florida, and Illinois) reduced their welfare caseloads by more than two-thirds between 1996 and 2006. Wisconsin's program instituted under Governor Tommy Thompson was heralded as a model for welfare reform and

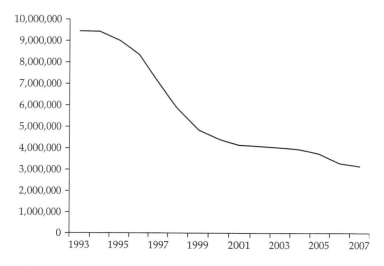

Figure 4.1 Number of Poor Children Receiving Welfare

provides a means of analyzing the results of reform in one state. Thompson himself called the program "the most dramatic change in social policy in 50 years," and proclaimed that "the welfare check is history."[25] His state took the lead in implementing major changes in program operation prior to the passage of reform at the federal level. In 1996, about 133,000 children in Wisconsin had been receiving welfare benefits. With the passage of welfare reform, the number of children fell to fewer than 43,000 (see Figure 4.2).

Yet during the same period, the number of children in poverty in the state increased from 167,000 to 192,000. Thus, while the number of children in poverty increased by 25,000, more than 90,000 children were dropped from the state's welfare rolls. As can be seen in Figure 4.2, removal of children from the welfare rolls had little to do with the actual lives the children were leading. After the passage of welfare reform, child poverty in Wisconsin increased during the first year. Child poverty declined for the following two years and then leveled off before rising to its highest level by 2004.[26] Since the enactment of welfare reform (Temporary Assistance for Needy Families, TANF), the total number of welfare recipients in Wisconsin declined more than three-quarters by June 2007. From 1996 to 2006, the number of children living in poverty in the state of Wisconsin increased

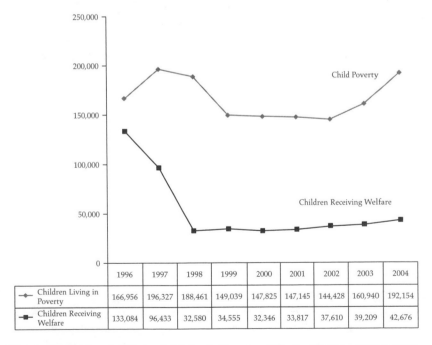

	1996	1997	1998	1999	2000	2001	2002	2003	2004
Children Living in Poverty	166,956	196,327	188,461	149,039	147,825	147,145	144,428	160,940	192,154
Children Receiving Welfare	133,084	96,433	32,580	34,555	32,346	33,817	37,610	39,209	42,676

Figure 4.2 Children in Wisconsin Living in Poverty and Losing Welfare, 1996 to 2004

by 14 percent from 169,000 to 192,000. Welfare reform did not end child poverty in Wisconsin, but it ended welfare benefits for most recipients even though poverty increased.[27]

Equating caseload declines with declines in child poverty, many have argued that welfare reform has improved the lives of children. But as we examine the states with the highest caseload reductions—those states that cut the number of children receiving welfare by more than two-thirds—we see no concomitant reduction in poverty. For the group of states in Table 4.1, more than 2 million children lost their welfare benefits; during this same period, fewer than half a million children were removed from poverty.

Like Wisconsin, Florida became a model state for welfare reform. During the period since the passage of welfare reform, more than 75 percent of poor children receiving income assistance—more than 300,000 children—lost their aid in Florida. Most of these children did not exit poverty; they simply lost their welfare benefits. Welfare reform did not end child poverty—it ended income assistance to many children living in poverty.

The reductions in people receiving aid could indicate that many single mothers and their children have achieved economic independence and are no longer in need of help. Yet in light of other figures, this optimistic interpretation seems misleading.[28]

Table 4.1 Changes in Welfare and Poverty, 1996 to 2004

	Child Poverty 1996	Child Poverty 2004	Change in Child Poverty	Children Removed From Welfare	Percentage of Children Removed From Welfare
Wyoming	19,000	15,492	–3,508	8,983	94.2
Virginia	276,151	221,675	–54,476	99,525	85.2
Illinois	591,749	539,394	–52,355	386,356	84.1
Idaho	56,860	56,562	–298	13,573	83.3
Louisiana	369,254	314,522	–54,732	127,246	77.3
Florida	784,588	699,280	–85,308	310,413	76.6
Connecticut	118,359	95,407	–22,952	77,674	71.8
New York	1,156,555	940,974	–215,581	539,288	69.1
North Carolina	357,716	398,952	41,236	133,198	68.8
Maryland	187,858	156,087	–31,771	97,744	68.5
Mississippi	232,548	212,865	–19,683	67,281	68.3
Wisconsin	166,956	192,154	25,198	90,408	67.9
South Carolina	223,387	217,509	–5,878	61,419	67.6
Total	4,540,981	4,060,873	–480,108	2,013,108	

Changes in Child Poverty After Welfare Reform

The United States provides a set of means-tested programs to aid children in poverty. Besides welfare, the most important program to provide aid to poor children is food stamps, which was introduced as part of the War on Poverty.[29] The 1996 Welfare reforms did not alter the previously established food stamp program.[30] Eligibility for food stamps is determined using separate federal program standards than welfare, even though there is often a great deal of overlap between the two programs. Food stamp recipients encompass children and adults and include senior citizens living in poverty.[31] In order to determine eligibility for food stamps, officials collect extensive income data. Although some states administer food stamps and welfare out of the same welfare office, eligibility for food stamps is independent of welfare eligibility and conforms to a uniform national standard.

Data from the food stamp program provide an independent measure of the economic situation of poor children after welfare reform. Because eligibility for the food stamp program is strictly enforced and has been developed and tested over several years, the administrative data from the program provides one of the best independent indicators of the economic condition of children post-welfare reform. The advantage of the food stamp administrative data is that it is based on a national standard that is consistently applied across the different states and is subject to federal audits to ensure reliability and is therefore likely to be one of the more reliable indicators of economic changes.

State agencies operating within the uniform guidelines established by the federal government determine food stamp eligibility. Therefore, if a mother with two children has a net monthly income of less than US$1306 (in 2005), then the family will be eligible for food stamps.[32] The amount of the food stamp benefit will be determined by the net income below this amount, with a maximum amount of US$393 a month. These same rules apply in each state.

Changes in the food stamp caseload have historically mirrored changes in the welfare caseload. As welfare caseloads decline, a parallel decline in the number of food stamp recipients follows, even though food stamps might still be provided to some welfare recipients even after they have ceased to receive welfare payments. Many recipients who leave welfare and go to work are employed at low paying jobs that may leave them eligible for continued food stamp assistance. The data in Figure 4.3 displays the number of children receiving food stamps and welfare in the United States.

The data in Figure 4.3 indicate that in the first few years after the passage of welfare reform, the number of children nationwide receiving food stamps

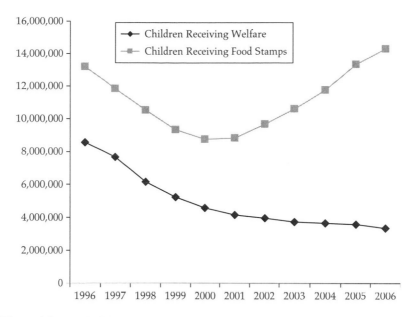

Figure 4.3 Poor Children Receiving Welfare and Food Stamps

declined along with the decline in children receiving welfare.[33] However, after 2000, the number of children receiving food stamps increased. By 2006, there were more children receiving food stamps than there had been prior to welfare reform. Nonetheless, these children who would have been entitled to welfare prior to reform were now no longer likely to receive assistance.

Decline in Food Stamps Varies by State

To understand what happened to food stamp recipients after the passage of welfare reform requires an examination of the change in caseloads at the state level.[34] For example, in Wisconsin, one of the most lauded state examples of welfare reform, the number of children receiving welfare fell by more than two-thirds, whereas the number of children receiving food stamps went in the opposite direction—it increased in excess of 10 percent (see Figure 4.4). Why such a difference? By 2004, the number of children receiving food stamps exceeded the number prior to welfare reform in 1996. Although the numbers of child food stamp recipients were exceeding their pre-welfare reform levels, the welfare caseload has remained at less than a third of their pre-1996 levels.

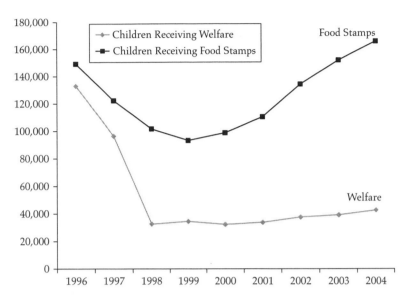

Figure 4.4 Children Receiving Welfare and Food Stamps in Wisconsin, 1996 to 2004

The data suggest that children have been taken off the welfare caseload, yet have remained reliant upon food stamps because Wisconsin was able to remove impoverished children with impunity from welfare but not food stamps. What happened in Wisconsin was repeated in most of the states that achieved sharp welfare caseload reductions. The food stamp statistics suggest the economic situation of poor children has not substantially improved since the passage of welfare reform—and thus calls into question the putative achievement represented by the dramatic and oft-cited state welfare caseload declines. In previous research, I have shown that the average monthly food stamp benefit per person has risen in the states with steep cuts in children receiving welfare. This indicates that the income of those still receiving food stamps in these states declined. Rather than providing assistance to more children with less need, food stamps served more children and the needs of these children had increased.[35] What is called upon as a justification of further cuts and an example of the success of reform, becomes questionable, especially with respect to the state of children who would once have been recipients of welfare.

It should be noted that the apparent inconsistency of an increase in the child food stamp caseload combined with a decline in the welfare caseload varied substantially among the states; however, the states with the greatest welfare caseload declines recorded the greatest discrepancy between the two figures suggesting that many children have been removed from the welfare program even though their poverty has remained or even worsened.

Perhaps there is some other explanation for this discrepancy that is unique to the administration of the food stamp program. Another source of information on the economic situation of poor children during the last decade is the school lunch program. As with food stamps, children from welfare families have also received a government-subsidized free lunch through the National School Lunch Program (NSLP) that was administered independently of the welfare program.[36]

Child Poverty Measured in the School Lunch Line

In 2008, the NSLP[37] provides lunches to 30.6 million children whose families are below 130 percent of the national poverty level (US$26,845 for a family of four in 2008).[38] The program includes a federally subsidized free lunch for poor children in school. In order to qualify for free lunches, the child's parent must complete an income verification application.[39] The advantage of using administrative data from this program to gauge child poverty is that the income verification application completed and signed by the parent provides information that is independent of TANF and the food stamp program.[40] However, the number of children receiving free lunch through the NSLP does not include infants and young children in poor families who are not enrolled in school. Thus, it is not a complete measure of child poverty but only a proxy measure of child poverty among school-age children.

National Trend

Figure 4.5 displays the national trend in terms of the number of children receiving welfare and the number of children receiving a subsidized free lunch throughout the United States. From 1977 to 1995 the difference between the number of children eligible for the free lunch program at school and the number of children on welfare was consistently about 2 million.[41] After the passage of welfare reform and the removal of children from the welfare caseloads, the spread between these programs increased to 8 million.

Millions of children continued to qualify for subsidized free lunch despite no longer qualifying for welfare. In fact, the number of children qualifying for subsidized free lunch increased from 12 to 15 million during the same

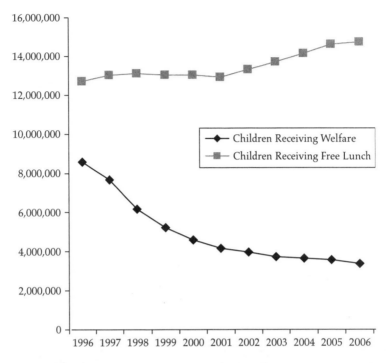

Figure 4.5 Poor Children Receiving Free Lunch and Welfare in the United States

time that the number of children receiving welfare was cut from roughly 9 million to 3 million. These data confirm what the food stamp program data have already suggested: that millions of poor children lost welfare benefits even though their economic situation had not improved.

In both cases, if poverty had truly been alleviated, the decline in the number of children receiving welfare would be consistent with a decline in the number of children receiving free lunches and with children receiving food stamps (see Figure 4.5).

If we are to believe the data from the free lunch program, then the number of children living in poverty continued to increase after the passage of the welfare reform legislation. Every year since 1996, the number of children receiving a free lunch has increased. By 2006, the number of children receiving free lunch had risen by more than 3 million, going from 12 to almost 15 million.[42]

With this data we can gain greater insight into exactly what has been happening at the state level. For instance, in the model state of Wisconsin the sharp reduction in children receiving welfare was heralded as evidence of the improving conditions of poor children as a result of welfare reform.

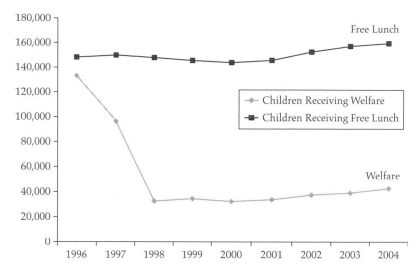

Figure 4.6 Children Receiving Welfare and Free Lunch in Wisconsin, 1996 to 2004

However, this rosy picture is belied by that which is provided by the free lunch data. During the time when children were being removed from the welfare rolls at a pace never seen before in history, they remained or were being added to the free lunch program.

In 1996, the number of children receiving welfare in Wisconsin was roughly equivalent to the number of children receiving a federally subsidized free lunch. Shortly after the passage of welfare reform, the number of children receiving welfare declined from over 120,000 to less than 40,000 in 2007. Yet the number of children eligible and receiving subsidized free lunch continued to increase. Reports from the NSLP indicate that the overall income characteristics of those eligible and receiving free lunch has not changed since the passage of welfare reform. Figure 4.6 displays a comparison of the number of children receiving free lunches with the decline in the number of children receiving welfare in Wisconsin.[43]

Women, Infants, and Children—and Welfare

The limitation of using data from the subsidized free lunch program to assess child poverty is that these figures do not include preschool age children. Data from the Women, Infants, and Children (WIC) Program allows us to supplement the data from the subsidized free lunch program to assess child poverty. The WIC program provides important nutritional and medical assistance to low-income mothers with children under 5. The program is means-tested but provides assistance to a larger group of poor mothers than the food stamps program. For instance, the income cutoff point for a mother with two children in 2005 was US$30,000. The program is particularly designed to provide food and medical services to pregnant women and women with infants and young children. When welfare reform was enacted, the WIC program was left untouched. Eligibility for WIC is separate from eligibility for welfare (TANF), although in most states mothers who are receiving welfare are automatically eligible for WIC.

Again, as with data from the federal food stamp program and the subsidized NSLP, the WIC numbers indicate that child poverty did not decline after the enactment of welfare reform.[44] In fact, the number of mothers enrolling in the WIC program has increased. As Figure 4.7 shows, although the number of children receiving welfare declined substantially, WIC enrollment increased almost one-third.

Twelve years after the passage of welfare reform we have the ability to assess its impact upon poor children. The indisputable fact that the number of poor children receiving income assistance through welfare has been greatly reduced led to conclusions that these sharp reductions was evidence that welfare reform had led to a reduction in child poverty and had actually resulted in improved economic conditions for poor children in the United

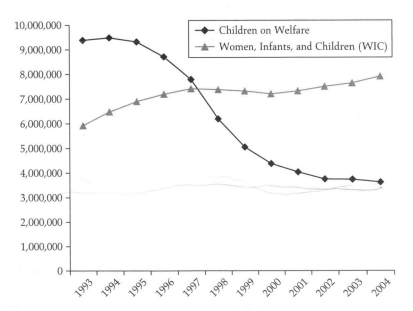

Figure 4.7 Women, Infants, and Children—and Welfare

States. It was difficult to refute this argument in the early years after the passage of welfare reform; however it is now clear that such conclusions were wrong or the result of partisan zeal.

There were more children receiving food stamps in 2006 than prior to welfare reform. Furthermore, over the last dozen years, the number of children eligible and participating in the subsidized free lunch program has increased. In virtually every state that removed more than two-thirds of poor children from their welfare rolls, these same children continued to remain eligible for free lunch. In fact, not only did the numbers remain constant, in most cases, the number of children eligible for subsidized free lunch increased. A final source of data, the WIC program that provides an independent indicator of the number of infants and preschool age children needing federal government assistance, also showed an increase in the number of eligible children; WIC participants have increased by one-third since 1996.

In the arguments prior to the passage of the Welfare Reform Bill, child advocates warned that welfare reform would lead to millions of children being dropped from the welfare rolls. The data examined in this chapter vindicate their prediction. It appears that as many as 6 million poor children have lost income assistance. Although no longer eligible for the welfare benefits, their economic situation has not improved but worsened, and they have had to adapt to a lower standard of living and a bleaker economic situation overall. The data from these federal means-tested programs indicate that the number of children living in poverty has increased since 1996 and demonstrate that the net effect of welfare was to end entitlement to income protection which the Social Security Act provided back in 1935.

What has been painfully ironic is that those who have promoted this change have argued that it was in done in the best interests of poor children. No doubt they are sincere. Tommy Thompson, Secretary of Health and Human Services for President George W. Bush argued,

Child poverty rates are at or near historic lows. This is one of the most important outcomes we could have hoped to achieve—and TANF has been a stunning success. The overall child poverty rate has fallen from 20.5% in 1996 to 16.3% in 2001—a 20% decline. The poverty rate for African American children is down 24% since 1996 and in 2001 reached it lowest level ever recorded.[45]

Melissa Pardue of the Heritage Foundation echoed these views claiming

In the almost seven years since the welfare reform law was enacted, economic conditions have improved dramatically for the United States's poorest families. Welfare rolls have plummeted, employment of single mothers has increased dramatically, and child hunger has declined substantially. Most striking, however, has been the effect of welfare reform on child poverty, particularly among black children.[46]

The publications by the conservative proponents of welfare reform rarely rely on peer-reviewed scientific publications, but rather stem primarily from publications of conservative think tanks and private foundations. The statements about welfare reform being responsible for the reduction of child poverty have not appeared in the scientific peer-reviewed literature. These assertions of a connection are not supported by credible scientific evidence. As we have seen earlier, when examined at the state level, there is no correlation between declines in children receiving welfare and children living in poverty.[47]

Beginning in 1995 the percentage of parents who were employed increased from 76 percent to 79.5 percent in 2000. From 2000 to 2004, however, this same parent employment fell back to 76.4 percent. In short, the supposed increase in work was largely the result of the improving economy.[48]

First precept: our overriding goal ought to be to save the children. Other goals—reducing the cost of welfare, discouraging illegitimacy, and preventing long-term welfare dependency—are all worthy. But they should be secondary to the goal of improving the life prospects of the next generation.

James Q. Wilson, From Welfare Reform
and Character Development[49]

The meager lives and hopelessness that these poor children endure on a daily basis is, after welfare reform, deeply and incontrovertibly more painful.[50] Between 2000 and 2006, child poverty increased by 11 percent. There has been an even greater increase in extreme poverty for children that increased by 20 percent between 2000 and 2004.[51] Black children in extreme poverty increased by 20.7 percent, whereas it increased by 24.9 percent for Latino children during this period.[52] Child poverty, after falling seven of the eight years of Clinton presidency, has increased during most of the George W. Bush presidency. By 2006, almost 40 percent of the nation's children—more than 28 million—lived in low-income families.[53]

Welfare Reform: The End of Income Assistance to Poor Children

By 2000, the economic boom had come to an end.[54] The "dot com" bubble burst and with it came financial stagnation.[55] What had seemed to work for everyone—to some degree—began to take on a less rosy hue. From 2000 to 2006, the prospects and realities for poor children grew bleaker. More children depended upon food stamps. More children relied upon subsidized free lunches from the federal government. During the summer when the state subsidized school breakfast and lunch programs were unavailable, many poor children no doubt went hungry.

Thus, the appearance of a decline in child poverty rates was false when viewed over the decade since the passage of welfare reform. The only indicator that the condition of poor children has not been worsening was the declining welfare rolls, but it was the wrong signal. By 2006, the number of children receiving welfare has been reduced by almost two-thirds. This decline has been cited repeatedly as an indicator of a decline in child poverty.[56] Yet the child poverty rate, according to the Census Bureau, declined from 20.5 percent in 1996 to 18.3 percent in 2006. As can be seen in Figure 4.8, the number of children living in poverty began declining in 1993 and continued until 2000, when the economic boom came to an end with the dotcom bust. Since 2000, child poverty has trended up and today there are about as many children in poverty as prior to welfare reform. For Black children the story was the same. By 2006, there were more Black children living in poverty than prior to welfare reform.

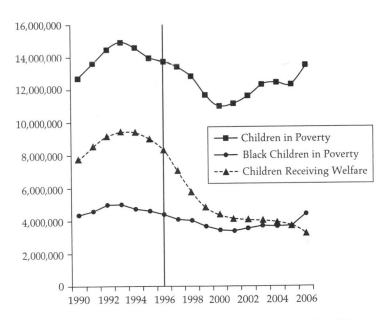

Figure 4.8 Children Living in Poverty and Receiving Welfare, 1990 to 2006

Source: Census Bureau.

In 1996 almost two-thirds of children in poverty received welfare. By 2006, less than one-quarter of children in poverty received welfare. Although there has been a small decline in the overall child poverty rate since welfare reform, it hardly accounts for the dramatic decline in children receiving welfare. The decline in children receiving welfare is primarily a result of states limiting access to benefits and dismantling their welfare programs.

What has replaced the income support for welfare provided to poor children? No major new programs replaced welfare. Children living in poverty simply adjusted to living on less income.

Although welfare reform was successful in dismantling the means-tested welfare program, it has not proved effective in achieving anything of import with regard to ameliorating the problem of child poverty. The need for extending public assistance to children in poverty has never been more pressing than since the original passage of the Social Security Act of 1935. Yet the responsibility for giving that assistance now falls to the states rather than the federal government. Welfare reform has allowed the states to step away from this responsibility and to essentially cease providing benefits to children. Most states have been taking advantage of this feature and have reduced their welfare rolls without providing anything else comparable for the children who had depended upon welfare.

As welfare reform was being debated, Donna Pavetti used a statistical model to predict the impact of the proposed program changes, including time limits.[57] Pavetti's research indicated that 3.5 million children would be dropped from income assistance by 2001 and that by 2005 that number would reach 4.9 million (and that more than two-thirds would be Black and Hispanic children).[58] Pavetti predicted that children would be dropped not because their economic situation improved but because the program would no longer be obliged to provide income support even if they lived in poverty. Her research was prophetic. The data examined in this chapter suggest this was close to what happened.

The essential lesson of this chapter is that welfare reform did not end child poverty or even contribute to its reduction.[59] What welfare reform did do, however, was to end the federal entitlement program of income assistance for poor children. It empowered the individual states to allocate funds elsewhere, including the right to cut off benefits, or to redirect welfare block grant money into a host of other activities.

Closing: Different Worlds of Childhood in the United States

It is hard to reconcile the heralded achievements of welfare reform with the Dickensian parsimony of our current TANF welfare program.[60] The conundrum compels us to consider anew the responsibilities of the nation toward its poor children? The findings in this chapter reveal that the program most responsible for providing income assistance to poor children—welfare—was fundamentally altered by welfare reform. A dozen years later, the number of children receiving welfare had been reduced to about 3 million from almost 9 million. Advocates of welfare reform cited this as an indicator of a decline in child poverty.[61] But it was not. In most states, children were simply denied benefits. Although they remained in poverty, their mother ceased to receive the meager welfare check. A dozen years after welfare reform, more children were living in poverty than before its enactment. Data from the food stamps program, the subsidized federal free lunch program, the WIC program all point to more children living in poverty and low-income families. As Senator Moynihan complained in 2002, "This is not [welfare] reform. This is repeal of Aid to Families with Dependent Children."

One of the indisputable outcomes of welfare reform is that it took children away from their mothers for longer periods of time. Since more than two-thirds of welfare mothers have children under the age of 6, the result is that more infants and toddlers are separated from their mothers at a critical stage in their growth and development. The employment rate of unmarried mothers increased from about 50 percent before welfare reform (1996) to about 63 percent in 2008. Welfare reform did little for these mothers and their children except demand that the mothers work 40 or more hours a week in low paying jobs. Even though single mothers worked longer hours after welfare reform, their overall economic situation did not improve; it declined. As we will see in the next chapter, their poverty has less to do with their failure to work—most of these mothers now work long hours at low paying jobs—than with the failure of essential economic support systems in the United States that serve single mothers.[62] In most other industrialized countries, these economic support systems, which include effective child support collection, an equitable children's allowance and universal free day care, are in place and are responsible for substantially reducing child poverty.

During the era of the wealthy class, tax policies were implemented that raised the fortunes of those at the top. During this same period, the floor of income protection for those at the other end—the low income and poor—was removed. In particular, income support for the poorest of the poor—children in poverty—was cut by two-thirds.

The welfare program is not coming back. It was a flawed program that provided relief from the pains of poverty but did little to move single mothers and children out of poverty and into independent self-sustaining careers. The reforms brought about by welfare reform effectively ended welfare but did not end the problem welfare was designed to alleviate. Child poverty in the United States remains at the highest levels in the industrial world. But as we pointed out in Chapter 1, child poverty is concentrated among Hispanic and African American children, where the child poverty rates are closer to 35 and 40 percent.

As we have seen in the case of poverty among seniors, there are policies and programs that could substantially reduce child poverty in the United States. These new policies and programs are universal—they would apply to all children—not just the poor. The benefits from these programs would not be clawed back as single mothers improved their situation. These programs essentially involve fixing the child support collection system and stream-lining our social policies toward children. In the next chapter we examine these programs and policies.

5

⟡

Eliminating Welfare
and Reducing Child
Poverty

The closest the United States has come to implementing a socialist economy has been the public welfare system. The premise of the socialist economy was "to each according to his/her need, from each according to his/her ability," which was more hope than was reality. In the United States, the welfare system gave rise to a far from nurturing environment. Although it provided a safety net, it neither sated the needs of its recipients nor challenged them to make use of their inherent strengths and talent. Rather than provide entry to the middle class or participation in the nation's economic prosperity, it fostered dependence and limited opportunity. So blatantly did the system fail its users, that although he held grave reservations about reforming welfare, Bill Clinton himself declared, "I will sign this bill—first and foremost, because the current system is broken."[1]

Has welfare reform fixed the welfare system? The welfare reform legislation replaced an entitlement program with a system of block grants to the states. With the federal government basically abdicating responsibility, the states have been given free reign to phase out their welfare programs. What remains in the broken shards of what was once welfare, are the problems that it was originally designed to address, most notably the problems of single mothers and their children.[2]

The major problem with the old welfare system was the means-tested premise upon which it was built. Means testing inadvertently rewards a lack of means sending the message that if you demonstrate that you do not have the means to take care of yourself, you can get help. There are no provisions for people who cannot completely take care of themselves or who need a small boost. Demonstrating self-sufficiency results only in penalty. The weakness of Communism was its failure to reward individual effort and ingenuity. Welfare similarly worked to punish anyone who had the desire if not the means to escape it. The restrictions of the means-tested approach rewarded failure in order to retain benefits. As Rector writes, "To 'earn' this welfare paycheck, the mother had to fulfill two conditions: She could not work and she could not marry an employed man."[3]

With the dismantling of welfare comes an opportunity to construct a new set of programs and policies more in accord with the fundamental premises of capitalism and the free enterprise market economy.[4] The principles of a Jeffersonian democracy emphasize the primacy of the common man and woman through ownership of personal property. The essential requirement of effective social programs is universal coverage, meaning that they should be available to all citizens, rather than limited to the poor.

The most successful social program that arose out of the New Deal has been Social Security. Whereas Social Security has led to the elimination of poverty among seniors, welfare that was a part of the Social Security program failed to lead to the elimination of poverty among single mothers and their children. Why was one part so successful and the other so flawed? The most salient difference between welfare and Social Security is that Social Security encompassed all citizens and provided them with a mechanism to set aside money for a time when they would need it—when they retire—whereas welfare was limited to those in desperate need. Social Security is a social insurance program that provides benefits to program participants irrespective of their income and wealth. Thus, if a senior citizen has saved money in a retirement fund, he or she will not experience any reduction in benefits.

The most intractable operational problem of welfare was that as a single mother worked she would have her benefits taken away—or clawed back.[5] The "claw back" feature of welfare meant that earnings from work were often taxed at high rates, sometimes exceeding 70 percent. Hence, a woman who worked could find herself no better off than one who did not. This is completely at odds with a capitalist philosophy that rewards work.

The Current State of the Welfare State

Despite the United States' broad and comprehensive set of universal social programs designed to protect the economic situation of seniors, there is no

Table 5.1 Major Income Support and Health Programs for
Young Children and Seniors (2006)

	Amount in Billions (US$)
Seniors (N = 41 million)	
Universal	
Social Security	461
Medicare	418
Medicaid	314
Prescription drug benefit (Part D)	75
Children 0–6 (N = 25 million)	
Universal	
None	
Means-tested	
TANF	12.7
Head start	6.9
Foster care	4.4
SCHIP	5.5
Medicaid	40.6

Source: Social Security Administration (2007); Urban Institute (2007).[8]

Note: The figures for children for Temporary Assistance for Needy Families (TANF),
Foster Care, SCHIP, and Medicaid cover children from 0 to 18.

similar set of benefits for children. Rather, in contrast to what is provided to
seniors, the federal government does relatively little for young children (see
Table 5.1). To put it bluntly, the main reason that the United States, the richest country in the industrialized world, has the highest child poverty rates
is that in contrast to what the elderly receive, social programs for children
under the age of six are a patchwork of means-tested plans geared far more
toward making sure mothers work than to protecting the economic condition of their children. In this regard, the United States stands apart from
nearly every other modern industrialized nation.

In this chapter, we explore three areas where universal programs and
policies that have been developed in other free market economies could be
implemented in the United States to fundamentally alter the impoverished
state of the typical single mother.

Over time, welfare became a bundled solution to address the following:[6]

1. The failure to provide government subsidized child care for children
   under six. The United States provides universal free public education for
   children from kindergarten to 12th grade (6 to 18 years of age) but fails to
   provide child care for the infants and toddlers.

2. The failure of America's children's allowance program—administered as a child tax credit—to provide coverage for poor and low-income children.

3. The failure of the current child support system to collect child support, especially for poor and low-income children.

In almost all modern industrial democracies, every child is covered by a state-administered child support collection system. In addition, almost all industrial democracies provide for a children's allowance to every child. Finally, almost all industrial democracies provide universal government subsidized child care.[7] If the United States provided a system of effective children support collection, a universal children's allowance, and publicly subsidized child care, then the need for welfare would be eliminated. All children would be guaranteed income protection through systems that would provide greater support than the current welfare program. As we have seen in Chapter 4, welfare is being essentially phased out. If policies that provide basic income protection for children along the lines outlined above are put in place, then welfare can finally be eliminated.

The Failure of Means-Tested Welfare

Lacking both adequate child support and a children's allowance, the United States has had to rely upon welfare as a "bundled benefit" to make up for the failings of the child support and children's allowance program. The term *bundled* indicates that rather than providing separate benefits to make up for an absence of child support for poor families and the denial of a children's allowance to the poorest children, welfare bundled all these otherwise separate needs into one lump sum benefit.

The bundled benefit combined child support and the children's allowance into one single payment which, as we have seen, failed to move poor children out of poverty, either before or after reform.

The early debate between Liberals and Conservatives often centered on how much cash to provide the poor.[9] With the publication of Charles Murray's ideological treatise, *Losing Ground*, came a questioning of the fundamental premise of providing income assistance in its entirety. From his book sprang the Conservative campaign that would bring an end to welfare as we knew it.[10] As each of the states selectively, but inexorably, dismantle income support for poor children and their mothers, it seems highly unlikely that the original welfare program will be restored, despite growing evidence that poverty among children continues at high levels.

Working and the Claw Back Effect

In ending welfare, the country took away their single largest source of income. They didn't march or riot. They made their way against the odds into wearying, under-paid jobs. And that does now entitle them to something—to "a shot at the American Dream" more promising than the one they've received.

Jason DeParle, *American Dream*[11]

Although critics of welfare argued correctly that welfare discourages work, they did not always understand the reasons for this. The inherent problem with welfare lay in the fact that it is taken away as its recipients improve their situation. A poor mother who receives welfare will lose either a portion or even all of the welfare payment. As the mother earns income, the government then "claws back" the welfare payment it provides. This claw back has the effect of taxing the wage income the mother receives.

Researchers from Brookings Institute compiled income data on the effects of welfare reform on single mothers. Mothers in the bottom 20th percentile increased their earnings from US$1774 in 1995 to US$3148 in 2000—a more than 75 percent rise.[12] However, during this same period their welfare payments decreased (got clawed back) from US$4758 in 1995 to US$3298 in 2000. This loss of US$1460 surpassed the amount they had gained through their increased earnings. Thus, even though these mothers had increased their earnings by 75 percent, they experienced a net loss after taking into account the claw back of means-tested benefits.

This same phenomenon occurred among female heads of households in the second-fifth of the study group. Between 1995 and 2000, these mothers increased their earnings from US$6898 to US$11,710 or by 70 percent, whereas their means-tested benefits declined from US$5678 to US$2636: a loss of more than US$3000.[13] As a result, the net benefit from increased earnings was more than cut in half by the claw back of welfare benefits.

In 2005, researchers from the Tax Policy Center of the Urban Institute and the Brookings Institution estimated the average effective marginal tax rate confronting single-parent families.[14] They calculated that single-parent families with income between US$10,000 and US$40,000 had an effective marginal tax rate of 88.6 percent[15] (taking into account food stamps, health programs, Temporary Assistance for Needy Families (TANF), housing, and child care subsidies), whereas families with an income from US$90,000 to US$230,000 had an effective tax rate of 33.2 percent.[16] The reason the low-to-moderate income families paid such a high effective marginal tax rate is because as they earned income, they lost a multitude of means-tested welfare benefits including food stamps, Medicaid, State Child Health Insurance, TANF (welfare),

Table 5.2 Net Effective Earnings Before and After Welfare[18]

	On Welfare (US$)	Off Welfare (US$)
Earnings	6500	16,100
Earned Income		
Tax credits	2300	5600
Payroll taxes	−500	−1200
Cash welfare	8400	0
Food stamps	4800	4400
Total income	21,500	24,900

public housing assistance, Women, Infants, and Children (WIC) subsidies, and child care subsidies. The problem with means-tested public aid is that it has to be clawed back as the individual works and earns income.

As the Brookings and Urban Institute data illustrate, providing income assistance to poor mothers using a means-tested welfare structure results in the unintended consequence of imposing an exorbitant tax on earnings, thus diminishing the financial rewards of work.

New York Times reporter Jason DeParle (2005) tells the story of Angie, a welfare recipient he followed during the period after welfare reform.[17] When Angie left welfare she got a job as a nursing aide that allowed her to earn US$16,100 (Table 5.2). Yet the net benefit from working as a nursing aide and earning US$9600 more than the previous year when she was on welfare was actually US$3400. This represents a net effective tax rate of 65 percent.

Although Angie appears to have improved her well-being by working, it may be less than these figures indicate. As DeParle notes, "The more she worked, the more her work expenses increased. There was bus fare, babysitting, work uniforms, and snacks from the vending machine. In Angie's case, the child care costs were minimal, since the kids mostly minded themselves."[19]

Proven Programs for Ending Child Poverty

So why not take the opportunity that the demise of AFDC now thrusts upon us? Why not start talking about broad new ways—a widening of the idea of social security—to help the majority of American working parents, with extra help for the poorest offered in the context of such an overall effort?

Theda Skocpol, The Next Liberalism[20]

Restoration of the pre-1996 welfare system is neither feasible nor desirable. Although both the public and the government agreed in condemning the old system of income support to poor mothers and their children, we are presented with a rare opportunity to restructure our approach to helping poor children.

It is important to develop income support programs that meet the needs that welfare provided without the limitations and harmful side effects that welfare created. Programs must ensure that poor mothers receive *both* child support and a children's allowance—subsidies that will not be taken back as wage income increases. If the welfare mother works and earns additional income, she will not lose the payments she receives from child support or a children's allowance as she does now with welfare.

The first step should be to make the nation's children's allowance program—currently provided by way of a tax deduction—fair, equitable, and available to *all* children. Second, we should provide a child support program along the lines of what is provided in other modern industrial democracies. If these two programs are then combined with universal child care, the problem of child poverty that has been with us for so long will start coming to an end, and we will have no need for any means-tested welfare program.

Publicly subsidized child care must be made available. Infants and young children should have access to prekindergarten in just the same way as their peers in Western Europe and their older brothers and sisters attending public school in the United States (see Table 5.3).

Table 5.3 Percentage of Children, Age 3 to School Age, Enrolled in Publicly Financed Child Care Facilities

Country	Percentage Provided
Austria	75
Belgium	95
Denmark	79
Finland	43
France	99
Germany*	100
Greece	64
Ireland	52
Italy	97
Netherlands	69
Portugal	48
Spain	84
Sweden	79
United Kingdom	53

Data Source: Gauthier (1999: table 5), updated by author.[21]
*Percentage for Germany represents those eligible but not necessarily enrolled.

If we are to follow the example of other industrialized nations beyond the institution of daycare, we find that for the most part the democracies of Europe provide income support programs to create a safety net for poor and disadvantaged children. These programs take the form of income support packages that include assured child support, a children's allowance as well as publicly subsidized child care.

Universal Children's Allowance

Children's allowance programs can be found in more than 70 nations, including all of Western Europe (see Table 5.4).[22] In these countries, children's allowance programs play a vital part in protecting the economic viability of many poor families. Recognizing the financial burden that parents shoulder in raising children, these direct payments are applied universally from the poorest families to the wealthiest. This approach presumes that children represent a society's future; thus, ensuring for their care and well-being

Table 5.4 Children's Allowance Programs

	Program Started	Annual Benefit (US$)		Means-Tested
		First Child	Second Child	
Belgium		933	793	No
Canada	1944	658	658	Sliding scale
Denmark*	1952	1747	1252	No
Finland§	1948	1242	1524	No
France	1932	1251	1251	No
Germany	1954	128	128	No
Greece	1958	86	172	No
Netherlands	1939	671		No
Norway**	1946	2536	2536	No
Spain	1938	249	249	Part is means-tested
Sweden	1947	1084	1084	No
United Kingdom	1945	1248	832	Part is means-tested
United States	None			Tax deduction

Source: Social Security Administration (2002).[23]

*Denmark provides a variable family allowance for children based on age. Data displayed are for children 0–2 years old. Benefit for school-age children (7–17) is US$1252 per year.

§Finland provides a variable single-parent supplement based on the number of children. The amount displayed here is for two children. Child care allowance for child under 3.

**Norway family allowance includes US$1053 supplement for children aged 1 to 3.

represents an investment in society itself. Just as Social Security plays a critical role for elderly citizens—particularly those with limited income—these children's allowance programs can provide families with children the possibility of escaping poverty.

The French version provides every family, regardless of income and without any requirements, an annual benefit of US$1200 for each child. The objective is to assure that all families have a minimal amount of money to provide for the needs of their children no matter how much money they earn. Several other countries in Europe achieve the same goal through a "negative income tax" program, which guarantees all families a minimal base income.

The Child Tax Credit Approach

In the United States, the current children's allowance takes the form of a child tax credit of US$1000 per child. Children in families earning between US$30,000 to US$110,000 in 2006 are assured the full benefit.[24] Children in families with incomes below US$12,000, however, receive nothing at all. Thus, a single mother working full-time all year at the federal minimum wage of US$5.85 an hour would earn less than US$12,000 a year, and so she and her children would receive no benefit through the child tax credit. In contrast, a family with an income of US$75,000 would receive a benefit of US$1000 for one child and US$3000 for three children (see Table 5.5). The tax credit benefits only those who pay a certain amount in taxes. According to the Urban Institute, about 14 million children from the poorest families receive no benefit from the child tax credit. As seen in Table 5.6, 28.1% of Hispanic children, 19.1% of Black children, and 8.8% White children received no benefit because their parent had so little income.[25]

Table 5.5 Value of the Children's Allowance Benefit Provided Through the Child Tax Credit (2005)

Family Income (US$)	One Child (US$)	Two Children (US$)	Three Children (US$)
11,000	0	0	0
20,000	1000	1000	1000
50,000	1000	2000	3000

Table 5.6 Composition of the 13.9 Million Children
Who Receive No Benefit From Child Tax Credit[26]

Race/Ethnicity	Percentage With No Benefit
White	8.8
Black	19.1
Hispanic	28.1

Guaranteeing the Child Tax Credit

If we were to extend the refundable tax credit to the poorest children, the inequity of the current child tax credit might be remedied. Currently, the poorest children are punished and denied basic income support simply because of their parent's income. By disconnecting the benefit from the work behavior of the parent, poor children as well as wealthy children receive an equal benefit. Implementing such a program would be a simple matter. This approach would prove an efficient distribution mechanism in terms of promoting equity and fairness for all children by ensuring that poor children receive the same benefits as children from upper-income families.

In addition to failing to provide a tax credit to children in the poorest families, another of the main tax advantages denied to poor families is the mortgage deduction. For the middle class, the mortgage deduction provides an essential support in allowing home ownership. For a family with a home mortgage of US$100,000, the deduction is more than US$1600 a year. A family with a home mortgage of US$200,000 receives an annual federal benefit of US$3250, an amount far in excess of the average annual welfare (TANF) benefit received by a mother with two children. The mortgage loan amount is capped at a million dollars. As seen in Table 5.7, this can lead to a US$16,250 benefit for this household. In 2002, there were more than 130 million tax returns filed of which 37 million claimed the mortgage interest deduction. More than half of the benefits went to the top 12 percent of taxpayers who had annual earnings above US$100,000.[27]

Fred Foldvary points out that to the owner of an expensive home, the value of the mortgage deduction is about US$450,000.

There is a bit of a problem when someone has recently bought a house for $1 million, expecting her $912,895 mortgage to be tax deductible. Suppose her mortgage rate was six percent . . . the deduction reduces her taxes by $18,000. To see the . . . value of this $18,000 subsidy, relative to other taxpayers, we need to get the real interest

Table 5.7 Value of the Mortgage Deduction at 25% Tax Bracket

Mortgage Amount* (US$)	Value of Exemption (US$)
50,000	812
75,000	1219
100,000	1625
200,000	3250
500,000	8125
1,000,000	16,250 Maximum Benefit

* Assuming a 6.5% mortgage interest rate.

rate. Suppose inflation is two percent. The real, after-inflation, interest rate is then 4 percent. Now divide $18,000 by .04; we get $450,000. A tax-free bond that paid $18,000 per year would have a market value of $450,000. [28]

Families with high-cost housing and mortgage payments, benefit substantially from the mortgage deduction. These families can deduct interest on up to US$1 million in mortgage indebtedness and interest payments on another US$100,000 in home equity loans. In 2008, the deduction amounts to US$89.4 billion and is likely to cost more than US$500 billion over the following five years.[29]

Because poor families are rarely able to benefit from a mortgage deduction, the deduction has had an unintended *dis*-equalizing effect. For a family lacking in the resources to buy a house, the tax advantage is effectively denied. But, even if such a family had managed to scrape together a down payment and acquire a mortgage, their tax benefit would be far less than that of a high-income family. The guaranteed child tax credit could be used to balance this disadvantage. For instance, if the custodial parent did not claim a mortgage deduction, the family should be entitled to a *double* guaranteed child tax credit. Permitting a double child tax credit would serve to more effectively equalize the distribution of tax benefits to all families.

Although deduction mechanisms in the current tax law have been used successfully to achieve a variety of socially desirable purposes, their main limitation, at least with regard to children, has been that they deny benefits to poor children. The cost of the Child Tax Credit in 2008 was US$32.3 billion. Again, like the other tax credits we have discussed, most poor families gain nothing from this deduction. Table 5.8 shows the cost of the major deductions available in 2008.[30]

Table 5.8 Major Deductions in the Income Tax Code Provided in 2008

Deduction	FY 2008 Value ($Billions)
Exclusion of employer provided medical insurance	160.2
Mortgage interest deduction	89.4
Charitable deduction	45.8
401 (k) plans	44.0
Exclusion of capital gains on home sales	38.9
Child tax credit	32.3
State and Local Tax Deduction (excluding property taxes)	27.9
Exclusion interest on tax-free municipal bonds	27.2
State and local property tax deduction	12.6
Earned income tax credit	5.3
Total value	483.6

Data Source: Dubay and Ahem (2007).

In 2008, the tax code provides for almost half a trillion dollars in tax deductions. Few of these deductions benefit low-income and poor families. As we will see in the next chapter, the bottom two-thirds of tax filers pay most of their taxes through the employment tax that is not reduced by most of these deductions. The only one of these deductions that primarily benefits low-income and poor families is the last one listed in Table 5.8, that is, earned income tax credit. It amounts to about 1.5 percent of the total value of all deductions. As seen in Table 5.9, it is primarily those in the highest income groups who benefit from these tax incentives for saving and investing and tax deductions.

As can be seen in Table 5.9, more than 80 percent of the benefit for the mortgage deduction goes to the top income group (quartile), whereas those in the bottom 60 percent of income earners received less than 5 percent of the benefits. The distribution of benefits through tax deductions is highly skewed in favor of the highest income groups. The one exception is the earned income tax credit, which is at the bottom of the list.

The guaranteed child allowance assumes that children should not be denied income security because of their parent's action or inaction. The guaranteed child tax credit is intended to ensure that poor children receive the same tax benefits that are already provided to upper-income children. Universally applied, it would guarantee children more equitable and fair treatment without the stigmatization associated with a means-tested benefit.

Table 5.9 Distribution of Benefits by Income Quintile for Selected Tax Deductions, 2006

Deduction	Lowest Quintile (%)	Second Quintile (%)	Middle Quintile (%)	Fourth Quintile (%)	Top Quintile (%)
Self-employed health insurance deduction	0.2	1.7	6.5	15.0	76.6
Home mortgage interest deduction	0.0	0.4	3.1	14.9	81.5
Exclusions and deductions for retirement savings	0.1	2.4	8.1	17.2	72.2
Child and dependent care credit	0.0	4.1	23.7	30.8	41.4
State and local property tax deduction	0.0	0.6	3.4	17.6	78.4
Student loan interest deduction	0.4	4.9	22.8	29.7	42.3
Preferential rates on capital gains and dividends	0.0	0.1	0.4	2.0	97.6
Earned income tax credit	27.7	52.0	19.4	0.6	0.1
All select federal tax expenditures	3.4	8.0	7.7	12.3	68.6

Data Source: Carasso, Reynolds & Steuerle (2007), Table 1.[31]

Child Support: Collecting What Is Due

> Research indicates that more than $34 billion in potential child support income goes unpaid each year and that almost two-thirds of single mothers receive no assistance.
>
> Center on Budget and Policy Priorities, 1998[32]

The most common scenario when a two-parent family breaks apart is that the income-earning parent heads off and starts afresh, freed of any labor-intensive child care responsibilities and, too often, free from financial responsibility.[33] The remaining parent becomes burdened with increased child care demands, limited employment opportunity, and reduced earning capacity. Rarely does the noncustodial parent provide adequate or equitable financial support for the child or children. If the custodial parent is a poor single mother, when she receives child support it is usually the second largest source of family income and accounts for almost one-third of the income for her and her children, but most often she will not receive any support.[34]

Historically, the child support collection system used in the United States evolved from the primary role that state courts play in domestic relations. When a husband and wife seek to divorce, they turn to the courts. If there are assets involved, the court will assist in the division of those assets. The court is also instrumental in deciding child custody questions if they are in dispute. Thus, it is only logical that the courts continue their involvement in issues of child support.

The methodologies the courts use for this determination, be it a standardized formula, a set of guidelines to be interpreted by a judge, or a combination of these, is legislated by the various states. Many states now provide a Web-based calculator to determine the amount owed based on a variety of inputs such as number of children, age of children, noncustodial parents income, and so on.

Although a court may stipulate a level of support, collecting that support has been another matter. Child support arrangements may be agreed to in court, but they are not always fully complied with. This is especially true for unmarried mothers. Despite the rhetoric about tracking down "deadbeat dads" and making sure they contribute to the support of their children, the United States has one of the industrial world's lowest levels of child support collection.

In 2007, 61 percent of child support was collected only when a child support order was in place.[35] Of course, in most cases there is no child support order.[36]

Blank reports that fewer than half of the children who live apart from their fathers receive a child support award from the courts.[37] Among those born out of wedlock, the likelihood of receiving a child support order is even slimmer: under 25 percent. During a time when the divorce rate and the number of children born out of wedlock were lower, substituting a bundled welfare benefit for lost or uncollected child support might suffice. However, over the years, with the increase in the number of children living in divorced or never-married families, the problem of uncollected child support has worsened.

In 1970, one-parent families comprised nearly 11 percent of all families. By 2006, one-parent families comprised 32 percent of all families.[38] The largest increase in the number of children in one-parent families derives from children born out of wedlock. This phenomenon has increased the importance of establishing paternity for children. In 2007, the 1.7 million paternities established in the United States represented a more than six-fold increase from 245,000 in 1986.[39] Although states varied in their effort to establish paternity, the national average was 88 percent in 2007, with many states achieving 100 percent.[40] To ensure child support, all states need to make sure that paternity is established for all children.

In 2005, of the 13.6 million single mothers or fathers who had custody of their children, about 6,810,000 were due to collect child support; however only 5,260,000, received anything. The median monthly child support payment was about US$200. Less than one-quarter received their full payment (3,192,000). Table 5.10 illustrates how fewer than 30 percent of Black custodial parents received any child support.

In 2005, the total amount of child support due through support orders—leaving out the children where no award has been established—was US$38 billion.[42] Of this, US$24.8 billion was collected. Despite several high-profile collection efforts, progress toward reducing the more than US$107 billion in delinquent child support has been slow.[43] The amount in arrears collected annually is about $7 billion. Sorenson and others have pointed out that the US$107 billion in delinquent child support figure is low and represents only arrearages for child support orders currently in place.[44] It is an underestimate by as much as 60 percent of what is potentially due.[45]

Much speculation has focused upon why most parents do not pay child support. The most obvious answer is: Why should they? Aside from any moral obligation, which has not proved sufficient motivation, many fathers sense they have little to fear from their refusal to pay. Many of these fathers are angry and feel betrayed by the mothers who would receive their money. Mothers lack the traditional reciprocity arrangements available to other creditors in civil court. Although a bank may collect on a car or house loan through confiscation or foreclosure, the mother cannot obtain a court order to repossess anything. Many fathers angrily believe that the mother who has custody of the children already possesses everything of value anyway. For fathers, anger and disillusionment over their custody arrangements may be

Table 5.10 Child Support Received by Custodial Parents (2005)

Race/ Ethnicity	Received No Child Support Payment*	Received Full Child Support Payment	Received Partial Child Support Payment	Total
White	4,228,000 (55.9)	2,096,000 (27.6)	1,246,000 (16.5)	7,570,000
Black	2,404,000 (70.1)	584,000 (17.0)	443,000 (12.9)	3,431,000
Hispanic	1,424,000 (66.4)	421,000 (19.6)	301,000 (14.0)	2,146,000

Source: U.S. Census Bureau (2007).[41]

Note: Numbers in parentheses represent percentage of population group.

*Includes both no award and no payment despite award.

a motivating factor. As for the mother, she cannot even register delinquent payments with credit bureaus that would be a way to force payment.

One of the more popular misconceptions about child support is that most noncustodial parents (primarily fathers) do not pay child support because they simply do not have the money. Having separated from their former spouse and children, it is argued, they incur new expenses and demands that prevent them from making adequate child support payments. This issue was carefully examined by Cassetty[46] using data from a longitudinal analysis of family income for 5000 families using the Michigan Panel Income Study.

Cassetty found that overall only 15 percent of expected child support payments are actually made. Absent fathers kept for themselves 85 percent of what they might otherwise be expected to pay (using Cassetty's conservative estimate of what the noncustodial parent should and could afford to pay). Although her research was completed some time ago, her findings are still salient. Through her initial study and subsequent research, it is reasonable to conclude that most children are being denied child support, not because the funds are unavailable but because the court-administered collection mechanism has proven ineffective. Two decades after Cassetty's research Cynthia Miller, Irwin Garfinkel and Sara McLanahan report, "We find that fathers on average are able to pay nearly five times more in child support than they currently pay, and also that low income fathers can afford to pay substantially more than they actually pay."[47]

Clearly, there are some fathers who have a difficult time providing adequate child support.[48] Nearly one-third of those owing child support reported earnings of less than US$10,000 annually. The Urban Institute reports that two-thirds of fathers who do not live with their children fail to pay child support. More than two-thirds of fathers who fail to pay child support "have no apparent financial reason to avoid this responsibility."[49] That still leaves a third of fathers who face difficulties paying child support. Blank (1997) reported that many unmarried fathers are homeless or otherwise in difficult financial situations.[50] The Urban Institute estimates that 2.5 million fathers who do not pay child support are themselves poor. However, 4.5 million who do not pay child support fail to do so even when they have the resources to pay.[51]

In the mid-1990s about 11 percent of unmarried fathers were under court supervision (i.e., in jail or on parole or probation).[52] Among Black fathers this figure jumps to 37 percent). Clearly, there are many children with fathers who are unlikely to pay child support. Should these children and their mothers be denied child support? Most of the advanced countries have answered *no*.

Even taking into account the fathers who are unable to pay, the fundamental problem of the child support system lies in the mechanism of collecting child support payments. Historically, this has been viewed as a civil matter in which the child-caring or custodial parent, usually the mother, is required to collect child support from the noncustodial parent, usually the father (approximately five out of six custodial parents are mothers) using the courts. These are the steps a mother must usually follow in order to extract child support from an unwilling father:

1. She must acquire the services of an attorney. Given the expense of retaining competent legal help, she must weigh the prospect of draining her limited resources in the present against the possibility of receiving child support in the future.
2. She will have to find time to meet the attorney. Although this may seem trivial, it can amount to a considerable burden to a woman already overburdened with a job, child care responsibilities, and maintaining a household.
3. She will have to provide all necessary documentation proving nonpayment, taking care to observe any technical requirements of the court designed to safeguard the rights of the father.
4. She will have to assist in locating the father who may have gone to another state. In order to do this, she may require the services of a private investigator.
5. She is required to identify the father and assist in establishing paternity.
6. The mother will find herself having to assume an adversarial stance toward the father. She could well aggravate an already tense and difficult relationship, thereby significantly undermining any hope of reconciliation and accord. She is also putting herself at odds with the man who is the father of her children. She may worry about jeopardizing custody agreements.

Even if she is able to do all of these things and gets the father into court and the court orders him to pay child support, there is no assurance that he will ever do so. If he does not pay, she can, if she wishes, turn to local civil authorities for help in forcing the issue. However, the amount of manpower and resources devoted to this endeavor is significant. Even with this enormous legal effort, the results are hardly encouraging; because the costs of such enforcement frequently amount to more than the amount of child support that the mother and her children would be entitled to in the first place.[53] Furthermore, in order to be cost-effective, child support enforcement programs select to pursue only the cases with a reasonable probability of success, even though such a policy is, by nature, unfair and counter to the legal doctrine that requires that the law be applied equally to everyone. So, it is children from the poorest families—the ones who are most in need of assistance—who are the least likely to be represented.

Faced with such an exhausting and costly legal gauntlet with no guarantees of success, it is easy to see why most single mothers conclude that it is easier to make ends meet without child support than to fight to collect it. The only mothers who can be certain that they are not going to spend all of their time and money in their collection efforts are the mothers receiving welfare. The state pays for the legal fees, however, when support payments have been secured by state courts; much of the money collected will be channeled back into the state child support collection system and applied against the legal and welfare costs. So even in such cases, there may be little benefit to the mother or her children in pursuing legal action against the delinquent father.

Developing a Reliable Collection System

Collecting child support payments is—like national defense, road building, social insurance for seniors, and public education—a far too important matter to assign to voluntary compliance or a cumbersome and inefficient legal system. An easy and reliable means of collecting child support payments from noncustodial parents, which does not intrude on the relationship between the noncustodial parent and the child needs to be instituted. The noncustodial parents must not be allowed to escape responsibility. Because emotions such as hurt and anger have surrounded the separation, parents often have difficulty speaking rationally to each other. An approach that separates the issue of child support responsibility from this volatile emotional context and assures regular payments would better support the needs of the children.

Nor should it be the mother's responsibility to collect child support. Clearly, she has little or no means of doing so. The father is responsible for paying child support and if he does not, it should be the government's responsibility to collect, because the mechanisms for effective and efficient collection lie there and not with individual mothers.

The United States has a hybrid child support collection system that combines both the courts and the federal-state child support enforcement system which was put in place with the creation of the Child Support Enforcement Program as Title IV-D of the Social Security Act in 1975. The program was originally designed to improve the collection of child support for mothers receiving welfare. Much of the cost of the early program was paid for out of collections.[54] Over the years, the program has grown substantially and expanded beyond serving welfare mothers.

Since its inception, the Child Support Enforcement program has undergone many changes. The 1996 welfare reform legislation included specific provisions to improve child support collections.[55] As a result of these

Table 5.11 Child Support Collections, 1994 to 2005

	1994	1996	1998	2000	2002	2005
Families	13,690,000	13,715,000	13,949,000	13,529,000	13,383,000	13,147,000
Received Nothing	56.8%	56.1%	57.5%	56.7%	56.3%	61.3%

Source: Census Bureau.[56]

changes, the government child support program has become the major way child support is collected in the United States. In 1978, less than one-fourth of child support payments were made through the government operated child support collection system. By 2001, the percentage had increased to 87. The primary mechanism the Child Support Enforcement program uses to collect child support is income withholding. Yet even with all of the advances in child support collection and stiff new penalties for those fathers who fail to meet their obligations, the record of hybrid child support collection system in the United States has been and remains disappointing. As seen in Table 5.11, during the last dozen years more children have received "nothing" from noncustodial parents.

As we have seen earlier, most single mothers, especially those with a child under 5, live below the poverty line.[57] According to an Urban Institute analysis of 2004 Census Bureau data, 57 percent of poor single mothers received no child support.[58] For the 43 percent who receive child support, it makes up about one-third of their family income. For these women and their children, child support is their second largest income source after earnings. If the United States could develop an effective system of child support collection that would insure child support to all mothers and their children, there would be a substantial decline in child poverty. As we shall see in the next section, in most European and other industrialized nations the collection of child support is a seamless activity that is the primary responsibility of the federal government. The result is to provide a reliable and substantial income support payment that is not taken away as the mother works, remarries or otherwise improves her economic situation.

Advanced Maintenance System

In almost all of the other developed countries, the government assures that a minimal child support payment is collected through an approach called advance maintenance payments. Under this approach, the mother receives a minimal child support payment from the government, which the state then collects from the father. With the authority and various collection strategies available to the government, the rates of collection are high and minimal administrative costs are incurred.

Germany, like most European nations, employs this advance maintenance payments program. If a single parent does not receive child support that is at least equal to the established amount, then the children receive an advance maintenance payment from the government. The children living with a single parent are eligible for an advance maintenance payment of up to US$185 a month for a period of up to six years. Once the government has advanced the maintenance payment, it goes about collecting that amount from the nonresident parent. Under this policy, all children in single-parent families in Germany are guaranteed to receive at least a minimal level of child support.

New Zealand provides a seamless system for child support.[59] There a single mother follows three steps in order to obtain child support:

1. The mother files an application for child support at the tax office (Inland Revenue).
2. The tax office uses a standard formula to determine the amount of child support due. A letter is then sent to both mother and father informing them of this amount.
3. The tax office collects the child support payment from the father and passes it to the mother.

Most European countries use some variation of the advance maintenance payment approaches employed in Germany, Australia,[60] and New Zealand, thus assuring that child support is paid (see Table 5.12). Within these various schemes, the single mother cannot be deprived of a minimal child support payment. The government then attempts to recoup this money usually by means of their national tax or revenue departments.

In the Netherlands single mothers are provided with a social assistance payment equal to 90 percent of the minimum wage.[61] The single mother is not required to seek employment until her youngest child is older than 5. Thus, the substantial social assistance payment obviates the need to provide an advanced maintenance payment.

For years, the United Kingdom operated a child support collection system similar to that in the United States. Like the United States, their record of collection was dismal. In 1998, a parliamentary study group published a green paper examining the low compliance of absent fathers and the ineffectiveness of the various enforcement strategies that Britain had employed.[63] After reviewing several approaches, the report recommended one similar to

Table 5.12 Countries That Take Public Responsibility
for Collecting Child Support

	Provide an Advance Maintenance Payment
Austria	Yes
Belgium	Yes
Denmark	Yes
Finland	Yes
France	Yes
Germany	Yes
Netherlands	No
Norway	Yes
Sweden	Yes
United Kingdom	Yes
United States	No

Data Source: Corden (1999, table 2.3).[62]

that employed in most of Europe, which would involve shifting the responsibility for collecting child support from the mother to the government.[64] Under the collection system that was proposed, the government would make an automatic payment to the single mother and then utilize the national tax system to collect the payment from the absent father.

Freeing the mother of the highly charged and volatile task of collecting child support, who herself cannot help but be a partisan in the marital divide, and placing it in the hands of the government makes it far more likely that the children, who are entitled to child support, will actually receive it. Removing the mother from the transaction also removes a great deal of the potential rancor and discord. Although proponents of the new system in Britain feared that the public might resist the proposal, they found that by and large it was embraced and received only limited resistance. It was subsequently enacted.[65]

The United States needs to consider a child support system operated through the federal tax system. The mechanism for collecting and redistributing child support is simple. At the time of separation, divorce, or establishment of paternity, fathers would be shifted to a child support tax table, thereby becoming subject to a slightly higher withholding tax rate calculated on their gross earnings and the number of children concerned. Employers would withhold the additional money for child support just as they withhold Social Security and other taxes.

Benefits to custodial parents or guardians would be decided according to a fixed national schedule. For example, noncustodial parents would pay an additional 7 percent in federal income tax. The single parent would receive a monthly sum of US$200 for the first child and US$150 for the second and for each additional child. This payment would be provided to every custodial parent regardless of income. The mandatory payroll deduction might be waived if a noncustodial parent obtained permission from the court because other appropriate payment arrangements had been made. In the case of wealthy and upper-income fathers, the deduction would not interfere with the mother obtaining additional support through civil litigation. The government advanced payment would hardly amount to a great deal for wealthy parents, but it would ensure that every custodial single parent received at least the minimal child support required to meet the financial needs of his or her children.

Several principles would govern the implementation of the advance maintenance payment program:

- The noncustodial parent should not be allowed to abandon responsibility for the economic well-being of their children.[66]
- The enforcement of child support payments should not prove a severe financial burden on the noncustodial parent or discourage participation in the labor force.
- The burden of ensuring collection of child support should no longer be shouldered entirely by the child-caring parent.[67]
- The payment of child support should have no connection to other issues, such as visitation rights.

The advance maintenance payment program suggested here assumes that responsibility for collecting child support is a public trust. The implication is that the future of society at large depends ultimately upon the health and well-being of its children. By transferring the responsibility of collecting child support from the mother to the state, the welfare of children is elevated and noncompliance is no longer tolerated. The government's role is one of enforcing this necessary obligation in as efficient a manner as possible.

Critics of a more efficient and effective child support collection system suggest it is inherently antifamily. Robert Rector of the Heritage Institute argues, "Child support has, at best, a marginal effect on the well-being of the child.... Why then, the pre-occupation with child support and the neglect in fostering marriage? The answer lies in the institutional hostility to marriage I alluded to earlier."[68] Fixing the child support system will be, as the United Kingdom demonstrated, relatively straightforward. But it will require political will to overcome the resistance of those who fear it may undermine the economic threat that binds a marriage together.

Initially, instituting the advance maintenance payment program might cause some disruption in the current child support arrangements. Parents who are presently paying child support might ask for reductions to reflect the tax levied against them. A consent order signed by the child-caring parent or mediated by the family court could easily counterbalance the deducted payments against the previously agreed upon monies. This program would not abolish the right of child-caring parents to take legal action in order to obtain standards of child support compatible with the noncustodial spouse's earning capacity. Rather, the substance of the program is to provide a base of support that could, through the courts, be augmented. Should two parents work out other mutually acceptable agreements for child support payments, such evidence could be used to release the noncustodial parent from the incremental tax rate.

The Final End to Welfare

If single mothers could be certain of receiving child support from their spouses and a children's allowance from the government, the United States could phase out welfare completely. The income provided by an advanced maintenance payment child support system in combination with a fully refundable child tax credit would equal or surpass what is currently provided by welfare. The advantage of substituting universal income support programs for the current means-tested system is that it allows a mother to work without seeing her benefits being clawed back. The mother would not have an incentive to be poor. She would have reason to pursue satisfaction through labor. She would not have to worry that remarriage might endanger her benefit. As it stands now, the single mother must suffer the indignity of being labeled welfare mother in order to receive welfare. She cannot work without worrying about losing means-tested benefits. It is difficult for her to build a career whereby she might possibly be able to earn more than minimum wage. She must pursue the father of her children in order to eke out some pittance from him—this only if she has the time and energy left over from her work, her child rearing, and her endless struggles with the bureaucracy associated with welfare.

Closing

The United States is the only country in the industrialized world that does not have a children's allowance that benefits all children. What is touted as a child-friendly policy, the current tax credit approach gives nothing to those in the direst circumstances, benefiting only families with modest or upper income. The United States is the only advanced economy that does not assure single mothers that they will receive child support. Instead, the hybrid court-based child support collection system provides limited assistance for low-income mothers attempting to get the fathers of their children to take fiscal responsibility. There may be situations where a court-administered payment collection system is appropriate, but the collection of child support for poor and low-income single mothers is not one of them. Cumbersome and unbearably slow moving, this system places the burden of collection on the mother, an approach that only serves to exhaust resources and further exacerbate strained relationships between separated parents. Rather than require court involvement, the United States should follow the approach used in most industrialized economies and provide a system of advanced payments of child support administered by the federal government.

The absence of support in these two areas—children's allowance and assurance of child support collection—largely explains America's historic reliance on means-tested welfare. Welfare has substituted for these two essential income support programs (in effect, a bundled benefit[69]). Yet the principal limitation of a means-tested benefit such as our current welfare program provides lies in the fact that it ultimately reduces incentives for both working and getting remarried. Furthermore, the means-tested benefit carries a stigma with it that can often feel demeaning to the beneficiary.

In most European countries, children receive both a children's (or family) allowance and an advance maintenance payment for child support. For the most part, these are provided as universal programs for the poor, middle class, and wealthy alike. Children continue to receive full benefits regardless of their mother's income, employment or marital status.

For poor children and their mothers, the combination of child support and a children's allowance would make the kind of difference that Social Security has made for the elderly. Together they would dramatically reduce the poverty and hardship of single mothers and their children, ending the disparity in child poverty rates that exists between the United States and other industrialized countries.

The programs examined in this chapter would allow the United States to sharply reduce child poverty. In the next chapter we examine an approach that would extend this effort on behalf of children toward providing opportunity for all young people to participate in the economic prosperity of the nation.

America is the wealthiest country in the world. It has achieved this status as a result of the investment and savings of its citizens. It is important for all citizens to participate in this process of saving and investment and there is no better time to begin than when a person is young.

6

⟡

Embracing Capitalism: Investing in Our Children

I think all of us know in our heart of hearts [that] America's biggest problem today is that too many of our people never got a shot at the American Dream.

President William Clinton[1]

[we need to increase] the ability of a young person entering adult life to control his or her own destiny. Children in many ways are the ultimate pawns in our society; and one of the tragedies of that society is that too many of them stay as pawns on becoming adults. Capital grants at the age of majority are one way of encouraging everyone to develop from a passive to an active citizen.

Julian Le Grand, Asset-based Welfare[2]

When speaking of poverty, one can easily lose sight of America's enormous economic achievements while dwelling upon what has not occurred. I do not want to do that here; America has emerged in the last century as the wealthiest country in the world. It has reached this economic zenith as a result of tax and social policies that encourage the entrepreneurial spirit, savings, and wealth creation. The United States has also become a welcome home for those who wish to build vast personal fortunes. It has harbored those who came across the Ocean in steerage with only the clothes on their backs but who managed to rise from out of penury into prosperity. In some cases, one generation of a family experienced the deprivations, whereas the next celebrated the riches. This country has become the place where equality and opportunity are linked and where the air is rife with possibility. Historically, America has represented the best hope with its ethos of *freedom and justice for all*.

America: Land of Opportunity

America is a country of extraordinary wealth. The Spectrem Group reported that from 1995 to 2004, the number of families in the United States with a net worth of at least US$1 million (not including personal residences) grew more than 50 percent to 7.5 million households.[3] Between 2001 and 2004 the number of households with a net worth of more than US$5 million (not including their residence) rose by 54 percent from 480,000 to 740,000. Edward Wolff estimates that the number of households with net worth more than US$5 million is over 1.25 million if personal residence is included. During the last decade, Merrill Lynch has published its annual *The World Wealth Report* with the Cap Gemini consultancy. The report indicates that about one-third of the wealthiest individuals in the world live in the United States, even though it makes up less than one-twentieth of the world's population. Looking at the United States, their research indicates that in 2006 there were 2,920,000 high net worth individuals (HNWI)—individuals with financial assets not including their primary residence in excess of 1 million dollars—and that the number of individuals considered "ultra rich,"— having more than US$30 million—had reached 37,000 in 2005.[4] The wealthiest 37,000 have greater wealth than the bottom 200,000,000 (two-thirds) of the population. Similarly, the Forbes 400 wealthiest Americans had seen their share of the nation's wealth triple between 1983 and 2000.[5] By 2007, the combined wealth of these top 400—US$1.54 trillion—was greater than the bottom half of the U.S. population.[6] Between them, these reports not only attest to economic growth, but to a growing inequality with regard to the nation's privately held wealth. According to the World Wealth Report, one-third of the nation's wealth is owned by 1 percent of the population.[7]

Don Weston used to feel special cruising the world in his 100-foot yacht. "I used to think I had a good-sized boat," sighs Mr. Weston. "Now it's like a dinghy compared to these others. How big are they going to get?"[8]

There are many in the United States who enjoy lives of great abundance. Even though most yacht orders placed are rather modestly outfitted craft—assuming there can be such a thing as a modest yacht—orders for yachts of mega and giga proportions (over 200 feet) have increased substantially. During 2005, 651 were under construction, whereas in 2004, 507 were commissioned, and only 482 in 2003.[9] The 416-foot *Octopus*, the world's second biggest yacht (a fact that probably rankles its owner, Microsoft cofounder Paul Allen[10]) includes a pool, a basketball court, a movie theater and its own mini submarine. The Oracle Software founder Larry Ellison's 487-foot *Rising Sun*, holds the distinction of being the biggest mega yacht in the world—for now. *Rising Sun* will soon be eclipsed by the latest *Titanic*, a 518-foot palace on water. The latest and biggest will set new standards in design, outfitting, and functionality. With an estimated 500 million dollar price tag, its new owners probably hope to sail the world's most luxurious craft for a while—but if trends are any indication, there will be another bigger and better monument to riches and luxury in short order.

The American Economy

As the wealthiest country in the world and a nation of almost boundless opportunity, America provides a high standard of living for large portion of its members. The Federal Reserve Board has estimated that there is more than 58.6 trillion dollars of privately owned wealth in the United States.[11] If that wealth were divided equally between all Americans, then every person in this country would have a net worth in excess of US$195,000.

$$\frac{\text{US}\$58,600,000,000,000}{300,000,000} = \text{US}\$195,333$$

The typical household would have a networth greater than half a million dollars. As Mark Perry observes, "Household wealth has increased by almost $20 trillion in the last five years, and the average American household now owns about $528,000 worth of stuff (assets, real estate, etc.), free and clear of any debt!"[12]

The Federal Reserve has reported that the average (or mean) U.S. household net worth was US$448,200 in 2004.[13] Yet, in the same year the *median* household net worth was nowhere close to US$448,200; it was US$93,100 (see Figure 6.1). Why the difference? The median represents the wealth of the person in the middle. Bill Heyman (2005) points out that "in a group of 1,000 families, if 999 families have zero net worth and one has a net worth

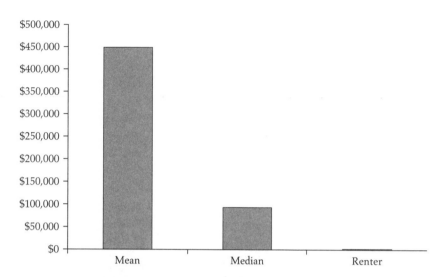

Figure 6.1 Household Net Worth in the United States (2004)
Source: Federal Reserve Board, 2006.[14]

of $400 million, the mean net worth is $400,000."[15] In short, the median figure serves not simply as an indicator of an average net worth, but points to
the failure of the average American family to share in the wealth generated
by the growing economy.

During the 1950s and 1960s, not only was the United States the showcase
of democracy and the standard of egalitarian achievement for the world, it
was also the wealthiest nation, producing an extraordinary 40 percent of the
world's wealth.[16] The U.S. free enterprise market economy produced such
affluence that its citizens were enjoying a level of material abundance unpar-
alleled in the history of civilization. Disease was receding, hunger, and want
were disappearing, and—thanks to technology, capitalism, and free enterprise, which appeared capable of accomplishing almost anything—life in
general was improving.[17] The overall expectation was that, except for a few
nagging social problems that would within a few years probably work themselves out, society was headed rapidly in the direction of something that
looked like utopia.[18]

Historically, incomes of Americans have fluctuated but mostly risen. From
1947 to 1979, the income share of the top one-fifth of wealthy Americans
increased by 99 percent (see Table 6.1). During this same period, the income
of the bottom one-fifth also increased by 116 percent. In other words, during
the almost three decades after World War II, the expanding economy
brought substantial income gains to Americans in all income categories.

Table 6.1 Change in Family Income From 1947 to 2005

Percentage Change in Income From 1947 to 1979 by Quintile		
Bottom one-fifth	116	
Middle one-fifth	111	All income groups participated
Top one-fifth	99	
Percentage Change in Income From 1979 to 2005 by Quintile		
Bottom one-fifth	−1	
Middle one-fifth	15	New income channeled to the top
Top one-fifth	53	

Source: Phillips (2002); Census Bureau (2007).[19] Online at: www.census.gov/hhes/income/histinc/f03.html and www.census.gov/hhes/income/histinc/f01.html

There was a widespread recognition therefore that living standards were improving. The education level of the American workforce increased as ex-servicemen, supported by the GI Bill, decided to go to college in expectation that learning would allow them to better themselves. During this time, young people could expect that they might have a higher standard of living than their parents.

Everyday, across America, millions of people head off to work. More than 142 million workers head off to jobs in factories, farms, hospitals, schools, airports, and all of the industrial and service sectors. Most of these workers will labor more than 40 hours, and they will do this all year long. At the end of the year, we can examine how the income generated by all these working people is divided. The distribution of income allows us to see how the fruits of all this labor are shared among the workers. The pie chart in Figure 6.2 shows how the nation's income was distributed in 1967.

The top quintile (or 20%) received 44 percent of the income distributed in 1967. In contrast, the bottom quintile received 4 percent of the income. Many of those in the bottom quintile were unemployed or did not work during the year, particularly in comparison to those in the top quintile. But the difference in work effort (i.e., in number of hours worked) was relatively small and accounted for only a very small part of the difference in income received. In fact, in 2004 more than one-ninth of the labor force consisted of individuals working full-time but who, nonetheless, earned income below the poverty line. The two major factors that explained the difference were the higher wages for those in the top quintile, and most important, income from capital investments. The top quintile received a substantial part of their income from capital gains, dividends, and interest. For those with income over US$10 million a year, capital gains and dividends account for more than 60 percent of their earnings, whereas for those with income

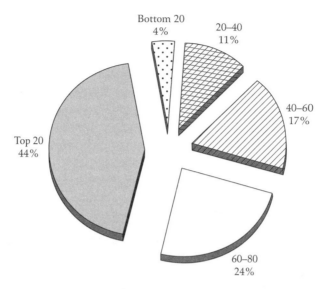

Figure 6.2 Distribution of Income in the United States (1967)
Source: U.S. Census Bureau, P60-229, August 2005, table A-3, p. 41.

below US$50,000 a year, capitals gains and dividends account for less than 3 percent of their earnings.

Tax policies during the last quarter of a century have resulted in substantial reductions in taxes paid on capital gains and dividends and have led to a substantial channeling of earnings and wealth to the top. The tax policies have essentially favored capital ownership over labor. The highest taxed income is that earned from working. Taking into account employment taxes, income from labor is taxed at three times the rate of income from capital gains and twice that for dividends. In a nine-part series in 2005, the *New York Times* examined the changing fortunes of American families.[20] In one of the articles in the series they reported the share of income received by American households as reported in federal tax filings in 2001, the latest data then available. As seen in Figure 6.3, the top quintile received 61 percent of all reported income. In contrast, the bottom quintile received 2 percent of all reported income. The bottom 60 percent of Americans combined received less than one-third of the income of the top 20 percent. These data provide a clear picture of the improving fortunes of the top income earners and the declining fortunes of the poor and middle class.

The growing inequality during the last two decades can be seen in the decline in the share of income received by the bottom half of income tax filings compared to the top 1 percent. In 1986, the top 1 percent received about

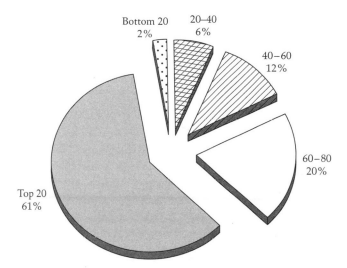

Figure 6.3 Share of Nation's Income From Tax Filings in the United States (2001)
Data Source: *New York Times*, June 5, 2005, p. 17.

two-thirds the income of the bottom 50 percent. By 2005, the top 1 percent received almost one-and-two-thirds the income of the bottom 50 percent (see Figure 6.4). According to the 2005 tax filings, the top 3.5 percent of tax filers, those with incomes greater than US$200,000, received more income than the bottom two-thirds (see Table 6.2).

In 2005, the bottom 60 percent of tax files reported income of less than US$50,000. The data on tax filers include only those who filed tax returns. Not everyone is required to file a tax return. For example, a married couple with income of less than US$16,000 is not required to file a tax return. Many retired individuals with low income do not file tax returns. Thus, the numbers in Table 6.2 understate the number of low-income households in the United States. What the data in Table 6.2 make clear is that the bottom 60 percent of tax filers in the United States are often in a difficult and precarious financial situation. In contrast, there is a small group of tax filers who receive a substantial share of all reported income.

In his 2002 keynote address at the annual meeting of the Institute on the Ethics of Journalism, Maxwell King, the retiring editor of the *Philadelphia Inquirer* asked, "What does it mean for a democratic society like ours, in which there has been a 25-year trend of the poor growing poorer, the rich growing richer, the divide between the have-more and the have-less growing steadily? A society in which 45 percent of those filing tax returns in 1993 met the federal government's definition of working poor? A society in

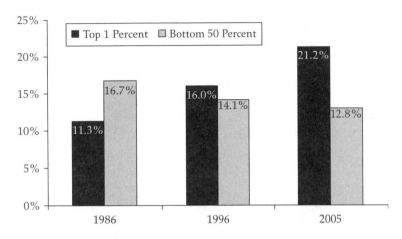

Figure 6.4 Changing Share of Income From 1986 to 2005
Source: Internal Revenue Service, 2007.

Table 6.2 Income in the United States in 2005 (From Tax Filings)

	Adjusted Gross Income	**Number of Filers***	**Pecentage of Filers**
Under 50,000	1,797,097,083,000	112,894,109	60.1
50,000–75,000	1,119,634,632,000	29,550,574	15.7
75,000–100,000	905,336,768,000	18,795,652	10.0
100,000–200,000	1,429,575,727,000	19,991,679	10.6
200,000+	2,112,995,921,000	6,633,282	3.5

Source: Internal Revenue Service, 2007.[21]
* Includes joint returns (joint return = two filers).

which the richest one percent of the population owns almost one-third of the nation's resources?"[22] Understanding the inequality in wealth and income in America today is central to understanding child poverty and developing strategies to alleviate it. In the discussion that follows we will examine how this inequality emerged and the resulting poverty that has become a by-product of the inequality.

The Wealthiest Country in the World

Individuals with financial assets greater than 1 million dollars are an elite group. They account for 0.2 percent of the global adult population, but

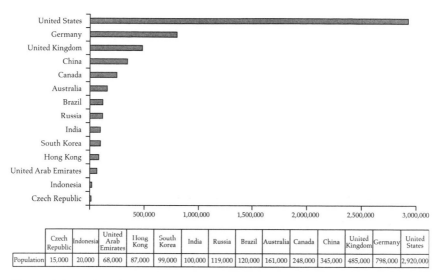

	Czech Republic	Indonesia	United Arab Emirates	Hong Kong	South Korea	India	Russia	Brazil	Australia	Canada	China	United Kingdom	Germany	United States
Population	15,000	20,000	68,000	87,000	99,000	100,000	119,000	120,000	161,000	248,000	345,000	485,000	798,000	2,920,000

Figure 6.5 Number of High Net Worth Individuals by Country (2006)

nearly one-quarter of the world's wealth. America is home to more of these individuals than any other country, making it the wealthiest nation in the world. According to Merrill Lynch's *World Wealth Report 2007*, there are more high net worth individuals in the United States than any other country in the world (see Figure 6.5).[23]

More than one-third of the world's high net worth individuals live in the United States. However, more than two-fifths of the world's ultra high net worth individuals (defined as having US$30 million or more in financial assets) live in the United States.

It is not surprising then that the United States leads the world in the number of millionaires, ultra millionaires and billionaires. What is surprising is this same country also leads the industrialized world in the number of children living in poverty.

The Highest Child Poverty Rates in the Developed World

Rates of poverty among children in other developed countries are often less than half that of those in the United States (see Figure 6.6). Most developed nations in Western Europe and Asia have essentially ended poverty among children and single parent families.[24] Vleminckx and Smeeding examined child poverty in the major industrial nations and found it highest

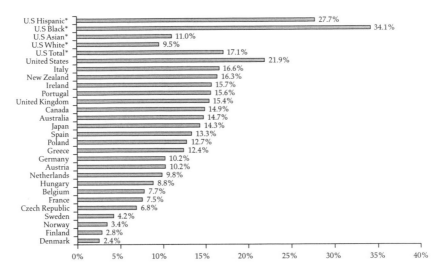

Figure 6.6 International Child Poverty Rates After Government Programs; Percentage of Children Living in "Relative" Poverty

Source: UNICEF, 2005.

*Percentage of children living in households below the poverty line. The poverty line is defined by the federal government in the United States and is lower than the definition of poverty used by the United Nations.

in the United States, observing that "the relative child poverty rate in New York is considerably higher than in any European country."[25] The first listings in Figure 6.6 display child poverty rates in the United States based on the poverty line used by the U.S. Census Bureau. This is a more restrictive measure than the measure of poverty used by the United Nations and most European countries. The Census Bureau poverty line is based on ability to meet basic needs, whereas the United Nations measure is equal to half the median income. Thus, the United Nations estimates that total child poverty in the United States is 21.9 percent, whereas the U.S. Census Bureau estimates total child poverty at 17.1 percent. Using the restrictive Census Bureau poverty line measure, the data in Figure 6.6 demonstrate the difference in child poverty rates for White, Black, Hispanic, and Asian children in the United States. As discussed in Chapter 1, child poverty in the United States reflects two worlds of childhood. The child poverty rate for Black and Hispanic children is about three times greater than for White children.

America then is a country of extremes. Both the wealth amassed in the hands of the few and the wants that have multiplied for the poor have been enabled by public policies and programs. President Reagan's administration may have ended the Cold War and seen the collapse of the Berlin Wall, but it also unleashed the powerful, nearly unfettered, free enterprise energies that channeled wealth in the United States to the top. The government policies of this era made certain to take care of business and wealth holders—the capitalists—but did very little to help the middle class or the poor and their children who too often lacked capital.

Children and Opportunity

America imagines itself as a country where the poorest can become the richest. The rags to riches dramas—now on television and in the celebrity magazines where they were once in the dime store novels of Horatio Alger a century ago—where newsboys through pluck, determination, and moral conviction worked their way up the rungs to achieve their fortunes. The truth of the matter, however, is rather less simple. The virtues of hard work do not always provide the way out of poverty. As we have seen, the opportunities in place that can make success possible are not distributed evenly throughout the society. Rather, opportunity knocks on only certain doors, and tends to linger in certain neighborhoods inhabited by certain types of people. America, in contrast to the persistent myth of equality, has become a highly stratified society where the class boundaries that divide rich from poor have widened and become far more rigid and unassailable.

To understand child poverty requires a broad examination of the distribution of wealth and poverty among America's children and their families. One of the central tenets of America's commitment to children has been the idea of ensuring equal opportunities to all, and in this book, I wish to examine the opportunities that are provided to children in the United States. Historically, this country has relied upon education as a great equalizer. It was here that the development of free public school education for all children beginning in 1632 was pioneered. The provision of public school education is credited with much of the dynamic economic success of the country. Yet, in recent years, education has almost served an opposite purpose. As Jonathan Kozol points out, "We put other people's children into an economic and environmental death zone. We make it hard for them to get out. We strip the place bare of amenities. And we sit back and say to ourselves, 'Well, I hope that they don't kill each other off. But if they do, it's not my fault.' "[26]

Children growing up in the United States experience very different opportunity structures and have quite different life trajectories depending on their parents' economic circumstances. There is considerable variation in how individual children perform within each of the income groups. However, the potential of economic mobility is meant to encourage poor children to work hard to escape poverty. Despite variations, however, the fact remains that those who have been left out and left behind share many traits.

For many, poverty continues to be viewed as a private affair. When single mothers are unable to adequately provide for their children, they are often blamed for circumstances that are beyond their control and find their values and judgment questioned. They are criticized for failing to spend time with their children while at the same time faulted for failing to adequately provide for their children. The failure of absent fathers to parent their children or even to pay child support is too often ignored when faulting the lone mother. Consequently, single mothers are only reluctantly provided with income assistance. There are constant nagging suspicions that the funds will be not be spent on the children. Will the mothers use the funds for nutritious food or just squander it on cigarettes, drugs, or alcohol? The behavior of single mothers is scrutinized to a degree and in a manner, that others, such as the elderly who are also recipients of public money, would find objectionable—an insult to their integrity and dignity. "This discourse," argues Polakow referring to the attitude toward single mothers, "serves to conceal the continuing mean-spirited treatment of poor people and legitimates the minimalist and degrading support policies for single mothers and their children, who suffer the snowball effects of class and race as well as gender discrimination."[27]

Many children grow up without the necessary preparation to enter a workforce that has become ever more competitive, let alone in possession of the tools to succeed in college (should they be lucky enough to have access to an affordable school). Yet the erosion of the public school system is not the only factor in the continuing decline of America's underclass. The tax policies of the recent decades have resulted in a more immediate shift of wealth from the middle and upper classes to the very top 1 percent of families. As the United States entered the new millennium, President George W. Bush accelerated the channeling of wealth upward through tax policies that favor asset holders. The Institute on Taxation and Economic Policy working with the Children's Defense Fund (2002) calculated the benefit that various income groups would receive as a result of the George W. Bush tax cut. The top 1 percent receives the greatest benefit. These families receive more in tax cuts than the remaining 99 percent combined. Families who boast annual incomes in excess of 1 million dollars a year will average US$342,000 in tax cuts over the coming decade. Commenting on this tax cut, Edelman observes that "something is out of kilter when just three of our wealthiest Americans possess greater wealth than the incomes of seven million American families."[28]

Finding a Way to Reverse Inequality Trends

America is a country of enormous wealth. Unfortunately, many children never have an opportunity to share in this wealth. The fundamental premise of this book is that this does not have to be. What is needed are strategies that allow all children to have a chance at sharing in the wealth of the nation. In this chapter, I examine an approach that holds the promise of not just ending severe child poverty in the United States, but of reversing the trends toward increasing inequality and particularly inequality of opportunity. The program is a child savings account. The idea for this program has been with us for many years. However, in the last 10 years this approach has received substantial support from the Committee for Economic Development (CFED). Building on the pioneering work of Michael Sherraden, CFED has teamed up with several partners, including the Ford Foundation, the Charles Stewart Mott Foundation, the New America Foundation, and others, to promote child savings accounts.

Ten years ago, the idea of a universal child savings account was not on the national agenda. CFED, with the leadership of Bob Friedman and Andrea Levere, has assembled a powerful coalition of supporters. The group was involved in supporting the passage of a Child Trust Fund in England. As of 2002, all children born in Great Britain have child savings accounts provided for them. The Child Trust Fund provides parents with a certificate so that they can open an account in their child's name. The 3 million accounts opened by 2008 allow all children to save and invest so that when they turn 18, they will have a substantial amount of money in a savings account that they can do with as they wish.

There are two major limitations with the Child Trust Fund in Britain. First, it provides the young people with the money when they turn 18 with no restrictions. This places a heavy burden on young people to prudently use their savings at a time when they may not have the experience necessary to wisely manage these funds. Furthermore, if young people use these funds to purchase a car or other consumer goods, then the real purpose of the account will have been undermined. It may leave too many young people regretting their inability to appreciate and properly manage their savings.

The purpose of the child savings programs is to provide young people, when they are leaving home and beginning an independent life as an adult, with an asset base. The hope is that this asset base will provide resources for expanding economic and educational opportunity. If a national program of child savings accounts is established with public funds, as any program of progressive child savings will require, then it is necessary that restrictions on use be put in place.

Second, the amount of funding needs to be large enough to make a difference. The British program is simply too meager.[29] It is not likely to lead to the growth of a sufficient asset base that a young person can use to take advantage of the educational opportunities that will be available when they reach their age of maturity. Most of the economists who have examined this question (including James Tobin, winner of the Nobel Prize in Economics, Lester Thurow, Robert Haveman, and Barbara Wolfe) have suggested that an asset base close to US$25,000 is the minimum.

Child savings accounts are modeled on the social savings approach of Social Security. Social Security does not provide unrestricted access to the value of the funds when a senior reaches retirement age. Seniors are not provided the option of a lump sum payment. They are not provided an opportunity to invest their savings in a variety of risky investments that might provide greater returns. Rather, the purpose of Social Security is to provide a base of income support to all seniors. The success of Social Security in this regard is unquestionable.

If we did not have in place a system of Social Security, life for seniors in the United States today would look very different.

If we put in place an effective child savings account, we will create a different world for children. We will create a different future for the children. Child savings accounts hold the promise of substantially reducing the inequality of opportunity and wealth, which is now the primary force shaping the future of children in the United States. By laying the foundation for all young people to begin building their own personal asset base upon which they can draw funds for college, for a down payment on a house or other allowed purposes, a child savings account will have put in place the essential infrastructure needed to broaden participation in the great wealth of the nation.

The purpose of the child savings account is to allow young people from the time of their birth to tap into the core element of the capitalist free enterprise system—and that is the ownership of capital, of assets.

Opening a child savings account at birth maximizes the child's opportunity to build wealth, to grow their account and take advantage of compounding interest. If an account is opened for a child at birth and 1000 dollars is put in the account, and then US$500 is added each subsequent year, by the time the child reaches 18 their account will have about 40,000 dollars (see Figure 6.10). Providing all children with a restricted savings account with this much money when they turn 18 has the possibility of fundamentally changing the futures of children.

In Chapter 1, we examined the vast inequality among children. There are many children in the United States, particularly Black and Latino children who have little opportunity. They leave home at 18 with little real prospect of going to college. Their families are unable to give them much support. It is as if they are beginning a *Monopoly* game but they start with no money, although most around them start off with strong economic support from their parents.

The outcomes for these poor children are not good for them or for the nation. We can change it. The child savings accounts represent the best approach available to truly make a difference, particularly on a large scale.

History of the Idea for a National Child Savings Account

The idea of providing the young person with the financial resources they need upon entering the free enterprise market economy as a capable and equipped participant is not new. In the early colonial period, Thomas Paine proposed that every person on their twenty-first birthday "should be entitled to receive [about US$20,000 in current dollars] each" funded from a 10 percent inheritance tax.[30] In 1970, James Tobin, Nobel Laureate in economics, proposed that every child should be provided roughly US$30,000 [in current dollars] upon graduation from high school.[31] His reasoning was as follows:

> This proposal has a number of important advantages. Individuals are assisted directly and equally, rather than indirectly and haphazardly, through government financing of particular programs. The advantages of background and talent that fit certain young people for university education are not compounded by financial favoritism. Within broad limits of approved programs, individuals are free to choose how to use the money the government is willing to invest in their development.[32]

In 1992, Lester Thurow, former dean of the Sloan School of Management at MIT, proposed:

> The Social Security system could be expanded beyond health care and pensions for the elderly to include training for the young. Upon birth, every young person would have a training account set up in his [or her] name for use after graduation from high school in which a sum of money equal to the amount of public money that is now spent on the average college graduate (about $17,500) would be deposited. Over their lifetime, individuals could draw upon this fund to pay for university training or to pay their employer for on-the-job skill training. Repayment would occur in the form of payroll tax deductions.[33]

In 1994, in my book, *The Welfare of Children*, I proposed a universal child savings account that would begin with US$1000 at birth and supplemented annually with US$500 until the child's eighteenth birthday.[34] Each account would be housed at a private bank or brokerage firm selected by the parent.[35]

In 1998, economist Robert Haveman in his book, *Starting Even*, proposed providing a US$20,000 universal personal savings account to youth on their eighteenth birthday.[36] The account restricted use of funds to educational and medical purposes.

In 2003, Ray Boshara proposed an American stakeholder's account that would begin with US$2000 at birth and an additional US$4500 over the years.[37]

The Ownership Society

The United States is a land of great opportunity. To take full advantage of it young people need to have an understanding of financial management and savings. They need to learn about investing and building their own personal asset base—an estate, but not in the sense of the great fortunes of the industrial barons, but in the sense of owning their own home and a portfolio of stocks, bonds, and other income producing assets. This is the central theme of the ownership society and the heart of capitalism. For the ownership society to take on real meaning and broad significance, we need to develop opportunities for all young people to participate in this vital part of American life.

Building an Asset Base

[P]roperty is so important to the free development of individual personality that everybody ought to have some...a propertyless person lacks crucial resources needed for self-definition. He can never taste the joys and sorrows of real freedom—and the possibilities of learning from his own successes and mistakes. He is condemned to a life on the margin, where the smallest shocks can send him into a tailspin. He can never enjoy the luxury of asking himself what he really wants out of life, but is constantly responding to the exigent demands of the marketplace.[38]

Ackerman and Alstot, *The Stake Holder Society*

An asset base provides young people with the needed savings account that can serve for accumulating income-earning assets. A young person's economic future is contingent on both income and assets. The importance of an asset base is that it provides the foundation for a young person to begin saving and accumulating income-earning assets, which will serve the young person throughout their adult life. In a sense, an asset base is like an estate except that it is narrower in scope and purpose. Estate is a term often associated with British royalty, large mansions, and expansive rolling hills. These estates represent the top echelon of wealth. However, all citizens have estates in the sense that they have accumulated net worth. It is just that most estates are small or empty, whereas a small number are immense. We all build our own asset base. In this chapter, we are concerned with the fact that everyone in the United States is building an asset base. However, most Americans have not been successful in building an asset base that represents their share of the wealth in the United States.

An asset base allows the individual to save and to accumulate income-earning assets. The goal is not to dwell in luxury and conspicuous consumption but rather to achieve financial independence. Thoreau observed, "There is no more fatal blunder than he who consumes the greater part of his life getting a living."[39] Financial independence, which is within reach for most Americans, can be achieved by careful spending, saving, and disciplined financial management. Most of all, it requires an understanding of how to invest and save in order to build an asset base. By providing a child savings account at an early age and taking advantage of the many years of childhood to build that asset base and have assets grow, taking advantage of cumulative and compounding interest, we teach young people both the power and importance of saving and of the inherent nature of capitalism.[40]

An Opportunity for All Children

The primary victims of poverty in the United States are children who grow up in circumstances devoid of hope and opportunity. The result has been a social misfortune whose proportions are deepening and which we are only beginning to appreciate. Although its physical form can be seen in the blighted neighborhoods of most major cities, its impact on the hopes and dreams of the poor, especially poor children is not so visible. Investing only the minimal amount in the development of poor children is unwise in the extreme because children represent one of society's most valuable human resources.[41]

To allow for children from disadvantaged backgrounds to succeed will require more than additional spending on education. Without question, adequate school funding is vital. But to alter the life trajectories of young people will require a fundamentally different approach.

Our first step is to acknowledge that a *structural problem* is the root cause of the continuing child poverty in our county. Our means-tested welfare approach to poor children and their needs says, in effect, that poverty is somehow the fault of the child who must demonstrate eligibility for public aid.

Although the child support and children's allowance reforms proposed in the previous chapter are important programs that will help reduce child poverty, they will not eliminate the underlying causes of child poverty. We need a bold new approach that implements fundamental reform—a Marshall Plan of sorts directed at child poverty that has the potential of substantially changing the socioeconomic status of poor children and the way society approaches their physical, emotional, psychological, educational, and social development.

To be effective, any program intended to rectify the problem of child poverty should be universally applied and must begin at birth. It must be progressive. That is, it must ensure participation of all children regardless of their parent's circumstances. Programs that provide opportunity during the child's transition to adult life, their emancipation from the family and embarkation into adult responsibilities, are essential ingredients for any comprehensive reform. Unless imaginative programmatic efforts to break the cycle of poverty are undertaken, that will provide children the *escape velocity* to break out of patterns established over years, even generations, we have little chance of ending poverty among children.[42]

Leaving Home Ready to Become Self-Sufficient

High school begins the young person's transition to adult life. At this stage, adolescents undergo major psychological and physiological growth and change. They develop a sense of personal identity[43] and begin to consider the career options and opportunities open to them when they leave home: college, vocational training, job apprenticeships, and so on.

When young people graduate from high school, they begin the most important and difficult transition in their lives. They embark on their adult career, which ideally, should be characterized by independence and self-sufficiency. If they have prepared for this transition and have the necessary resources, then they will likely become productive and contributing adults. If not, they will be vulnerable to dependency and failure in a society that demands independence and self-reliance. In a free market economy, the passage from adolescence to adulthood requires more than years of physical, intellectual, and emotional development. It requires that young people have the financial resources that will permit emancipation from nearly two decades of dependence on their family and that will enable them to sever ties with home and family and to embark successfully on an independent life.

Currently, only children from upper middle class and wealthy families can safely rely on such resources. For children from poor and low-income families, the resources, and hence opportunities, are too often absent. The Corporation for Enterprise Development points out, "More than a third of the four million children born each year—and more than half of minority children—are born into families with negligible savings to weather emergencies or invest in their [children's] futures."[44] Too many children, realizing as they grow up that they will not have the resources and opportunities to move into productive adulthood, turn to or allow themselves to be exposed to early childbearing and public assistance, or worse, to drugs and crime. The Children's Defense Fund examined this issue with data from the National Longitudinal Survey of Young Americans.[45] They compared teenage girls from poor families who lacked basic academic skills with those from affluent families and more skilled peers. They found that the poor teenage girls were nearly six times more likely to become pregnant. With little confidence in their future, teenagers living in poverty lacked the incentives to delay parenthood.[46] How can the situation of these young people be changed? How can these young people gain confidence in their future?

Education has been the route of social mobility in the United States for most of the last century. The reforms of the progressive education leaders in the early part of the last century have led to universal education all the way through high school. During the great expansion of the middle class during the 1950s and 1960s, the majority of young people graduated from high school. Opportunities for higher education opened up to the broad middle class and numerous programs to ensure access to higher education for low-income and poor students were created.

Today, access to higher education has been largely stripped of financial barriers. For low-income and poor students, there are a multitude of state and federal loan programs. Most states offer access to community colleges and four-year state universities at tuition levels that are within their reach. As a result, for most young people education has been available as an important avenue of social mobility, but with a growing loan burden upon graduation, especially for low-income and poor students.[47]

Higher education provides one of the most promising avenues to success for young people who are disproportionately afflicted with destitution. In today's world, a college education has become an important building block for a successful career and has substantial impact on lifetime earnings (see Figure 6.7). Most states have developed public universities that are largely subsidized through public expenditures. Although there is great variation in median income for different racial and ethnic groups, much of the difference can be explained by educational attainment. The variation is largely the result of education and, to a lesser degree, by race and ethnicity.

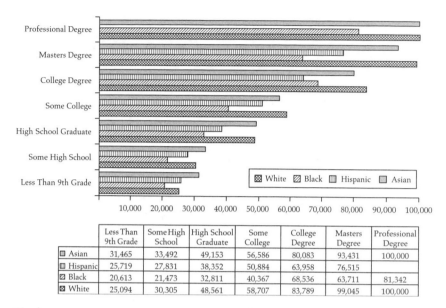

	Less Than 9th Grade	Some High School	High School Graduate	Some College	College Degree	Masters Degree	Professional Degree
Asian	31,465	33,492	49,153	56,586	80,083	93,431	100,000
Hispanic	25,719	27,831	38,352	50,884	63,958	76,515	
Black	20,613	21,473	32,811	40,367	68,536	63,711	81,342
White	25,094	30,305	48,561	58,707	83,789	99,045	100,000

Figure 6.7 Income, Race/Ethnicity, and Education (2004)
Source: U.S. Census Bureau, 2005.

Access to Higher Education

Education, particularly higher education, has been one of the main avenues of social mobility in modern America. During the 1950s and 1960s, the number of young people going to college increased sharply and, no doubt, contributed to the rising median income during this period. In recent decades, growth in the percentage of young people graduating from college has slowed considerably. Access to college has leveled off. The opportunity to attend one of the top universities in the United States is largely determined by the economic status of a child's family. Anthony Carnevale and Stephen J. Rose studied the economic diversity at 146 top colleges in the United States and found that more than three-quarters come from the richest quarter of families, whereas less than one-tenth come from the bottom half of families ranked by income.

Ross Douthat (2005) observed that the odds of obtaining a bachelor's degree by age 24 are substantially determined by family income (see Table 6.3).

Ensuring a Better Chance for Success

Ackerman and Alstott proposed a program that would provide all children a major stake in U.S. society, "a one-time grant of eighty thousand dollars

Table 6.3 Family Income and the Likelihood of Obtaining a Bachelor's Degree by Age 24

Family Income (US$)	Odds of Graduating From College
Greater than 90,000	1 in 2
Between 61,000 and 90,000	1 in 4
Between 35,000 and 61,000	1 in 10
Less than 35,000	1 in 17

Data Source: Douthat (2005).

as the child reaches early adulthood.'[48] The only requirement to gain access to their stake is that the child graduate from high school. Ackerman and Alstott suggested that without such a program, it is unlikely that disadvantaged young people will ever have a chance to achieve the American dream.

Ackerman and Alstott proposed that the grant be viewed not as a gift but rather as the initial stake needed for a chance at success in the free enterprise market economy in the United States. They provide for a number of conditions for accessing the grant. The young person would be limited to accessing US$20,000 a year. They would be obliged to pay back the money received later in life, as their earning power and ability to pay back increased.

E. F. Denison has suggested that much of the great economic achievement of the United States during the half century between 1930 and 1980 can be credited to the idea of universal free education pioneered in the United States.[49] Hence, the stakeholder proposal, though seemingly impractical and expensive, is not without precedent. When first adopted, many viewed such a public education stakeholder program as too costly and idealistic; however, now public school education is taken as a right of citizenship and viewed as a key to providing equal opportunity to all children.

529 College Savings Plan

If you start with $100 and contribute the same amount monthly to your child's account, you'll have accumulated over $60,000 at 10% interest over 18 years.[50]

If you are wealthy and married, consider contributing up to $100,000 to each of your grandchildren's 529 savings plans.[51]

In 1995, the General Accounting Office (GAO) conducted a study of the college savings plans the various states offered to parents.[52] Several years later, Congress relied on the experience of the states and the GAO Report in drafting the 529 section of the tax code. The 529 plan allows a parent (or any relative) to invest money tax free in a college savings account so that when the child is ready to go to college the money will be there. In essence, the 529 College Savings Plan is a government subsidized child savings account. It has the following features:

- The 529 plans allow money deposited by the parent to grow tax free.[53]
- Withdrawals used to cover college costs are not taxable.
- The parent (or account owner) maintains control of the account until the child reaches age 18, 21, or 25.
- The account can accumulate as much as US$300,000 per child.[54]
- If the child opts not to go to college, the parent can transfer the funds to another beneficiary.
- Because assets in the account are considered to be the property of the account owner, only 6 percent of the account balance will be considered in the financial aid eligibility calculation if the account is held by a grandparent or other relative.
- Most states provide identical tax breaks on state income taxes for 529 withdrawals, but 23 states go further and provide upfront tax deductions.

As of June 30, 2002, a total of US$21.8 billion was invested in 529 plans, compared to US$11 billion a year earlier in June 2001.[55] The *New York Times* reported that by 2005 more than US$68 billion was invested in 529 plans (see Figure 6.8).[56] The Financial Services Corporation estimates that by 2010 more than 225 billion will be saved in these accounts. Susan Dynarski examined the 2001 Survey of Consumer Finances data on 1533 families and found that less than 3 percent of households had a 529 or Educational Savers Account (ESA). By 2008, there were 7 million 529 accounts opened, covering roughly 10 percent of all children, primarily children from the wealthiest families.

In the small group of 46 households studied by Dymnaski, the 529 account holders were an elite group. More than 90 percent had a bachelor's degree (compared to 37% in the sample). The median income was 80 percent higher than for the rest of the sample and the net worth of those who had opened a 529 account was US$281,200 (more than four times the median net worth of the rest of the sample).

The cash value of the 529 savings plan for those who participate is substantial. If the parent sets aside about US$5000 a year for five years it will grow to $36,983. If this fund were taxed, it would have grown to about US$25,083 (see Figure 6.9).[57] Thus, the government subsidy for the child in this example is US$11,900. If the same amount were contributed over

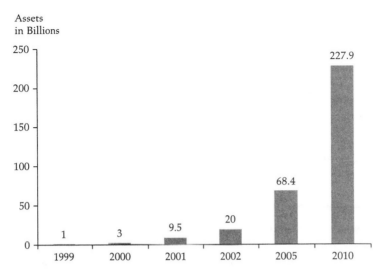

Figure 6.8 Assets in 529 College Saving Plans

Data Source: Kristof, 2002.
Note: The estimate for 2010 is from Financial Services Corporation.

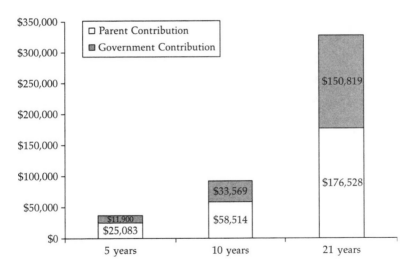

Figure 6.9 Government Contribution to the Growth of a 529 Account Over the Years

10 years the account would grow to US$92,083, of which US$33,569 would be the government's subsidy.[58] Finally, if same amount were contributed over 21 years, the child would have an account balance of US$327,347. The government's contribution to this account would be over US$150,000.[59]

Children from low-income and disadvantaged families are essentially excluded from the benefits of this major federally subsidized college savings plan. After all, you cannot save money you do not have.

Programs such as the 529 College Savings Plan are a great idea, but unless there is a mechanism that allows middle class, low-income, and poor children to participate, these plans simply accelerate and extend the inequality that already exists. What was meant to have a positive impact on society ends up having a negative impact if some way is not found for all children to fully participate. The gulf between children who have and children who do not will widen even more.

Child Savings Account

In recent years, Michael Sherraden, Ray Boshara, Robert Friedman,[60] and others have proposed a shift in social welfare policy from the means-tested income transfer approach (welfare) to an assets-based approach (investment and saving). The focus of an asset-based approach is to provide individuals with the assets and savings needed to succeed in a free enterprise market economy. Rather than focusing on providing the minimal resources to ensure the daily needs of the poor, an asset-based approach focuses on encouraging individuals to build up an asset base that will ensure their long-term well-being. This is the underlying assumption of Social Security.

Whereas the original Social Security Act provided a social insurance and social savings approach to provide income assistance to the elderly, the same Social Security Act provided a means-tested income transfer program to provide income support to poor mothers and their children. Over the years the social insurance approach has proven effective for seniors. The program is widely credited with ending poverty among seniors. In contrast, the means-tested income transfer program for poor mothers and their children (Aid to Families with Dependent Children, AFDC) has been viewed as a failure and even credited by some with making the situation of those it served worse.

Forging a New Approach

The old welfare system provided needed income support to poor children, but it was also an impediment to fundamental reform. The old welfare system was a means-tested program that served at times to foster dependency. More important, it failed to focus on building a foundation for recipients to exit poverty. This limitation was addressed by Michael Sherraden in his pioneering work on assets-based social policy.[61] In addition to providing income assistance targeted to income deficits, Sherraden argued that policies and programs needed to consider the importance of asset development and savings for the poor. The comprehensive series of studies on asset development and savings and the testing of Individual Development Accounts (IDAs) have been instrumental in refocusing discourse in the field and contributed to a shifting paradigm in the social welfare field.[62]

The assets-based approach to social policy combined with the essential demise of the conventional means-tested welfare set the stage for a bold new approach to ending child poverty. What might this new approach look like?

Just as Social Security requires citizens to prepare for their retirement years by setting up a social savings account, a similar child savings account might be created that would provide a savings account for junior citizens to ensure they have the funds necessary at the age of 18 to embark successfully on adult life, regardless of the economic situation they are born into. It would provide poor children an opportunity to break free of the cycle of poverty by ensuring that they would have money for a college education or some other training opportunity.

How might this work? One approach is that at birth, every child, regardless of the economic status of their family, would have a custodial account—a child savings account—opened in their name with an initial deposit of US$1000 assured by the government. The funds would be deposited in a registered brokerage firm account selected by the parent. Each year the account would receive an additional US$500 deposit assured by the government from funds collected in the same fashion used by Social Security. In a sense, the child savings account would be a 529 plan guaranteed for all children.

The child's parents could, if they wished, contribute privately to the account, as could the child through his or her earnings, although such contributions would not diminish the government contribution. At age 18, the accumulated funds would be made available to the young person for approved career program expenditures, such as college tuition, vocational training, job-readiness programs, and so on. By the time the child reaches 18, a typical child savings account might have an accumulated balance of nearly US$40,000 (see Figure 6.10).

Cost of the Program

Given roughly 4 million births a year in the United States, new child savings accounts would cost an estimated US$4 billion annually. Maintaining the annual contribution to the accounts for the other roughly 74 million children

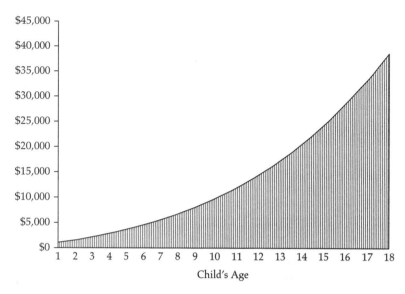

Figure 6.10 Projected Growth of a Child Savings Account

under the age of 18 would add another US$37 billion, for a total annual cost of roughly US$41 billion.

Following a start-up expense, the program could be funded entirely by children *repaying* their benefits during adulthood, using a collection mechanism similar to that used by the Social Security Administration, in which a payroll contribution of less than one-half of 1 percent would be made by employee and employer.

Parents would contribute to the cost of a child savings account of their child through a graduated tax schedule and thus reduce the cost incurred. For instance, parents with income above US$35,000 might be asked to contribute at the rate of 1 percent of all taxable income above US$35,000 (with appropriate adjustments for family composition).

Such an approach, which shares the cost of the child savings account with parents, would fund more than half the total cost of the program. Thus, the remaining cost of the program that would need to be funded would be less than US$20 billion (or less than one-half of 1 percent from both employer and employee).

Child Trust Fund in Britain

The Child Trust Fund is a groundbreaking new initiative which will strengthen financial education, promote positive attitudes to saving and ensure that all children, regardless of family background, will benefit from access to a stock of financial assets when they start their adult lives. It is based around the Government's belief in progressive universalism—benefiting every child while offering more help to those in most need.[63]

In 2003, Prime Minister Tony Blair and Chancellor of the Exchequer Gordon Brown launched a progressive universal children's savings account for the United Kingdom.[64] In Consultation with Michael Sherraden and others, the prime minister started a program to create a child trust fund for every child in the United Kingdom.[65] The program provides all children in the nation a savings and investment account for their future.

The British plan provides every child born in the United Kingdom since September 2002 with a Child Trust Fund account opened at birth. The initial endowment is £250 (about US$500). Children from low-income families will qualify for £500 (US$1000), although estimates are that about two-thirds of families will be eligible for the £500 amount. Parents, family members and friends will be able to contribute up to an additional £1200 (US$2400).

Accounts are made available through a certificate the parent uses to open their child's account. Children will not be able to access the funds until they are age 18. Funds can be used for any purpose or may be rolled over into other savings accounts.

It is estimated that if parents "paid their weekly child benefit into the fund (£10 or US$20.00), the fund would have grown to a substantial £27,000 (US$54,000) by age 18, presuming 7 percent annual growth."

In many respects, the Child Trust Fund is similar to the child savings account proposed in this chapter. The funding for the Child Trust Fund is less than proposed for the child savings account but, as Fred Goldberg (2002) observes, it is important "to put the plumbing in place" that will provide all children with an account.[66] Sherraden continues that once "the accounts are in place, there will be creative policy making and private initiative, impossible to define or predict ahead of time, to fund accounts."[67]

It is reasonable to expect that with the development of this program in the United Kingdom, other nations in Europe will follow. The premise of the asset-based social policy approach discussed above is that it builds the foundation for fundamental change of the economic circumstances of poor and disadvantaged children. This approach beckons a new approach to child policy that holds the potential of transforming life for children now mired in poverty. With the opening of a child trust fund for every child, the United Kingdom is at the inflection point for change for disadvantaged children. It may take a number of years for the program to take effect, but, as with

Social Security in the United States (see Figure 3.1, where there was also an inflection point for the program), once the program takes hold, it will produce fundamental change for all children and lead to a long-term decline in child poverty.

Encouraging Assets Accumulation

There is evidence that homeownership and asset development is associated with improved access to credit, social and political involvement, reduced domestic violence, marital stability, and higher educational attainment.[68] Unfortunately, the importance of asset building has often been overlooked in antipoverty policy. Wealth inequality outstrips income inequality by large margins—in 2005, the wealthiest 10 percent held more than 70 percent of privately held assets in this country, whereas the bottom half of the nation held less than 3 percent of the total net worth. Racial asset inequality is great; in 2004 White households had a median net worth 7 times more than Hispanic and Blacks.[69]

This disparity is no accident; during the era of the wealthy class, government policy has encouraged asset development for the upper middle and wealthy classes through tax incentives. In 2003, the federal government spent over US$335 billion on asset-building policies, but approximately 84 percent of those benefits went to the top one-fifth of individuals earning more than US$80,000 annually. The poor and middle class rarely receive benefits from these programs. The bottom 80 percent of individuals received about 16 percent of the benefits from these asset-building programs.[70] The bottom two-thirds of income earners in the United States pay most of their federal taxes through the employment tax, which, in most instances, does not offer deductions for these asset-building purposes. Employment taxes (Social Security and Medicare) are not eligible for the major categories such as mortgage deduction and investment expenses. The top-income earners, for whom the individual income tax is their main federal tax liability, are the ones who are able to benefit most from the current asset-building tax policies. In other words, because low- and middle-income families pay most of their federal taxes through the employment tax, they are effectively prevented from benefiting from participating in the asset-building tax deductions (see Table 5.9).

During the era of the middle class, the personal savings rate in the United States fluctuated around 8 percent. Most middle class families were able to save and invest. However, during the era of the wealthy class, the personal savings rate has consistently declined (see Figure 6.11).[71] When the era of

Figure 6.11 Personal Savings Rate between 1950 and 2008

the wealthy class began with the administration of President Reagan, the personal savings rate was about 10 percent. By 2006, the personal savings rate had slipped into negative territory, the lowest it had been since the Great Depression.[72]

The child savings account proposed in this chapter is designed to reverse the long-term downward trend in the personal savings rate. It is designed to teach children about saving and investing at an early age so that they will continue saving and investing as they grow older. In this sense, the child savings account represents a social investment approach to safeguarding the futures of all children. The program conforms to and takes advantage of the inherent nature of the capitalist free enterprise market economy. It does not rely on a means-tested targeted assistance approach but attempts to prevent the need for services by building a structure that reduces the number of children unable to achieve economic self-reliance. The intent is to provide children with the essential asset base of savings required to build upon in order to achieve economic self-sufficiency. The child savings account would guarantee all children the resources required at a critical stage in their lives to make the difficult transition to effective, self-reliant, and productive citizenship. It would permit them to realize opportunities in the free enterprise market economy without reference to the economic status of their parents, thereby ensuring all an equal opportunity and a fair start. It would be the fulcrum of opportunity that frees all children to fully engage their potential.

As with Social Security for the elderly, the child savings account would be paid for by the beneficiaries themselves during their working lives, the assumption being that young people who had the resources to properly prepare themselves for a career or occupation would earn more income and, thus, pay into the program throughout their working life. The program would, within a generation, significantly reduce poverty among children, at least to the extent we have seen it reduced among the elderly. Many of the social problems currently attendant upon that poverty would vanish.

The Case for Social Security

The landscape of poverty for seniors has been fundamentally altered by Social Security. It can be fairly argued that Social Security is responsible for essentially ending high rates of poverty among seniors. Before Social Security began to provide coverage for most seniors, they constituted the group with the highest poverty rates in the nation. When Molly Orshansky first began compiling data using the poverty line measure she developed for the federal government, the group with the highest poverty rate was seniors. The poverty rate for children was about one-third less. Today the situation for children and seniors has reversed. Children now have the highest poverty rates in the nation, whereas seniors have among the lowest.

Today about 35 million seniors receive a monthly Social Security check approaching 1000 dollars. For about a third of seniors in the United States, Social Security represents more than 90 percent of the income they receive. For two-thirds of seniors, Social Security is the main source of their retirement income. The Social Security Administration estimates that without Social Security almost half of all seniors in the United States would be living in poverty. By just about any measure, Social Security has been a resounding success for seniors.

Discussion and Closing

I've been rich and I've been poor. Believe me, rich is better.

Sophie Tucker[73]

In contrast to the success of Social Security for seniors, the part of the Social Security Act that provided income assistance to poor single mothers—what we commonly refer to as the welfare program—has essentially been a failure. The depth of that failure was showcased in the welfare reform debates that preceded the major welfare reform legislation that was signed into law by President Bill Clinton in 1996.

With the passage of welfare reform, the main program in the United States established to help poor single mothers and their children has been essentially dismantled. As a result, we have a situation where single mothers and their children represent the core of poverty in the United States today. Nothing in the welfare reform legislation has led to a change in this situation. In fact, on balance, welfare reform has deepened and made more difficult the plight of poor single mothers and their children in the United States.

What can be done to change the economic blight for most single mothers in the United States? Is it possible to make progress against child poverty? In this book, I have argued that it is possible to make progress. More importantly, it is imperative that we make progress against child poverty if we want to provide a better future for all our children. Today in the United States, we have essentially two childhoods. The one experienced by mostly White and Asian children is one of abundance and opportunity. It is a childhood rich with educational opportunities and excellent school systems. The other childhood experienced by almost half of all African-American and Latino children is one of low-income, jobs that provide limited health care, and schools that track children to bleak futures. The schools these children attend are too often underfunded, poorly staffed, and signal failure from the start.

Today children from these low-income and poor families have little chance of going to college and getting a good job. Less than 1 in 17 children from households with family income below US$35,000 a year will get a four-year college degree by age 24. More than half of all African-American and Latino children are growing up in homes with incomes below US$35,000 a year. In contrast, children growing up in households with incomes above US$75,000 a year—about 40 percent of all White and Asian children—are five times more likely to go to college. We can argue that all children have equal opportunity but to do so is disingenuous. Opportunity is effectively tied to family wealth and the ability of the child's parent(s) to promote his or her success.

After World War II, there was a renaissance in U.S. education. Educational opportunities expanded and encompassed almost all children. Children of the middle class and the working class experienced growing opportunities to finish high school and go on to college. But those days are in the past. Education is no longer serving to provide opportunities to enter the American mainstream that it once did.

If we want to improve the opportunities available to poor, low-income and middle class children, then we will need to revisit the purpose Social Security had for children. Social Security has met its obligation to seniors, but because of the fundamental limitations of the approach to assisting poor mothers and children that were built into the welfare component of Social Security, the part of Social Security that served poor mothers and their children was a failure.

What actions need to be taken? In the previous chapters, I have demonstrated that we have an ineffective child support collection system in the United States. For poor and low-income children, it could reasonably be said that for the most part, we essentially do not collect child support. In most other countries, the federal government collects child support and provides an advanced maintenance payment to the parent caring for the child—more often than not—the mother. In these countries, every child not living with both biological parents receives child support. The child support payment is thus a universal benefit and is not means-tested. Thus, if the mother works, she and the child do not lose the benefit.

Child support is the major component of missing income for poor and low-income children in the United States. If we had an effective child support collection system using something like the advanced maintenance payment model found in most other industrialized nations, we could cut child poverty in the United States by more than half. It is simply a matter of making this a national priority and of finding the will to make the necessary change.

The other major income disadvantage faced by poor and low-income children in the United States is the regressive nature of the child tax credit. In most other countries, families are provided with income assistance for their children in the form of a children's allowance. In the United States, the children's allowance has taken the form of a child tax credit. For poor and low-income children, this approach has meant that they are denied the benefit. As the Urban Institute study of this issue has pointed out, almost 14 million of the poorest children in the United States are essentially denied any benefit. I have proposed approaches to change the children's allowance scheme in the United States. If we adopted a progressive universal model, we could again substantially reduce the number of children living in poverty. Furthermore, the approaches I have suggested are universal and thus are not taken away if the mother works or remarries.

Both reforming child support collection and the child tax credit in the United States would substantially reduce child poverty. They will provide the foundation required to insure opportunity for all children. With these reforms in place, single mothers and their children would have greater opportunities to better themselves and to exit poverty.

In this book the central argument, however, has been the need for an asset-building program for poor and low-income children. If we want to fundamentally alter the limited life trajectories that await most poor and low-income children, then we need to find a way to let these children have the tools and resources required to enter the American mainstream. These children need to be able to begin building an asset base that will serve them during their adult lives. I have suggested a child savings account program like the one implemented in Great Britain. When children are born, we should open an account in their name and deposit 1000 dollars in the account. We should do this for all children. Furthermore, we should provide for contributions of US$500 a year to these accounts over the child's first 18 years.[74] This may seem like a great expense, but keep in mind that we will likely spend about US$10,000 a year on these children once they enter school. The result of the investment in a child savings account will be a substantial asset base that the young person should be able to use for education or a down payment on a house or other activities that increase their asset base. The funds should be restricted to asset-building purposes. The young person should not be able to withdraw more than 20 percent of the principal in any year. The goal is to provide every child the capital required to fully engage and participate in a capitalist society.

Such an account would provide young people with an asset base at the age of emancipation. When young people leave home and embark on their adult lives, they would have the necessary asset base that would allow them to begin building up a savings base that they can use throughout their life. Professor Lingxin Hao has shown that young people begin building assets at the age of emancipation and that it occurs over their lifetime.[75] It is vital that young people have a sufficient base or foundation to begin this building process. As seen in Figure 6.12, young people start with a small difference that becomes accentuated over their lifetime. If all young people could start with at least a sufficient base, then we would likely reduce the growing inequality in wealth seen in Figure 6.12 and also the inequality in income discussed earlier in this chapter.

In a sense, the child savings account proposed here could provide the rough equivalent of what Social Security has provided for seniors. The child savings account allows participants to begin building the savings they will need at a critical time in their life. For seniors that time is retirement, whereas for children that time is the age of emancipation—when they leave home and begin their own lives as self-supporting adults in a capitalist free enterprise economy. When Social Security was first signed into law, it included a social savings program for seniors that over time has proven effective in securing a base of economic support during retirement years.

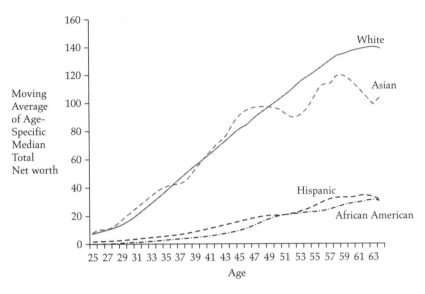

Figure 6.12 Growing Racial Wealth Gap Over the Lifecycle
Data Source: Hao, 2007.

Unfortunately, that same Social Security program implemented a different approach to providing Social Security for single mothers and their children. The residual means-tested program did not prove effective. Welfare reform essentially ended this program. But it did not provide a substitute approach to end poverty among those the program was originally designed to serve. In a sense, the child savings account program and other reforms proposed in this book are meant to correct the limitations in the original Social Security Act so that we not only provide Social Security to seniors but also to children.

The purpose of the child savings account is to insure that all children have the financial resources needed to fully participate in a free enterprise market economy when they reach their age of maturity or emancipation from home. Most middle and upper class children have parents who will provide them with the resources they need when they leave home and start life on their own. These young people know their parents will provide them with assistance needed to attend college or pursue career goals. However, for many low-income and poor children, these assurances are absent. The asset base provided and built through a child savings program will change this. These children would be assured of the resources they need. The assets saved in these accounts will provide the required infrastructure for economic and educational opportunity for all children.

Today we have a crisis in opportunity for children but particularly for poor and low income—and even middle class—children. The ideas and proposals set forth here are intended to move us toward finding and building a foundation for opportunity so that we can restore the American dream for all children.

The economic security of seniors that architects of Social Security achieved can be replicated for children. Imagine what the United States would look like if all children had an opportunity to participate in the wealth and prosperity of the nation. Imagine what this would do for the nation's future—our children.

7

Closing: The World We Leave Our Children

The ideas of economists and political philosophers, both when they
are right and when they are wrong, are more powerful than is commonly understood. Indeed the world is ruled by little else. Practical
men [and women], who believe themselves to be exempt from
any intellectual influences, are usually the slaves of some defunct
economist.

John Maynard Keynes, General Theory

Over the last half century, the United States has undergone fundamental
change. The change has been slow and imperceptible at first. It is sometimes
difficult to see change when you are in the middle of experiencing it, but it
now reveals itself. The United States has gone through an economic meta-
morphosis unlike any in its previous history. The country we live in today
is very different than the country we lived in a half century earlier. At the
center of this change has been growing inequality and unrelenting concentrated child poverty.

Coming out of World War II, the nation awoke to the brutal reality of
racism and discrimination as it was embedded in the segregated South.
With the advent of television, the brutality of the struggle for civil rights was
brought into our living rooms. As the country entered the 1960s, it elected a
president who was committed to ending the barriers to opportunity and civil
rights. The national economy was expanding, and the new wealth created
by the expanding economy was shared by most. Public policy was focused

on ending the scourge of child poverty. In the span of a decade, the child poverty rate, particularly among children of color, was cut in half.

The optimism of the 1960s ended with the war in Vietnam. President Johnson, who had pushed through the Civil Rights Act, Medicaid, and major programs for the War on Poverty, saw his presidency eroded by a Vietnam War that seemed to consume ever more resources to achieve less and less. Finally, President Johnson simply withdrew his name for reelection. The ensuing fight for leadership of the Democratic Party resulted in deep divisions that paved the way for the election of Richard Nixon.

The country that had been leading the world toward expanding civil rights and economic opportunity began to stall. Programs inherited from the War on Poverty and Great Society were systematically ended.

In 1980, the nation elected Ronald Reagan as president, who proclaimed that it was morning again in America. President Reagan entered his presidency with deeply held beliefs and theories on how to get America back on track. President Reagan was committed to removing what he viewed as the barriers to wealth accumulation that progressive social policy had put in place. The central focus of Reagan's presidency was to reduce and remove the progressive income tax policies. During his two terms in office, the tax liability of the wealthiest Americans was reduced by more than half, while the middle class saw small change. It was argued that this reduction would lead to increased economic activity and, eventually, to increased revenue and benefits trickling down to all segments of the economy. However, the consequence of Reagan's policies was a dramatic increase in the national debt. Increased economic activity did not pay for his tax reductions. Rather, the cost was shifted to an ever-expanding national debt. During his time in office, the personal savings rate began a decline from above 10 percent to a historic negative rate in recent years. The policies also led to an acceleration of inequality and decline of the middle class.

The consequence of the increasing national debt is a financial burden that will be left to the next generation—our children. They will need to pay the interest on this debt, which now approaches US$10 trillion. This debt exacerbates the most disappointing consequence of the Reagan era economic policies: the increase in inequality both in terms of income and wealth. During the last three decades, the disparities in wealth and income have been substantially increased. Today, the top 1 percent own more financial assets than the bottom 90 percent combined. In 2005, according to the Internal Revenue Service, the top 4 percent received more income than the bottom two-thirds combined. Public policies have been put in place that ensure the prosperity and opportunity for those already wealthy but do little for the vast majority of citizens who have limited assets.

The children of wealthy have new benefits, including the 529 child savings plans. Children of those in the top-income brackets now have greater opportunity than at any previous time in history. The financial infrastructure to ensure their future well-being has been set firmly in place.

What propelled me to write this book is the declining economic opportunity for middle class, working class, and poor children. The quality of educational opportunities has been greatly reduced for many children in low-income communities. They attend schools where they are virtually assured of being unable to go on to college. They have seen the quality of jobs available to them decline. They have seen the gap between their economic opportunity and possibility widen when compared with their cohorts from prosperous households.

We are leaving these children a world of diminished opportunity and hope. We are leaving them a world where their parents' economic achievements are the single most important determinant of their economic future—more important than any effort that they might personally make to better themselves.

The inequality is now leading slowly but inexorably toward a caste system of the haves and have-nots. We need to change this. We need to restore the sense of hope and opportunity that guided the country in earlier decades. We cannot allow greed to overwhelm our sense of decency.

I recall one summer while kayaking in the waters off Pender Bay in British Columbia, paddling by a modestly outfitted 25-foot cabin cruiser. It was an older boat that was obviously cared for. But there in the distance was a mega yacht, one of the 200-foot plus variety I talked about in the previous chapter. The comparison between these two vessels could hardly be more striking. I particularly liked the name painted on the back of the modest cabin cruiser—*It'll do.*

It seems that the extremes of wealth that have flourished in the new era of the wealthy class have gone too far. How can we feel good about hundreds of millions being lavished on mega yachts and custom-outfitted jetliners for a wealthy few when millions of children live in debilitating poverty? These children go without the basic necessities of life. They are deprived of any real opportunity from the day they leave the delivery room. Their deprivation in a land of such great abundance is difficult to reconcile.

In this book, I have argued that we can substantially reduce child poverty in the United States. I doubt many experts in the field would disagree with this premise. After all, child poverty has been essentially ended in most industrial nations that have wealth comparable to ours. But to reduce child poverty will require a commitment, and the development and enactment of policies to achieve this.

The core of child poverty in the United States comprises single mothers trying to raise their children, working full-time in low-paying jobs outside the home, maintaining a household, and providing the intensive parent–child nurturing essential to raising young children. As a result of welfare reform, the major federal program to provide income assistance to these families has been essentially eliminated. Nothing was developed as a replacement. The early result of welfare reform was more single mothers working longer hours outside the home. A dozen years later, we can see that the most salient consequence of welfare reform has been the persistence of poverty for children in single-parent families.

More needs to be done to protect the economic opportunities of single-parent families. We should develop universal income support policies that reduce barriers to remarriage and employment, and we should encourage marriage. It is vital to implement policies that assure child support. Most advanced economies ensure child support collection for children in single-parent households through a variety of government collection systems. These programs assign the burden of collecting child support to the government, rather than the mother, because the government has the tools and resources to achieve compliance. In the United States, most eligible children never receive child support—particularly children living below the poverty line. Reforming child support to ensure full compliance would do more to end child poverty in the United States than any other policy reform.

We also need to ensure that poor children are not denied benefits by our system of child tax credits. Child tax credits currently provide the greatest benefits to children of the upper-income groups and no benefits to the poorest children. I have outlined ways we could reform these policies to achieve equity and fairness for all children. If we are to reduce child poverty, we will need to reform these policies and programs.

The effort of this book, however, is more ambitious. It is not enough to develop policies that reduce child poverty; rather, we need to restore economic opportunity for all children. This will require a bold effort.

By reducing child poverty, we would be removing one of the greatest contributors to the growing inequality in the nation. It is the destiny of capitalism to extend economic opportunity, and the freedom and liberty that makes this possible, to all young people.

Child poverty is the life blood of severe inequality. It is critical to develop strategies to end child poverty. I close with a proposal for a child savings account. I argue that just as Social Security was primarily responsible for the great reduction in poverty among the elderly in the United States, so would a universal child savings account lead to a major reduction in child poverty. The Social Security Act passed in 1935 laid the foundation for true social security for seniors. This same Social Security Act also produced the welfare program that, in contrast, proved far less successful for children. We owe it to children to provide them with a workable social security program based on the social savings and social insurance models of social security that we provide seniors. Social security for children can be achieved with a progressive child savings account. A child savings account would be an investment in making the great opportunities provided by the capitalist economic system available to a large group of children who would otherwise never know the possibilities and opportunities which our economic system offers.

I have urged that our public programs and policies for children embrace the spirit of capitalism. The essence of capitalism is not found in the arrogant opulence of half billion dollar yachts or tax policies that erode the middle class. Rather, the spirit of capitalism is unleashed by the widespread ownership of income earning assets. The proposal for a child savings account is directed toward that end. It would allow children of the middle class and the poor an opportunity to participate in the true spirit of capitalism.

The future of a nation can be viewed by examining how it provides for its children. In the United States, we are providing different opportunities and different life trajectories for our children. Many youth are born into prosperity and great opportunity. But many, too, are born into poverty and despair. In earlier periods during the nation's history all children could rely on access to opportunity. In recent years, however, opportunity and access to the American Dream has diminished for children of poor and low-income families, and increasingly, even for children of the middle class. Unless we take a different direction in our policies toward child poverty, we will continue to move toward greater inequality. One of the best ways to reduce the growing inequality is to pursue policies toward children that increase opportunity and full participation in the capitalist economic system.

Notes

Introduction

1. Jonathan Kozol (1991). *Savage Inequalities*. New York: HarperCollins; *The Shame of the Nation: The Restoration of Apartheid Schooling in America*. New York: Crown, 2005.
2. See Chapter 3, Figure 3.5. Online at: http://www.census.gov/hhes/www/income/ histinc/f05.html, accessed December 11, 2007. The median family income increased from $22,792 in 1950 to $45,240 in 1976 (in 2005 dollars). The median income increased from US$48,804 in 1980 to US$56,587 in 2006 (in 2005 dollars). See *Income, Poverty, and Health Insurance Coverage in the United States: 2006*. P60–233. Washington, DC: U.S. Census Bureau.
3. Isaac Shapiro (2005). New IRS Data Show Income Inequality Is Again On The Rise. *Center on Budget Priority*. Online at: http://www.cbpp.org/10–17-05inc. htm, accessed December 17, 2007. See Figure 3.6 in Chapter 3.
4. Greg J. Duncan & Jeanne Brooks-Gunn (eds.) (1997). *Consequences of Growing Up Poor*. New York: Russell Sage.
5. Andrew Hacker, *Two Nations: Black and White, Separate, Hostile, Unequal*. New York: Scribner, 1992. Also see Douglas Massey & Nancy Denton (1994). *American Apartheid: Segregation and the Making of the Underclass*. Cambridge, MA: Harvard University Press; and the earlier study by Michael Harrington (1974). *The Other America: Poverty in the United States*. New York: Macmillan.
6. See Chapter 1, Table 1.1.
7. See Stephen Shames (1991). *Outside the Dream: Child Poverty in America*. New York: Aperture Books. Also see Koen Vleminckx & Timothy M. Smeeding (eds.) (2000). *Child Well-Being, Child Poverty and Child Policy in Modern Nations*. Bristol, UK: The Policy Press.
8. UNICEF. Child Poverty in Rich Countries 2005. *Innocenti Report Cards*.
9. Merrill Lynch, Cap Gemini Ernst, & Young (2007). *World Wealth Report 1997–2007*. New York: Merrill Lynch. Online at (requires registration): http://www.us.capgemini.com/DownloadLibrary/files/Capgemini_FSI_ WorldWealthReport2007_062707.pdf, accessed July 7, 2007.
10. Ross Douthat, Does Meritocracy Work? *Atlantic Monthly*, November 2005.
11. Internal Revenue Service, table 2. *Individual Income and Tax Data, by State and Size of Adjusted Gross Income, Tax Year 2005*, from the Internal Revenue Service. Online at: http://www.irs.gov/pub/irs-soi/05in53us.xls, accessed October 22, 2007.

12. Theda Skocpol (2000). *The Missing Middle: Working Families and the Future of American Social Policy*. New York: W.W. Norton.
13. Thomas Taliaferro (2007). Baby Boomers Opt To Live Longer, Play Harder. *EzineArticles* (October, 16), http://ezinearticles.com/?Baby-Boomers-Opt-To-Live-Longer,-Play-Harder&id=785397, accessed January 2, 2008.
14. In recent years home equity loans have allowed middle class home owners a sense of increasing income but at the expense of drawing down their main asset—their home. In these instances, increased middle class income has come at the expense of declining middle class wealth.
15. Source: Wojciech Kopczuk & Emmanuel Saez (June 2004). *Top Wealth Shares in the United States, 1916–2000: Evidence From Estate Tax Returns, National Tax Journal*, LVII, no. 2, Part 2, figure 12. Online at: http://www.cbpp.org/3–29-07inc.htm#_ftn1; http://www.forbes.com/2007/03/07/billionaires-worlds-richest_07billionaires_cz_lk_af_0308billie_land.html, accessed July 7, 2007. Also see Edward Wolffe's report online at: http://www.levy.org/vdoc.aspx?docid=929, accessed July 7, 2007.
16. Isaac Shapiro & Joel Friedman, *Tax Returns. A Comprehensive Assessment of the Bush Administration's Record on Cutting Taxes*, Center on Budget and Policy Priorities, April 14, 2004; Lynnley Browning, U.S. Income Gap Widening, Study Says. *New York Times*, September 25, 2003.
17. Paul H. Douglas (1971). *Social Security in the United States: An Analysis and Appraisal of the Federal Social Security Act*. Cambridge, MA: Da Capo Press.
18. Sarah Fass & Nancy K. Cauthen, (November 2007). *Who are America's Poor Children? The Official Story*. New York: National Center for Children in Poverty, Columbia University.
19. Charles Murray (1994). *Losing Ground: American Social Policy 1950–1980*. New York: Basic Books; and Robert Rector & Patrick F. Fagan, The continuing good news about welfare reform, *Heritage Foundation Backgrounder* No. 1620, February 6, 2003.
20. The latest data on welfare recipients can be found online at: http://www.acf.hhs.gov/programs/ofa/caseload/caseloadindex.htm, accessed December 21, 2007.
21. See Vleminckx & Smeeding, note 7.
22. Duncan Lindsey (2004). *The Welfare of Children, 2nd Edition*. New York: Oxford University Press, 313–336.
23. Adam Carasso & C. Eugene Steuerle (October 10, 2005). *The True Tax Rates Confronting Families with Children*, Tax Policy Center, Urban Institute and Brookings Institution.
24. Lisa Keister (2005). *Getting Rich: A Study of Wealth Mobility in America*. New York: Cambridge University Press.
25. Robert T. Kiyosaki & Sharon L. Lechter (2000). *Rich Dad, Poor Dad: What the Rich Teach Their Kids About Money—That the Poor and Middle Class Do Not!* New York: Warner Books. Also see fact sheet about teaching children about money online at: http://www.prosperity4kids.com/statistics.shtml
26. Michael Sherraden (2002). *Asset-Based Policy and the Child Trust Fund*. St Louis: Center for Social Development, Washington University.

27. Anna Bernasek, In a 529 savings plan, the number to watch may be 2010. *New York Times*, May 7, 2006.

Chapter 1

1. UNICEF. *Child Poverty in Rich Countries 2005*. Innocenti Report Cards. The United States Census Bureau calculates poverty using a different approach. The Census Bureau reports that in 2005 the child poverty rate in the United States was 17.1 percent. Online at: http://pubdb3.census.gov/macro/032006/pov/new03_100_01.htm

2. Ibid.

3. Robert B. Reich, The great divide. *The American Prospect*, 11 no. 12 (2000).

4. Census Bureau (2005). *People in Families with Related Children Under 18 by Family Structure, Age, Sex, Iterated by Income-to-Poverty Ratio and Race.* Online at: http://pubdb3.census.gov/macro/032005/pov/new03_100.htm

5. U.S. Census Bureau (August 2005). *Income, Poverty, and Health Insurance Coverage in the United States: 2004. U.S. Department of Commerce, Economic and Statistic Administration.* Online at: http://www.census.gov/prod/2005pubs/p60–229.pdf

6. Ibid.

7. The child poverty measure used by the United Nations is one-half of the median income. Poverty assessed in this manner thus refers to *relative* poverty. The poor child in the United States will thus have greater income than the poor child in the Czech Republic. The poverty measure reported here and used by the federal government is the *poverty index* developed by Molly Orshansky for the Department of Agriculture and is based on having sufficient resources to provide for basic human needs.

8. Daniel T. Lichter, Diane K. McLaughlin, George Kephart, & David Landry. Race and the Retreat from Marriage: A Shortage of Marriageable Men? *American Sociological Review* 57 (1992): 781–799.

9. In 2004, the waiting lists for child care contained 550,000. See *The State of America's Children® 2005. Washington, DC: Children's Defense Fund, 16.* Online at: http://www.childrensdefense.org/publications/greenbook/default.aspx

10. Tom Waldron, Brandon Roberts, & Andrew Reamer (2004). *Working Hard, Falling Short: America's Working Families and the Pursuit of Economic Security.* AnneE. Casey Foundation. Online at: http://www.aecf.org/publications/data/working_hard_new.pdf

11. Reich, *The Great Divide.*

12. Barbara Ehrenreich (2001). *Nickel and Dimed: On (not) Getting by in America.* New York: Metropolitan Books.

13. Beth Shulman (2003). *The Betrayal of Work: How Low-Wage Jobs Fail 30 Million Americans and Their Families.* New York: Free Press.

14. Valerie Polakow (1993). *Lives on the Edge: Single Mothers and Their Children in the Other America.* Chicago: University of Chicago Press; Sharon Hays (2003).

Flat Broke With Children: Women in the Age of Welfare Reform. New York: Oxford University Press.

15. Ann Mooney & June Statham (Eds.) (2003). *Family Day Care: International Perspectives on Policy, Practice and Quality.* London: Jessica Kingsley Publishers.

16. Kathryn H. Porter & Allen Dupree (2001). *Poverty Trends for Families Headed by Working Single Mothers.* Washington, DC: Center on Budget and Policy Priorities.

17. Congressional Budget Office (May, 2007). *Changes in the Economic Resources of Low-Income Households with Children.* Online at: http://www.cbo.gov/ftpdoc.cfm?index=8113&type=0&sequence=1

18. Cynthia Cready, Mark A. Fossett, & Jill K. Kiecolt, Mate Availability and African-American Family Structure in the U.S. Nonmetropolitan South, 1960–1990. *Journal of Marriage and the Family* 59 (1997): 192–203; Lichter and others, Race and Retreat from Marriage.

19. Sara McLanahan & Gary Sandefur (1994). *Growing Up With a Single Parent.* Cambridge, MA: Harvard University Press.

20. Ibid.

21. Ibid.

22. Kathryn Edin & Laura Lein (1997). *Making Ends Meet: How Single Mothers Survive Welfare and Low-Wage Work.* New York: Russell Sage.

23. Lynn Meersman, The end to social promotion is scaled back. *Los Angeles Times.* December 1, 1999, A26.

24. Richard J. Herrnstein & Charles Murray (1994). *The Bell Curve: Intelligence and Class Structure in American Life.* New York: Free Press.

25. Robert Rosenthal & Lenore Jacobson (1968). *Pygmalion in the Classroom.* New York: Holt, Rinehart & Winston.

26. For a discussion of these matters see Richard Thompson Ford (2008). *The Race Card: How Bluffing About Bias Makes Race Relations Worse.* New York: Farrar, Straus and Giroux; Cornell West (1993). *Race Matters.* Ann Arbor, MI: University of Michigan Press; Philomena Essed & David Theo Goldberg (Eds.) (2001). *Race Critical Theories.* New York: Wiley.

27. Betty Hart & Todd Risley (1995). *Meaningful Differences in the Everyday Experience of Young American Children.* Baltimore, MD: Brookes Publishing Company.

28. Ibid.

29. Ibid.

30. Ibid.

31. Ibid.

32. Sara McLanahan, Ron Haskins, Christina Paxson, Cecilia Rouse, & Isabel Sawhill (Eds.) (2005). *School Readiness: Closing Racial and Ethnic Gaps.* Washington, DC: Brookings; Annette Lareau (2003). *Unequal Childhoods: Class, Race and Family Life.* Berkeley and Los Angeles: University of California Press.

33. Jonathan Kozol (1991). *Savage Inequalities: Children in America's Schools.* New York: Crown Books; Jonathan Kozol (2005). *The Shame of a Nation.* New York: Crown Books.

34. The Civil Rights Project, Harvard University. Gary Orfield & Chungmei Lee (2005). *Why Segregation Matters: Poverty and Educational Inequality.* January 13, 2005; Erica Frankerberg, Chungmei Lee & Gary Orfield (2003). *A Multiracial Society With Segregated Schools: Are We Losing the Dream?* Online at: http://www.civilrightsproject.harvard.edu/

35. Barry A. Gold (2007). *Still Separate and Unequal: Segregation and the Future of Urban School Reform.* New York: Columbia University Press.

36. Kozol, 2005, *Shame of a Nation*, 45.

37. Ibid.

38. Saul Geiser (1998). *Redefining UC's Eligibility Pool to Include a Percentage of Students from Each High School.* University of California, Office of the President. Online at: http://www.ucop.edu/sas/researchandplanning/simulations.pdf
Saul Geiser with Roger Studley (2001). *UC and the SAT: Predictive Validity and Differential Impact of the SAT I and SAT II at the University of California.* Oakland, CA: University of California, Office of the President. Online at: http://www.ucop.edu/sas/research/researchandplanning/pdf/sat_study.pdf
There has been limited empirical research on critical issues surrounding the SAT and much of it is funded and/or sponsored by the College Board and the Educational Testing Service that owns the SAT and receives millions of dollars from the more than 2.3 million students who take the various tests each year.

39. Geiser, 1998, *Redefining UC's Eligibility Pool*, figure 5.

40. Kozol, 2005, *Shame of a Nation*, 53.

41. Ibid, p. 100.

42. James Fallows, The Tests and the "Brightest": How Fair are the College Boards? *Atlantic Monthly*, February 1980.

43. In one of the few peer-reviewed empirical studies of the SAT Jesse Rothstein finds, "the SAT's contribution is about 75% lower that the usual estimates, a result equally attributable to the two innovations. One important implication is that the SAT functions as a proxy for omitted background characteristics in sparse prediction models, and that this serves to inflate the SAT's apparent contribution." Jesse M. Rothstein, (2002). *College Performance Predictions and the SAT.* Berkeley, CA: Center for Labor Economics, University of California, Berkeley. Online at: http://www.nber.org/~confer/2002/hieds02/rothstein.pdf

44. Francis Galton (1889). *Natural Inheritance.* London: Macmillan; Edward L. Thorndike (1904). *An Introduction to the Theory of Mental and Social Measurements.* New York: The Science Press.

45. Arthur Jensen (1973). *Genetics and Education.* London: Methuen; Arthur Jensen with Martin Deutsch & Irwin Katz (1968). *Social Class, Race, and Psychological Development.* New York: Holt; Herrnstein & Murray (1994). *The Bell Curve*, note 24.

46. Pat Moore & Pete Wilson, SFGate.com (February 23, 1998). *What is Race?* Online at: http://www.sfgate.com/cgi-bin/article.cgi?file=/kron/archive/1998/02/23/race_part1.dtl&type=special

47. Ibid.

48. Walter Lippmann, The Mental Age of Americans, *New Republic* 32, no. 412 (October 25, 1922): 213–215.

49. Nicholas Lemann (1999). *The Big Test: The Secret History of the American Meritocracy*. New York: Farrar, Straus and Giroux. This history of the SAT discussed in this chapter derives from this book.

50. Ibid.

51. According to Carl Campbell Brigham, author of the first SAT, "There were three distinct white races in Europe—in descending order of intelligence, Nordic, Alpine, and Mediterranean—and that the United States was initially and successfully populated by the highest but was now being filled up with the lowest." Lemann, The Big Test, note 49, page 30. Eugenicists feared that the unintelligent (or southern Europeans in Brigham's research) "were reproducing at a more rapid rate than intelligent ones" and eventually the entire nation would suffer."

52. Ibid.

53. *The Use of Admissions Tests by the University of California*. Oakland, CA: University of California Office of the President and Academic Senate. Online at: http://www.universityofcalifornia.edu/senate/committees/boars/admissionstests. pdf

54. James Fallows, The Tests and the Brightest. *Atlantic Monthly*, September 1995.

55. Geiser (2001), *UC and the SAT*.

56. Geiser (2001), *UC and the SAT*. The focus here is on the SAT I, which is the main SAT test. The SAT II provides a number of subject matter tests which have been found to be more useful than the SAT I tests. In fact, the large scale University of California study found the SAT I did not provide statistically significant predictive information when disaggregated by separate year cohorts.

57. Peter Sacks, The Geography of Privilege. *Encounter* 17, no. 1 (2004): 5–9.

58. Ibid.

59. Ibid.

60. Saul Geiser (2001), note 70, above; State of California, Department of Finance, *Population Projections for California and Its Counties 2000–2050, by Age, Gender and Race/Ethnicity*, Sacrament, California, July 2007. Online at: http://www.dof.ca.gov/html/DEMOGRAP/ReportsPapers/Projections/P3/P3.php, accessed May 10, 2008.

61. David G. Sansing (1990). *Making Haste Slowly: The Troubled History of Higher Education in Mississippi*. Jackson: University Press of Mississippi, 148–154.

62. Ross Douthat, College Admissions 2005, *Atlantic Monthly*, November 2005, 120–126.

63. Peter Sacks (June 24, 2002). Testing Times in Higher Ed. *The Nation*.

64. I have not seen the SAT Interactive Handheld Tutor Advertised Elsewhere. *Wall Street Journal*, December 15, 2005, p. D4.

Chapter 2

1. John F. Kennedy, Remarks at Androy Hotel Reception, Superior, Wisconsin, March 18, 1960. Online at: http://www.jfklibrary.org/Historical+Resources/Archives/Reference+Desk/Speeches/JFK/JFK+Pre-Pres/1960/002PREPRES12 SPEECHES_60MAR18.htm, accessed May 10, 2008.

2. Theda Skocpol (2000). *The Missing Middle: Working Families and the Future of American Social Policy.* New York: W.W. Norton.

3. In the first presidential debate of 1960 with Nixon, Kennedy observed that Black children were substantially more likely to be poor, to end up in prison, and to attend inferior schools compared to their White counterparts. Irving Bernstein (1991). *Promises Kept: John F. Kennedy's New Frontier.* New York: Oxford University Press.

4. Doris Kearns Goodwin (1991). *Lyndon Johnson and the American Dream.* Boston: St Martins Press; Robert A. Caro (2002). *Master of the Senate: The Years of Lyndon Johnson.* New York: Knopf.

5. The data in Table 2.3 report the "financial wealth" of households in the United States. This measure reflects the accumulation of stocks, bonds, treasury notes, cash, and other financial assets.

6. Stephen E. Ambrose (1988). *Nixon* Volume I. New York: Simon and Schuster.

7. James Cannon (1998). *Time and Chance: Gerald Ford's Appointment With History.* Ann Arbor, MI: University of Michigan Press.

8. Burton I. Kaufman (1993). *The Presidency of James Earl Carter, Jr.* Lawrence, KS: University of Kansas Press.

9. Douglas G. Brinkley (1999). *The Unfinished Presidency: Jimmy Carter's Journey to the Nobel Peace Prize.* New York: Penguin.

10. Brinkley, *The Unfinished Presidency.*

11. Michael K. Deaver (2005). *Why I Am a Reagan Conservative.* New York: Morrow; Craig Shirley (2005). *Reagan's Revolution: The Untold Story of the Campaign That Started It All.* New York: Nelson.

12. Tom Wicker & Arthur M. Schlesinger (2002). *Dwight D. Eisenhower 1953–1961* (The American Presidents Series). New York: Times Books.

13. Barbara Ehrenreich (1990). *Fear of Falling: The Inner Life of the Middle Class.* New York: Perennial, 145.

14. Edmund Morris (1999). *Dutch: A Memoir of Ronald Reagan.* New York: Randon House.

15. Michael Schaller (1994). *Reckoning With Reagan: America and Its President in the 1980s.* New York: Oxford University Press.

16. Austan Goolsbee (1999). *Evidence on the High-Income Laffer Curve From Six Decades of Tax Reform* (ABF working paper). Washington, DC: American Bar Association.

17. *Income Tax Theories—The Laffer Curve—Who Pays How Much?* Online at: http://www.bized.ac.uk/virtual/economy/policy/tools/income/inctaxth5.htm, accessed July 7, 2007; William Gale & Peter Orszag, An Economic Assessment of Tax Policy in the Bush Administration, 2000–2004. *Boston College Law Review* 45, no. 4 (2004).

18. A. Smith (1937). *An Inquiry Into the Nature and Cause of the Wealth of Nations.* [first published in 1776]. New York: Modern Library.

19. Ray Boshara, The $6,000 Solution. *Atlantic Monthly,* February 1, 2003.

20. Lester C. Thurow (1975). *Generating Inequality: Mechanisms of Distribution in the U.S. Economy.* New York: Basic Books.

21. Robert T. Kiyosaki & Sharon L. Lechter (2000). *Rich Dad, Poor Dad: What the Rich Teach Their Kids About Money—That the Poor and Middle Class Do Not!* New York: Warner Books.

22. Edward N. Wolff (May, 2004). *Changes in Household Wealth in the 1980s and 1990s in the U.S.,* Jerome Levy Economics Institute; Lisa Keister (2005). *Getting Rich: A Study of Wealth Mobility in America.* New York: Cambridge University Press.

23. Stephen J. Rose (2007). *Social Stratification in the United States.* New York: The New Press. From tables 13 and 14, pp. 33–34.

24. G. William Domhoff (2006). *Wealth, Income and Power.* Online at: http://sociology.ucsc.edu/whorulesamerica/power/wealth.html, accessed October 21, 2007.

25. Lisa A. Keister (2005). *Getting Rich: America's New Rich and How They Got That Way.* New York: Cambridge University Press, 20.

26. Ibid; Meizhu Lui (2006). *Closing the Racial Wealth Divide. Santa Barbara, CA: Closing the Racial Wealth Gap—2006 Convening.* Data from Survey of Consumer Finances, Federal Reserve Board, 2006. Online at: http://www.insightcced.org/uploads///publications/assets/Panel%201a%20Lui%20Closing%20Racial%20 Wealth%20Gap.pdf, accessed May 7, 2008.

27. In 1960 individual income taxes were roughly 45 billion dollars, whereas employment taxes were 11.2 billion dollars (*Internal Revenue Service*, Table 7—Internal Revenue Gross Collections, by Type of Tax, Fiscal Years 1960–2000.) Online at: http://www.irs.gov/pub/irs-soi/05db07co.xls, accessed October 21, 2007.

28. Data for income tax liability drawn from table 2—Individual Income and Tax Data, by State and Size of Adjusted Gross Income, Tax Year 2005, from the *Internal Revenue Service.* Online at: http://www.irs.gov/pub/irs-soi/05in53us. xls, accessed October 22, 2007. Employment tax extrapolated from total provided in table 7—Internal Revenue Gross Collections, by Type of Tax, Fiscal Years 1960–2000. Table 7 also accessed from *Internal Revenue Service* Website at the same time table 2 was accessed. Using data from above, table 2 the employment tax was assigned to the income groups by multiplying the reported income by the appropriate tax rates for each group. Extrapolated data available from the author.

29. Ibid. The effective individual income tax rate was computed by dividing the total taxable income for each income group by the total taxes paid.

30. The Institute on Taxation and Economic Policy provides a concrete illustration of this. The average annual tax cuts as a result of the 2001–2003 tax reductions introduced by President Bush were US$80 for the bottom 20 percent, US$655 for the middle 20 percent, US$4,192 for those in the top 20 percent, and US$42,618 for the top 1 percent. Meizhu Liu, Institute on Taxation and Economic Policy, July 2005.

31. Warren Buffett has pointed out that his tax rate was 17.7 percent on the US$46 million he earned in 2006, whereas his secretary, who earned US$60,000 paid a tax rate of 30 percent. The reason is her earnings were from labor (and thus she paid employment tax on the full amount), whereas his was from capital (gains). See TimesOnline at: http://business.timesonline.co.uk/tol/business/money/tax/article1996735.ece, accessed April 21, 2008.

32. Thomas I. Palley (2000). *Plenty of Nothing: The Downsizing of the American Dream and the Case for Structural Keynesianism.* Princeton, NJ: Princeton University Press.

33. U.S. Department of the Treasury (2008). *Monthly Statement of the Public Debt and Downloadable Files.* Online at: http://www.treasurydirect.gov/govt/reports/pd/mspd/mspd.htm, accessed March 7, 2008. Also see: http://www.treasurydirect.gov/govt/reports/pd/histdebt/histdebt.htm, accessed March 7, 2008.

34. President Ronald Reagan, March 28, 1982. Address to the National Association of Realtors. Online at: http://johnshadegg.house.gov/rsc/Reagan%20and%20Tax%20Relief.pdf, accessed May 10, 2008.

35. Quoted in BNA Daily Tax Report, March 17, 2004. Richard Kogan, David Kamin, & Joel Friedman (March 22, 2004). *Too Good To Be True.*

36. Ronald Reagan is credited with defeating the Soviet Union. During his presidency, defense spending was increased and the Berlin Wall came down. The defeat of the Soviet Union was an economic defeat. The declining socialist economies came to realize the futility of the socialist regimes. The broad public support for change in Eastern Europe led to the move toward market economies and democracy. In 2008, the failing housing market and the increasing federal debt leads to serious concerns about the health of the American economy that only eight years earlier had been producing a federal government surplus and been the leading economy in the world. See Kevin Phillips (2008). *Bad Money.* New York: Viking.

37. Boshara, The $6,000 solution.

38. See note 27.

39. Leonard E. Burman & David L. Gunter (May 26, 2003). *17 Percent of Families Have Stock Dividends.* Washington, DC: The Urban Institute. Online at: http://www.urban.org/publications/1000488.html, accessed May 10, 2008.

40. William D. Zabel (1995). *The Rich Die Richer and You Can Too.* New York: William Morrow, vii–viii.

41. Schaller, *Reckoning With Reagan*; Goolsbee, *Evidence on High-Income Laffer Curve.*

42. U.S. Census Bureau (2007). *Race and Hispanic Origin of Householder*—Families by Median and Mean Income: 1947 to 2005, table F-5. Washington, DC: U.S. Census Bureau. Online at: http://www.census.gov/hhes/www/income/histinc/f05.html, accessed May 10, 2008.

43. Sources: For disposable income, online at: http://www.bea.gov/bea/regional/spi/drill, accessed March 10, 2008; for Census data see: http://www.bea.gov/bea/regional/spi/drill, accessed March 10, 2008; for income data see: http://pubdb3.census.gov/macro/032007/faminc/new01_001.htm, accessed March 10, 2008; and for Consumer Price Index data (to adjust for inflation) see online at: http://inflationdata.com/inflation/Consumer_Price_Index/HistoricalCPI.aspx?rsCPI_currentPage=4, accessed March 11, 2008.

44. Paul Krugman, Losing Our Country. *New York Times*, June 10, 2005.

45. Edward N. Wolff (May, 2004). *Changes in Household Wealth in the 1980s and 1990s in the U.S.*, Jerome Levy Economics Institute; Isaac Shapiro (October 17,

2005). *New IRS Data Show Income Inequality Is Again on the Rise.* Washington, DC: Center on Budget and Policy Priorities.

46. Isaac Shapiro (March 7, 2005). *What New CBO Data Indicate About Long-Term Income Distribution Trends.* Center on Budget and Policy Priorities; Congressional Budget Office, *Historical Effective Federal Tax Rates: 1979 to 2002,* March 2005. Paul Krugman writes, "Between 1973 and 2000 the average real income of the bottom 90 percent of American taxpayers actually fell by 7 percent. Meanwhile, the income of the top 1 percent rose by 148 percent, the income of the top 0.1 percent rose by 343 percent and the income of the top 0.01 percent rose 599 percent. (Those numbers exclude capital gains, so they're not an artifact of the stock-market bubble.)" Online at: http://www.thenation.com/doc/20040105/krugman, accessed May 10, 2008.

47. Bruce Ackerman & Anne Alstott (1999). *The Stake Holder Society.* New Haven, CT: Yale University, 2.

48. Robert Perrucci & Earl Wysong (2002). *New Class Society: Goodbye American Dream?* 2nd Edition. New York: Rowman & Littlefield Publishers.

49. Frank Levy (1987). *Dollars and Dreams: The Changing American Income Distribution.* New York: W.W. Norton, p. 14–16; Frank Levy (1999). *The New Dollars and Dreams: American Income and Economic Change.* New York: Russell Sage; Edward N. Wolff & Ajit Zacharias (2006). *Wealth and Economic Inequality: Who's at the Top of the Economic Ladder?* New York: Levy Economic Institute of Bard College.

50. David Leonhardt, Defining the Rich in the World's Wealthiest Nation. *New York Times,* January 12, 2003. Section 4, pp. 1 and 16.

51. Sar A. Levitan (1990). *Programs in Aid of the Poor.* Baltimore, MD: The John Hopkins University Press.

52. UNICEF (2000). *Child Poverty in Rich Nations.* Florence, Italy: United Nations Children's Fund (www.unicef-icdc.org).

53. Online at: http://www.forbes.com/lists/2007/54/richlist07_The-400-Richest-Americans_Rank.html, accessed April 21, 2008.

54. Thomas Piketty & Emmanuel Saez, The Evolution of Top Incomes: A Historical and International Perspective, *American Economic Review* 96 no. 2, (2006): 200–205.

Chapter 3

1. Brooking Institution Center on Urban and Metropolitan Policy (January, 2000). *The Value of Investing in Youth in the Washington Metropolitan Area.* Washington, DC: Brookings Institution.

2. Joan Hoff Wilson & Oscar Handlin (1992). *Herbert Hoover: Forgotten Progressive.* Waveland Press. Online at: http://www.americanpresident.org/history/herberthoover/biography/LifeinBrief.common.shtml, accessed July 7, 2007.

3. John Kenneth Galbraith (1954). *The Great Crash 1929.* New York: Houghton Mifflin.

4. In 1929, the worldwide economic collapse hit Germany particularly hard and led to widespread strikes, unemployment and demonstrations. The Communist Party began to gain strength and threaten the wealthy industrialists and land holders. The wealthy elite began to support the Nazis, in large part, because they challenged the Communists. The Nazis turned to brutal clashes with the Communists and were supported by police who ignored the clashes. The Nazis increased their strength in the elections of 1933 and appointed Hitler as Chancellor and later as Fuhrer of the Third Reich, and thus began one of the darkest periods of the history of civilized nations.

5. Franklin Delano Roosevelt (1937). *One Third of a Nation. Second Inaugural Address.* Online at: http://historymatters.gmu.edu/d/5105/, accessed July 7, 2007.

6. William E. Leuchtenburg (1963). *Franklin D. Roosevelt and the New Deal.* New York: Harper & Row; Arthur M. Schlesinger, Jr. (1958). *The Coming of the New Deal: 1933–1935, The Age of Roosevelt, Volume II.* New York: Houghton Mifflin.

7. Arthur M. Schlesinger, Jr. (1960). *The Politics of Upheaval: 1935–1936, The Age of Roosevelt, Volume III.* New York: Houghton Mifflin.

8. The original Social Security Act included four programs. Because many elderly, in 1935, were still suffering the ravages of the continuing depression, the Social Security Act also offered Old Age Assistance (OAA). This was a means-tested welfare program that provided a welfare payment to those who were 65 or older and unable to care of themselves. The OAA was a means-tested public assistance program. Another part of the Social Security Act was a program called Aid to the Permanently and Totally Disabled (APTD). Like OAA, this was a means-tested program that provided income assistance to disabled and blind individuals who were unable provide for themselves. In 1971, these two programs—APTD and OAA—were replaced with the Supplemental Security Income (SSI) program; Paul H. Douglas (1971). *Social Security in the United States: An Analysis and Appraisal of the Federal Social Security Act.* Cambridge, MA: Da Capo Press.

9. Social Security Administration, *Annual Statistical Supplement, 2004* (released August 2005). Online at: http://www.ssa.gov/policy/docs/statcomps/supplement/2004/index.html#toc, accessed July 7, 2007.

10. Henry Aaron (1982). *Economic Effects of Social Security.* Washington, DC: Brookings Institution.

11. Social Security Administration, *Social Security Programs in the United States* (released July 1997). Online at: http://www.ssa.gov/policy/docs/progdesc/sspus/index, accessed July 7, 2007.

12. U.S. Census Bureau (August, 2007). *Income, Poverty, and Health Insurance Coverage in the United States: 2006.* P60–233, table 3. Online at: http://www.census.gov/prod/2007pubs/p60–233.pdf, accessed March 10, 2008.

13. Charles F. Westoff & Norman B. Ryder (1977). *The Contraceptive Revolution.* Princeton, NJ: Princeton University Press; George A. Akerlof & Janet L. Yellen, An Analysis of Out-of-wedlock Childbearing in the United States, *Quarterly Journal of Economics* 2 (1996): 277–317.

14. Nancy F. Cott (2000). *Public Vows: A History of Marriage and the Nation.* Cambridge, MA: Harvard University Press; Julie DaVanzo & M. Amar Rahman, American Families: Trends and Correlates, *Population Index* 59 (1993): 350–386.

15. Wilson & Handlin. *Herbert Hoover.*

16. Duncan Lindsey (1994). *The Welfare of Children.* New York: Oxford University Press, p. 269.

17. James T. Patterson. (1994). *America's Struggle Against Poverty, 1900–1994.* Cambridge, MA: Harvard University Press.

18. Michael B. Katz (1989). *The Undeserving Poor: From the War on Poverty to the War on Welfare.* New York: Pantheon Books; Joel Handler & Yeheskel Hansenfeld (1991). *The Moral Construction of Poverty: Welfare Reform in America.* Newbury Park, CA: Sage.

19. Martin Rein & Lee Rainwater, Patterns of Welfare Use. *Social Service Review* 52 (1978): 511–534.

20. Ibid.

21. Ewie Becker, Elizabeth Rankin, & Annette U. Rickel (1998). *High Risk Sexual Behavior: Interventions with Vulnerable Populations.* New York: Plenum Press; K. A. Moore, C. W. Nord, & J. L. Peterson, Non-voluntary Sexual Activity Among Adolescents. *Family Planning Perspectives* 21 (1989):110–114.

22. Child Trends (August, 2001). Teen Birth Rate. *CTS Facts at a Glance.*

23. National Center for Health Statistics (2001). *Teen Pregnancy Rate Reaches a Record Low in 1997.* Hyattsville, MD: Author.

24. Leuchtenburg, *Roosevelt and New Deal*; Schlesinger, Jr. (1958). *Coming of the New Deal.*

25. Council of Europe (1999*). Recent Demographic Developments in Europe, 1999.* Council of Europe Press; Kathleen Kiernan (2000). *European Perspectives of Union Formation.* In Linda Waite, Christine Bacharach, Michelle Hindin, Elizabeth Thompson, & Arland Thompson, eds., *Ties That Bind: Perspectives on Marriage and Cohabitation.* New York: Aldine de Gruyter; P. B. Smith & John Poertner, Enhancing the Skills of Adolescents as Individuals and as Parents. *Children and Youth Services Review* 15 (1993): 275–280; Stephanie J. Ventura, NCHS & Christine A. Bachrach (October 18, 2000). Nonmarital Childbearing in the United States, 1940–99, *National Vital Statistics Reports* Vol. 48, No. 16. Hyattsville, MD: National Institute for Child Health and Human Development, National Institutes of Health. Online at: http://www.cdc.gov/nchs/ pressroom/00facts/nonmarit.htm, accessed April 30, 2008.

26. Stanley K. Henshaw & Jennifer Van Vort, Teenage Abortion, Birth and Pregnancy Statistics: An Update. *Family Planning Perspectives* 21 (1989): 85–88; Stephanie J. Ventura & Christine A. Bacharach. Nonmarital Childbearing in the United States, 1940–99. *National Vital Statistics Reports* 48, no. 16 (2000): 11; Stephanie Ventura, Joyce Abma, William D. Mosher, & Stanley K. Henshaw, Estimated Pregnancy Rates by Outcome for the United States, 1990–2004. *National Vital Statistic Reports* 56, no. 15 (April 14, 2008): 1–26.

27. George A. Akerlof & Janet L. Yellen (August, 1996). An Analysis of Out-of-wedlock Births in the United States. *Policy Brief #5*. Washington, DC: Brookings Institution.

28. Schlesinger, Jr. (1960). *The Politics of Upheaval,*

29. Brady E. Hamilton, Joyce A. Martin, & S. J. Ventura (2007). *Births: Preliminary Data for 2006*. National Vital Statistics Reports; Volume 55, Hyattsville, MD: National Center for Health Statistics, table 1. Online at: http://www.cdc.gov/nchs/data/nvsr/nvsr56/nvsr56_07.pdf, accessed March 11, 2008.

30. Committee on Ways and Means of the U.S. House of Representatives. *The 2000 Green Book*. 17th Edition. Online at: http://aspe.hhs.gov/2000gb/, accessed July 7, 2007.

31. Douglas J. Besharov, Escaping the Dole: For Young Unmarried Mothers, Welfare Reform Alone Can't Make Work Pay. *Washington Post*, December 12, 1993, C3, 51.

32. Andrew Hacker (1992). *Two Nations: Black and White, Separate, Hostile, Unequal*. New York: Ballantine Books.

33. Frederica Mathewes-Green, Pro-life Dilemma: Pregnancy Centers and the Welfare Trap. *Policy Review* (1996): 40–44; James Q. Wilson (2002). *The Marriage Problem: How Our Culture Has Weakened Families*. New York: HarperCollins.

34. Aria Davis Crump, Denise L. Hynie, Sigrid J. Aarons, Elissa Adair, Kathy Woodward, & Bruce G. Simons-Morton, Pregnancy Among Urban African-American Teens: Ambivalence About Prevention. *American Journal of Health and Behavior* 23 (1999): 32–42; Isabel V. Sawhill (November, 1998). Teen Pregnancy Prevention: Welfare Reform's Missing Component. *Policy Brief #38* Washington, DC: Brookings Institution.

35. National Center for Health Statistics. *Teen Pregnancy in 1997.*

36. Maureen Baker (1985). *What Will Tomorrow Bring? A Study of the Aspirations of Adolescent Women*. Ottawa: Canadian Advisory Council on the Status of Women.

37. Ventura & Bacharach. Nonmarital Childbearing in United States, figure 22.

38. Ventura & Bacharach. Nonmarital childbearing in United States, p. 9; Christine Bacharach. Adoption Plans, Adopted Children and Adoptive Mothers. *Journal of Marriage and the Family* 48 (1986): 243–253. These data need to be viewed with caution. The data used by Bacharach came from the National Survey of Family Growth conducted by the National Center for Health Statistics in 1982. Interviews were completed with 7,969 women between 15 and 44 years of age. Only 60 women in the sample had placed one or more babies for adoption (p. 244). Thus, the rates of placement may not be reliable estimates of national rates. In Ontario, a provincial government report indicated that 30.1 percent of unwed mothers kept their children in 1968, but that 10 years later the number had increased to 88.3 percent [Ontario (1979). *The Family as a Form for Social Policy*. Toronto, Canada: Provincial Secretary for Social Development: p. 19, table 2].

39. William D. Mosher & Christine A. Bacharach . Understanding U.S. fertility: Continuity and Change in the National Survey of Family Growth, 1988–1995.

Family Planning Perspectives, 28, no. 1 (1996): 4–12); Christine A. Bacharach, Kathy Shepherd Stolley, & Kathryn A. London. Relinquishment of Premarital Births: Evidence from the National Survey Data. *Family Planning Perspectives* 24 (1992): 27–32 and 48.

40. More than 60 percent children born out of wedlock currently living with a single mother are poor. See Ariel Halpern (1999). *Poverty Among Children Born Outside of Marriage—Preliminary Findings From the National Survey of America's Families.* (UI Report No. 99–16). Washington, DC: The Urban Institute; Dalton Garis, Poverty, Single-parent Households, and Youth At-risk Behavior: An Empirical Study. *Journal of Economic Issues* 32 (1998): 1079–1106.

41. Richard Wertheimer (2001). *Working Poor Families With Children: Leaving Welfare Doesn't Necessarily Mean Leaving Poverty* (Research brief). Washington, DC: Child Trends.

42. Given that unwed teenage mothers have an average annual income of less than $7,000 a year, an unintended consequence of current social and economic policy is to impose severe economic hardship on those who elect to keep their children and try to raise them as best they can. Those who are opposed to abortion would be wise to focus on improving the circumstances of the single mothers who elect to keep their child. For many who carry their child to term, the consequence is a life in poverty for both the mother and the child extending for many years. Frank Levy (1987). *Dollars and Dreams: The Changing American Income Distribution.* New York: W. W. Norton, 151.

43. The poverty rate for female-headed families was 54.7 percent for African-American children, 59.6 percent for Hispanic children, and 40 percent for White children (U.S. Census Bureau, 1999, Current Population Reports, Series P-60).

44. Sara S. McLanahan (1997). Parent Absence or Poverty: Which Matters More? In Greg Duncan & Jeanne Brooks-Gunn, eds., *Consequences of Growing Up Poor*, 38–45. New York: Russell Sage Foundation; P. F. Fagan (1999). *How Broken Families Rob Children of Their Chances for Future Prosperity.* Backgrounder No. 1283. Washington, DC: Heritage Foundation.

45. Amy Butler. The Changing Economic Consequences of Teenage Childbearing. *Social Service Review* 66 (1992):1–31, 5.

46. V. Joe Hotz, Susan Williams. McElroy, & Seth G. Sanders (1997). The Impacts of Teenage Childbearing on the Mothers and Consequences of those Impacts for Government. In Rebecca E. Maynard, ed., *Kids Having Kids: Economic Costs and Social Consequences of Teen Pregnancy.* Washington, DC: Urban Institute Press, 55–90); Sara McLanahan & Gary Sandefur (1994). *Growing Up With a Single Parent: What Hurts, What Helps.* Cambridge, MA: Harvard University Press.

47. David Ellwood & Christopher Jencks (2004). The Uneven Spread of Single-parent Families: What Do We Know? Where Do We Look for Answers? In Kathryn M. Neckerman, ed., *Social Inequality*, New York: Russell Sage Foundation, 3–118; Ralph Segalman & Asoke Basu (1981). *Poverty in America: The Welfare Dilemma.* Westport, CT: Greenwood Press.

48. Sara McLanahan, Diverging Destinies: How Children Are Faring Under the Second Demographic Transition, *Demography* 41 (2004): 607–627; Diane K. McLaughlin & Daniel T. Lichter, Poverty and the Marital Behavior of Young Women. *Journal of Marriage & the Family* 59 (1997): 589.

49. Robert I. Lerman, Married and Unmarried Parenthood and Economic Well-Being: A Dynamic Analysis of a Recent Cohort, Working Paper (Washington, DC: Urban Institute, July 2002); Stephen G. Bronars & Jeff Grogger, The Economic Consequences of Unwed Motherhood: Using Twin Births as a Natural Experiment, *American Economic Review* 85, no. 5 (1994): 1141–1156).

50. Social Security Beneficiary Data, Updated May 15, 2007. Online at: http://www. ssa.gov/OACT/ProgData/benefits.html, accessed December 12, 2007.

Chapter 4

1. Jason DeParle (2004). *American Dream: Three women, Ten Kids, and a Nation's Drive to End Welfare.* New York: Viking.

2. James Truslow Adams (1933). *The Epic of America.* Boston: Little Brown.

3. Adams, *The Epic of America*, 214–215.

4. Sylvia Bashevkin (1998). *Women on the Defensive: Living Through Conservative Times.* Chicago: University of Chicago Press; Gary Bryner (1998). *Politics and Public Morality: The Great American Welfare Reform Debate.* New York: Norton.

5. Gilbert Yale Steiner (1976). *The Children's Cause.* Washington, DC: Brookings.

6. Frances Fox Piven & Richard Cloward (1971). *Regulating the Poor: The Functions of Public Welfare.* New York: Vintage.

7. Gordon L. Berlin, Rewarding the Work of Individuals: A Counterintuitive Approach to Reducing Poverty and Strengthening Families. *The Future of Children* 17 (2007): 17–42.

8. James Q. Wilson (2002). *The Marriage Problem: How Our Culture Has Weakened Families.* New York: HarperCollins.

9. Sharon Parrot & Robert Greenstein (1995). *Welfare, Out-of-Wedlock Child bearing and Poverty: What is the Connection?* Washington, DC: Center on Budget and Policy Priorities.

10. John Hospers, *The Two Classes: Producers and Parasites,* Reason, Sept. 1975 at 12, 14–15.

11. Mimi Abramovitz (1989). *Regulating the Lives of Women: Social Welfare Policy from Colonial Times to the Present.* Cambridge, MA: South End Press, 226–227.

12. Joel F. Handler & Ellen Jane Hollingsworth (1971). *The "Deserving Poor": A Study of Welfare Administration.* Chicago, IL: Markham Publishing Company; Kathryn Edin & Maria Kefalas (2005). *Promises I Can Keep: Why Poor Women Put Motherhood Before Marriage.* Berkeley, CA: University of California Press; Kathryn Edin & Laura Lein (1997). *Making Ends Meet: How Single Mothers Survive Welfare and Low Wage Work.* New York: Russell Sage.

13. Clarence Page, This Drug Crackdown Targets Color. *Chicago Tribune*, December 31, 1989.

14. Charles Murray (1984). *Losing Ground*. New York: Basic Books; Richard J. Herrnstein & Charles Murray. (1994). *The Bell Curve: Intelligence and Class Structure in American Life*. New York: Free Press.

15. Congressional Record, 104th Congress, 1st Session, 1995, 141, pt. 7:9194, 9200. From Robert Asen (2002). *Visions of Poverty: Welfare Policy and Political Imagination*. East Lansing: Michigan State University Press.

16. 141 Congressional Record, H3766.

17. Dorothy Gilliam, Ugly Ways on the Hill, *Washington Post*, March 25, 1995, B1.

18. Nina J. Easton, Merchants of Virtue: By Shifting Their Party's Longtime Focus from Money to Values a Trio of Thinkers Hopes to Win Over the Agenda—and the Soul—of the GOP, *Los Angeles Times*, August 21, 1994, 16, 20.

19. Asen, *Visions of Poverty*.

20. George Will (September,1993). Quoted in Daniel Partrick Moynihan (1996). *Miles to Go: A Personal History of Social Policy*. Cambridge, MA: Harvard University Press.

21. Moynihan, *Miles to Go*.

22. M. W. Edelman, Say No to this Welfare Reform: An Open Letter to the President. *Washington Post*, November 3, 1995.

23. Washington Post (1995). The Welfare Fade (Editorial). *Washington Post*, November 3, 1995.

24. The latest data on welfare recipients can be found online at: http://www.acf.dhhs. gov/news/stats/recipients.htm, also see: http://www.acf.hhs.gov//programs/ofa/ caseload/2007/tanf_recipients.htm, accessed March 11, 2008.

25. Tommy Thomson, *New York Times*, May 19, 1996.

26. United States Census Bureau (2004). *Poverty in the United States: 2004. Current population reports,* Series P60–219. Washington, DC: U.S. Government Printing Office (see www.census.gov); United States Department of Health and Human Services, Office of Family Assistance, Temporary Assistance to Needy Families Separate State Program-Maintenance of Effort Aid to Families with Dependant Children: Caseload Data. Online at: http://www.acf.hhs.gov/programs/ofa/ caseload/caseloadindex.htm, accessed May 11, 2008.

27. *Wisconsin Council on Children and Families, "Poverty Rates Rise Substantially in Wisconsin."* August 28, 2007. Available online at: http://www.2020wi.org/ pdf/povertyrates_082807pr.pdf, accessed December 11, 2007. Welfare recipient data available online at: http://www.acf.hhs.gov/programs/ofa/caseload/2007/ tanf_recipients.htm, accessed December 11, 2007.

28. Most of the research and analysis supporting the "good news" about welfare reform derives from the conservative think tanks (Heritage, American Enterprise Institute, Manhattan Institute, and Cato) that provided much of the research that supported the legislation. See Lucy A. Williams (1997). *Decades of Distortion: The Right's 30-year Assault on Welfare*. Williams observes, "The Manhattan Institute hired a public relations expert to run the 'Murray campaign," spent US$15,000 to send 700 free copies of the book to "influential politicians,

academics, and journalists," booked Murray on talk shows, and paid a US$500–1500 honoraria to "intellectuals and journalists influential in policy circles" who attended a seminar on Murray's ideas." Online at: http://www.publiceye.org/welfare/Decades-of-Distortion.html

This is one area where partisan/advocacy research has carried far more influence than peer-reviewed scholarship.

29. Dean Jolliffe, Craig Gundersen, Laura Tiehen, & Joshua Winicki (2005). Food Stamp Benefits and Child Poverty. *American Journal of Agricultural Economics* 87 no. 3 (2005): 569. This report indicates that food stamps are important in reducing the poverty gap or depth of poverty experienced by children.

30. The welfare reform legislation did include provisions that reduced or eliminated food stamp assistance for legal immigrants (although some of this was later restored) and established time limits for able-bodied adults without children.

31. U.S. Department of Health and Human Services, Indicators of Welfare Dependence, *Appendix A: Program Data: Food Stamp Program, Annual Report to the Congress.* Online at: aspe.hhs.gov/hsp/indicators02/appa-FS.pdf; U.S. Department of Agriculture, Food and Nutrition Service, Program data (2005). Online at: http://www.fns.usda.gov/pd/fspmain.htm, accessed July 7, 2007.

32. *Food Stamp Eligibility.* Online at: http://www.fns.usda.gov/fsp/applicant_recipients/fs_Res_Ben_Elig.htm, accessed July 7, 2007.

33. Avis Jones-DeWeever reports that "For all poor children in single-parent families, access to food stamps declined between 1996 and 2000. The proportion of children whose families received no food stamps rose from 36 percent to 47 percent for poor children and from 27 percent to 37 percent for extremely poor children." p. 2. Online at: http://www.iwpr.org/pdf/D457a.pdf, accessed July 7, 2007.

34. Food stamp data at the state level are based on sample sizes designed to provide reliable estimates at the state level.

35. Duncan Lindsey (2004). *The Welfare of Children*, 2nd Edition. New York: Oxford University Press, table 10.6.

36. Nancy E. Wemmerus, Elyse S. Forkosh & Douglas Almond (May, 1996). *Characteristics of National School Lunch and School Breakfast Program Participants.* Washington, DC: U.S. Department of Agriculture, Food and Consumer Service, Office of Analysis and Evaluation.

37. The National School Lunch Act was passed in 1946. By 2007, the National School Lunch Program (NSLP) cost the Department of Agriculture about US$8.3 billion annually. Income eligibility guidelines for the NSLP are derived from the federal poverty guidelines and are updated annually. To participate in the NSLP, schools and institutions must agree to operate food service for all students and to provide free and reduced price lunches to students unable to pay the full price based on income eligibility criteria. See Carol Pogash, Free lunch isn't cool, so some students go hungry, *New York Times*, March 1, 2008.

38. *U.S. Department of Agriculture (USDA), Food and Nutrition Service (FNS), National School Lunch Program. National Level Annual Summary Tables: Fiscal Years 1969–2001.* Online at: www.fns.usda.gov/pd/slsummar.htm, accessed May 10, 2008. State information is also available in the Food Research and

Action Center's *State of the State: A Profile of Food and Nutrition Programs Across the Nation.* Washington, DC: FRAC, 2002. Online at: www.frac.org, accessed May 10, 2008.

39. Alberta Frost (March, 2002). *Free and Reduced Price Certification: An Update.* Washington, DC: U.S. Department of Agriculture.

40. Frost, *Free and Reduced Price Certification.* This report suggests that reductions and terminations have increased from 11 percent in 1986–87 to 18 percent in 2000–01.

41. The eligibility standards for the subsidized free lunch did not change during this period, and the studies of the characteristics of NSLP subsidized free lunch recipients indicate no major change in the recipient population during this period.

42. Food and Nutrition Service, U.S. Department of Agriculture, National Level Annual Summary Table. Washington, DC: U.S. Department of Agriculture. For 2006, average participation in the reduced price lunch program was 3.0 million, whereas average participation in the government subsidized full price lunch program was 12.6 million. Online at: http://www.fns.usda.gov/pd/slsummar.htm accessed May 10, 2008.

43. *U.S. Department of Agriculture (USDA), Food and Nutrition Service (FNS), National School Lunch Program. National Level Annual Summary Tables: Fiscal Years 1969–2002.* Online at: www.fns.usda.gov/pd/slsummar.htm. State information is also available in the Food Research and Action Center's *State of the State: A Profile of Food and Nutrition Programs Across the Nation.* Washington, DC: FRAC Publications, 2002. Online at: http://www.frac.org, accessed June 10, 2007.

44. *WIC Program: National Level Annual Summary.* Online at: http://www.fns.usda. gov/pd/wichome.htm, accessed July 7, 2007.
    WIC Participant and Program Characteristics 2002. Online at:
    http://www.fns.usda.gov/oane/MENU/Published/WIC/FILES/PC2002.htm

45. See note 24.

46. Pardue, note 28.

47. Lindsey (2004) reported a spearman rank order correlation of changes between 1996 and 2001 for children receiving welfare and children in poverty for 50 states of 0.03. See note 35, p. 286.

48. *The State of America's Children® 2005.* Washington, DC: Children's Defense Fund, p. 9. Online at: http://www.childrensdefense.org/publications/greenbook/ default.aspx, accessed May 11, 2008; Gregory Acs & Pamela Loprest (2004). *Leaving Welfare: Employment and Well-being of Families that Left Welfare in the Post-Entitlement Era.* Kalamazoo, MI: W.E. Upjohn Institute.

49. James Q. Wilson, *From Welfare Reform and Character Development,* July 1995, from the Wriston Lecture at the Manhattan Institute, New York.

50. Deanna Lyter, Melissa Sills, & Gi-Taik Oh, *The Children Left Behind: America's Poorest Children Left in Deeper Poverty and with Fewer Supports after Welfare Reform.* Online at: http://www.iwpr.org/pdf/D457a.pdf, accessed May 10, 2008.

51. Sarah Fass & Nancy K. Cauthen (November 2007). *Who are America's Poor Children? The Official Story.* New York: National Center for Children in Poverty, Columbia University.

52. *The State of America's Children® 2005,* note 48.

53. Fass & Cauthen, *Who Are America's Poor Children?*

54. Austin Nichols, *Understanding Recent Changes in Child Poverty,* Series A, No. A-71, August 2006. Washington, DC: Urban Institute. Online at: http://www. urban.org/uploadedpdf/311356_A71.pdf, accessed May 12, 2008.

55. John Iceland, Why Poverty Remains High: The Role of Income Growth, Economic Inequality, and Changes in Family Structure, 1949–1999, *Demography* 40 (2003): 499–519; Daniel T. Lichter, Poverty and Inequality among Children, *Annual Review of Sociology* 23 (1997): 121–145.

    John Iceland (2006). *Poverty in America: A Handbook.* Berkeley, CA: University of California Press.

56. Tommy G. Thompson, *Testimony Before the Committee on Finance—United States Senate, Welfare Reform: Building on Success.* March 12, 2003; J. Hein, Taming the welfare state: New York City, once America's "welfare capital," has become the epicenter of reform. *American Outlook,* May/June 2001; Melissa G. Pardue (2003). Sharp reductions in Black child poverty due to welfare reform, *Backgrounder No. 1661.* Washington, DC: Heritage Foundation; Robert Rector & Patrick F. Fagan (2003). The continuing good news about welfare reform, *Backgrounder No. 1620.* Washington, DC: Heritage Foundation; June E. O'Neill and Sanders Korenman (2004). *Child Poverty and Welfare Reform: Stay the Course.* Online at: http://www.manhattan-institute.org/html/cr_44.htm, accessed July 7, 2007.

57. Donna Pavetti, Urban Institute calculations, reported by Daniel Patrick Moynihan, *Miles to Go.*

58. Daniel Patrick Moynihan & Carol Moseley-Braun, Letter to President Clinton, dated March 4, 1996. Cited in Moynihan's, *Miles to Go.*

59. JiYoung Yoo & Younghee Lim, The Trend in the Income Status of Children in Female-headed Families: A Replication and Update, *Children and Youth Services Review,* forthcoming; Martha N. Ozawa & R. Y. Kim, The Trend in the Income Status of Children in Female-headed Families. *Children and Youth Services Review* 21 (1999): 527–547.

60. Joel F. Handler & Yeheskel Hasenfeld (2007). *Blame Welfare, Ignore Poverty and Inequality.* New York: Cambridge University Press.

61. Thompson, 2003; Pardue, 2003, note 56.

62. Rebecca Blank & Brian Kovak, The Growing Problem of Disconnected Single Mothers. *Focus* 25 (2007–2008, Fall–Winter): 27–34.

Chapter 5

1. Jason DeParle (2004). *American Dream: Three Women, Ten Kids, and a Nation's Drive to End Welfare.* New York: Viking, 154.

2. Max B. Sawicky (2004). The Mirage of Welfare Reform. In Louise B. Simmons, ed., *Welfare, the Working Poor, and Labor.* Armonk, NY: M.E. Sharpe, 11–23. Sawicky observes, "Welfare reform's achievements are uncertain and ambiguous, and its harm to a significant minority of poor families is manifest. Contrary to the complacency of a wide assortment of politicians, the debate over welfare reform is not over. It is just beginning" (p. 21).

3. Robert Rector (2001). *Implementing Welfare Reform and Restoring Marriage.* Washington, DC: The Heritage Foundation.

4. Theda Skocpol (2000). *The Missing Middle: Working Families and the Future of American Social Policy.* New York: W.W. Norton.

5. Claw back is a term used in Canadian and European discussions of means-tested welfare schemes. See Leah F. Vosko (2002). Mandatory "Marriage" or Obligatory Waged Work: Social Assistance and Single Mothers in Wisconsin and Ontario. In Sylvia Bashevkin, ed., *Women's Work Is Never Done: Comparative Studies in Caregiving, Employment, and Social Policy Reform.* New York: Routledge, 165–200 and 170.

6. For discussion of bundled benefits see, Herbert Obinger (2005). Federalism and the "New Politics" of the Welfare State. In Herbert Obinger, Stephan Leibfried, & Francis G. Castles, eds., *Federalism and the Welfare State: New World and European Experiences.* New York: Cambridge University Press, 209–218. Also see R. Kent Weaver (2000). *Ending Welfare As We Know It.* Washington, DC: Brookings Institution Press.

7. Sheila Kamerman & Alfred J. Kahn (2000). Innovations in Toddler Day Care and Family Support Services: An International Overview. In Bruce Hershfield & Karen Selman, eds., *Child Day Care.* New Brunswick, NJ: Transaction Publishers, 237–256. Kamerman and Kahn observe, "Advanced industrialized countries have almost unanimously elected universal but voluntary preschool for children from the ages of two, two-and-one-half, or three until six, or seven, varying with a country's age of compulsory schooling" (p. 240).
Suzanne Wiggans Helburn, & Barbara R. Bergmann (2003). *America's Child Care Problem: The Way Out.* New York: MacMillan, 39.

8. Social Security Administration, *A Summary of the 2007 Annual Social Security and Medicare Trust Fund Reports.* Adam Carasso, C. Eugene Steuerle, & Gillian Reynolds (2007). *Kids' Share 2007.* Washington, DC: Urban Institute. Online at: http://www.urban.org/publications/411432.html. Additional data online at: http://www.cms.hhs.gov/NationalHealthExpendData/downloads/proj2006.pdf

9. The great welfare debate, *Nation's Business*, April 1970.

10. Bruce J. Shulman (2000). *The Seventies: The Great Shift in American Culture, Society, and Politics.* New York: De Capo Press. In 1982, President Reagan declared, "Government began eating away at the underpinnings of the private enterprise system. The big taxers and big spenders in the Congress had started a binge that would slowly change the nature of our society and, even worse, it threatened the character of our people .... By the time the full weight of Great Society programs was felt, economic progress for America's poor had come to a tragic halt" (p. 236).

11. DeParle, *American Dream*, p. 330.
12. Brookings Institute (2002). *Brookings Welfare Reform and Beyond Initiative.* Washington, DC: Brookings Institute.
13. Ibid.
14. Adam Carasso & C. Eugene Steuerle (October 10, 2005). *The True Tax Rates Confronting Families With Children.* Tax Policy Center, Urban Institute and Brookings Institution.
15. If this percentage, 88.6, causes you to stop and question whether it could really be this high, you are not alone. These mothers are paying an almost 90 percent tax on income.
16. Ibid.
17. DeParle, *American Dream*.
18. Ibid., p. 283.
19. Ibid., p. 283.
20. Theda Skocpol, The Next Liberalism. *Atlantic Monthly*, 279 (1997): 118–120.
21. Anne H. Gauthier, Historical Trends in State Support for Families in Europe (post-1945). *Children and Youth Services Review*, 21 (1999): 937–965. Also see Kamerman and Kahn, note 7.
22. United Nations Children's Fund (1998). *Generation in Jeopardy: Children in Central and Eastern Europe and the Former Soviet Union.* Armonk, NY: M.E. Sharpe; Evelyn Mahon (1998). Changing Gender Roles, State, Work and Family Lives. In Eileen Drew, Ruth Emerek, & Evelyn Mahon, eds., *Women, Work and the Family in Europe.* New York: Routledge, 153–158; Anthony Barnes Atkinson (1995). *Incomes and the Welfare State: Essays on Britain and Europe.* New York: Cambridge University Press.
23. Social Security Administration (2002). *Social Security Programs Throughout the World: Europe*, 2002. Online at: http://www.ssa.gov/policy/docs/progdesc/ssptw/2002–2003/europe/
24. National Women's Law Center (December 2006). *Questions and Answers About the Child Tax Credit Tax Year 2006.* Washington, DC: National Women's Law Center. Online at: http://www.nwlc.org/pdf/CTC_Q&A_2007.pdf, accessed May 14, 2008. The benefit for Married taxpayers filing jointly. For a single taxpayer the income limit is US$30,000 to US$75,000 for maximum benefit. A sliding scale reduces the benefit above these amounts; Jason DeParle, Study Finds Many Children Don't Benefit from Credits. *New York Times*, October 2, 2005, 16; Carasso & Steuerle, *Tax Rates Confronting Families*.
25. Leonard E. Burman & Laura Wheaton, Who Gets the Child Tax Credit. *Tax Notes*, (October 17, 2005): 387–393. Washington, DC: Urban Institute, data from Table 3.
26. Ibid.
27. Edmund L. Andrews. Echoes of 1986? Not in Bush's Tax Reform Panel. *New York Times*, November 8, 2005.
28. Fred E. Foldvary (2005). *Tax Reform Panel Says: Cut Mortgage Tax Deduction.* Online at: http://www.progress.org/2005/fold426.htm

29. Curtis S. Dubay & William Ahern, *President's 2008 Budget Reveals Massive Holes in Tax Code.* Tax Policy Blog, February 6, 2007. Online at: http://www.tax-foundation.org/blog/show/2197.html, accessed May 11, 2008; *Joint Committee on Taxation, House Committee on Ways and Means and the Senate Committee on Finance, Estimates of Federal Tax Expenditures for Fiscal Years 2005–2009.* January 12, 2005. Washington, DC: U.S. Government Printing Office. Online at: http://www.house.gov/jct/s-1-05.pdf, accessed May 11, 2008.

30. Dubay & Ahem, 2007, *President's 2008 Budget.*

31. Adam Carasso, Gillian Reynolds, & C. Eugene Steuerle (2008). *How Much Does the Federal Government Spend to Promote Economic Mobility and for Whom?* Philadelphia, PA: *Pew Charitable Trusts, Economic Mobility Project.* Online at: http://www.economicmobility.org/assets/pdfs/EMP_Mobilty_Budget.pdf, accessed May 14, 2008. Note that the categories used in Table 5.7 and Table 5.8 are different and not directly comparable. Further, the data in Table 5.7 are for Fiscal Year 2008, whereas the data in Table 5.8 are for Fiscal Year 2006. See the precursor to the above Pew study prepared by CFED, Corporation for Enterprise Development (2004). *Hidden in Plain Sight: A Look at the $335 Billion Federal Asset-Building Budget.* Washington, DC: CFED.

32. Center on Budget and Planning Priorities (1998). *Developing Innovative Child Support Demonstrations for Noncustodial Parents.* Washington, DC: Author.

33. Patricia A. McManus & Thomas A. DiPrete, Losers and Winners: The Financial Consequences of Separation and Divorce for Men. *American Sociological Review,* 66, no. 2 (2001): 246–268.

34. Vicki Turetsky (June, 2007). *Basic Facts About Child Support.* Washington, DC: Center for Law and Social Policy. Online at: http://www.firstfocus.net/Download/CSBF.pdf, accessed May 12, 2008; The data source for the finding that child support is 31 percent of family income of poor single mothers when they receive it is the Urban Institute analysis of the March 2006 Current Population Survey.

35. Office of Child Support Enforcement (April 2008). *Child Support Enforcement, FY 2007: Preliminary Report.* Washington, DC: U.S. Department of Health and Human Services. Online at: http://www.acf.hhs.gov/programs/cse/pubs/2008/preliminary_report_fy2007/table_5.html, accessed May 15, 2008.

36. Office of Child Support Enforcement (2004). *Child Support Enforcement FY 2003 Preliminary Data Report.* Online at: http://www.acf.hhs.gov/programs/cse/pubs/2004/reports/preliminary_data/

37. Rebecca Blank (1997). *It Takes a Nation: A New Agenda for Fighting Poverty.* Princeton, NJ: Princeton University Press.

38. House Ways and Means Committee (2004). Child Support Enforcement Program. *Green Book.* Section 8, p. 8–3. Online at: http://frwebgate.access.gpo.gov/cgi-bin/getdoc.cgi?dbname=108_green_book&docid=f:wm006_08.pdf, accessed May 8, 2008; Kids Count Data Center, " Children in Single-Parent Families, by Race: Percent: 2006", updated January 2008. Online at: http://www.kidscount.org/data-center/compare_results.jsp?i=722, accessed May 8, 2008.

39. Office of Child Support Enforcement, note 30.

40. Bureau of Child Support, State of Wisconsin, (2005). *Facts About Establishing Paternity*. Online at: http://www.dwd.state.wi.us/dwd/publications/dws/child_support/pdf/dwsc_770_p.pdf, accessed April 21, 2008.

41. Timothy S. Grall (2007). *Custodial Mothers and Fathers and Their Child Support*: 2005. P60–234, August 2007. Washington, DC: U. S. Census Bureau. Online at: http://www.census.gov/hhes/www/childsupport/chldsu05.pdf, accessed April 21, 2008; Kathryn Edin, Single Mothers and Child Support: The Possibilities and Limits of Child Support Policy, *Children and Youth Services Review* 17 (1995): 203–230. Online at: http://www.sciencedirect.com/science/article/B6V98-3Y6HS7G-13/1/573271bfcf67f34ee6230f841ff1fde0

42. The findings on child support reported by the Census Bureau are quite different from those reported by the Office of Child Support Enforcement. Whereas the Census Bureau reported 38 billion in child support awards in 2005, the Office of Child Support Enforcement reported 31 billion in child support due in 2007.

43. Office of Child Support Enforcement, note 35.

44. Elaine Sorensen, A National Profile of Nonresident Fathers and Their Ability to Pay Child Support. *Journal of Marriage and the Family 59*, (1997): 785–797.

45. Ibid. The 60 percent estimate is based on the earlier calculation of Sorenson.

46. Judith Cassetty (1978). *Child Support and Social Policy*. Lexington, MA: DC Heath; Cynthia Miller, Irwin Garfinkel, & Sara McLanahan, Child Support in the U.S.: Can Fathers Afford to Pay More? *Review of Income and Wealth* 43, no. 3 (1997): 261–281; Judith H. Cassetty & Royce Hutson, Effectiveness of Federal Incentives in Shaping Child support Enforcement Outcomes, *Children and Youth Services Review* 27, no. 3 (2005): 271–289.

47. Ibid., p. 261; also see Maureen A. Pirog & Kathleen M. Ziol-Guest, Child Support Enforcement: Programs and Policies, Impacts and Questions. *Journal of Policy Analysis and Management* 25, no. 4 (2006): 943–990.

48. Elaine Sorensen & Chava Zibman. (2001). *Poor Dads Who Don't Pay Child Support: Deadbeats or Disadvantaged?* Washington, DC: Urban Institute. Online at: http://www.urban.org/UploadedPDF/anf_b30.pdf, accessed July 7, 2007.

49. Ibid.

50. Blank, *New Agenda for Fighting Poverty*.

51. Urban Institute, note 50 ; Maureen Waller & Robert Plotnick (1999). *Child Support and Low-Income Families: Perceptions, Practices, and Policy*. San Francisco, CA: Public Policy Institute of California.

52. For an earlier study of this issue see the classic study by David Chambers (1979). *Making Fathers Pay: The Enforcement of Child Support*. University of Chicago Press.

53. Irwin Garfinkel (2000). The Limits of Private Child Support and the Role of an Assured Benefit. In J. Thomas Oldham & Marygold S. Melli, eds., *Child Support: The Next Frontier*. Ann Arbor: University of Michigan Press, 183–189.

54. This group of delinquent fathers are often poor themselves and many have great difficulty in making payments. For the low-income fathers in this group the child support collection system is often viewed as unduly burdensome and insensitive to their inability to pay. See David L. Chambers (1979).

55. Jessica Yates, Child Support Enforcement and Welfare Reform. *Welfare Information Network* 1, no. 5 (May 1997): 1–4. Online at: http://www.financeproject.org/Publications/childsupportresource.htm, accessed May 11, 2008; *Green Book* (2004), Section 8, note 39.

56. Data for child support awards and payment: Child Trends Calculations (2003). *Custodial Mothers and Fathers and Their Child Support: 2001*, Current Population Reports P60–225, table A. Available online at: http://www.census.gov/prod/2003pubs/p60-225.pdf; Data for non-cash payments: U.S. Census Bureau, Child Support: Detailed Tables. Available online at: http://www.census.gov/hhes/www/childsupport/cs01.html. See tables 8 and 10.

57. See Table 1.1 in Chapter 1 of this book.

58. See note 55.

59. For a description of the child support system in New Zealand see online at: http://canada.justice.gc.ca/en/ps/sup/cspo/expedited.html#New%20Zealand%20A, accessed July 7, 2007.

60. For a description of the child support system in Australia see online at: http://canada.justice.gc.ca/en/ps/sup/cspo/expedited.html#Autralia%20A, accessed July 7, 2007.

61. For a description of the child support system in the Netherlands see online at: http://www.childpolicyintl.org/childsupporttables/1.105Netherlands.html, accessed July 7, 2007.

62. Arthur Corden (1999). *Making Child Maintenance Regimes Work*. London: Family Policy Studies Centre.

63. Child Support Agency (1998). *Children First: A New Approach to Child Support*. Green Paper (www.csa.gov.uk).

64. Child Support Agency On-Line (2002). *A new contract for welfare: children's rights and parents' responsibilities: A Summary*. White Paper (www.csa.gov.uk).

65. Ibid.

66. Geoffrey P. Miller (2004). Parental Bonding and the Design of Child Support Obligations. In William S. Comanor, ed., *Law and Economics of Child Support Payments*. Northampton, MA: Edward Elgar Publishing, 210–240.

67. Robert A. McNeely & Cynthia A. McNeely (2004). Hopelessly Defective: An Examination of the Assumptions Underlying the Current Child Support Guidelines. In William S. Comanor, ed., *Law and Economics of Child Support Payments*. Northampton, MA: Edward Elgar Publishing, 160–177.

68. Robert E. Rector, "The Fathers Count Act of 1999," Testimony before the Subcommittee on Human Resources/Committee on Ways and Means. October 5, 1999. Online at: http://www.heritage.org/Research/Welfare/Test100599.cfm?renderforprint=1, accessed May 12, 2008.

69. Bundled benefit is a payment that essentially bundles into one payment the amount needed to safeguard against the failure to collect child support and to make up for the exclusion of poor children from participating in the "tax deduction" based children's allowance program.

Chapter 6

1. William Jefferson Clinton, February 3, 1993, cited in Jason DeParle (2004). *American Dream: Three Women, Ten Kids, and a Nation's Drive to End Welfare.* New York: Viking, inside front page.

2. Julian Le Grand (2003). *Asset-Based Welfare in Theory and Practice: Notes on the British Experience.* Capital Hill Briefing, October 29. Sponsored by SEED (Savings for Education, Entrepreunership, Downpayment) and Corporation for Enterprise Development (www.cfed.org).

3. Robert Frank, Millionaire Ranks Hit New High. *Wall Street Journal* May 25, 2005, P. d1 and d2. See online report for Spectrem Group at: http://www.hnw. com/intelligence/market-sizeandgrowth.jsp

4. Merrill Lynch, Cap Gemini Ernst, & Young (2007). *World Wealth Report 1997–2007.* New York: Merrill Lynch. Online at (requires registration): http://www.us.capgemini.com/DownloadLibrary/files/Capgemini_FSI_ WorldWealthReport2007_062707.pdf, accessed July 7, 2007.

5. Wojciech Kopczuk & Emmanuel Saez (June 2004). Top Wealth Shares in the United States, 1916–2000: Evidence from Estate Tax Returns. *National Tax Journal*, LVII, no. 2, Part 2, figure 12. Online at: http://www.cbpp.org/ 3-29-07inc.htm#_ftn1; David Rothkopf (2008). *The Global Power Elite and the World They Are Making.* New York: Farrar, Straus, Giroux.
   See Lisa Keister (2005). *Getting Rich: A Study of Wealth Mobility in America.* New York: Cambridge University Press. Also see the Forbes 400 Richest Americans online at: http://www.forbes.com/2002/09/13/rich400land.html; also see online at: http://www.forbes.com/2007/03/07/billionaires-worlds-richest_07billionaires_cz_lk_af_0308billie_land.html, accessed July 7, 2007. See Edward Wolffe's report online at: http://www.levy.org/vdoc.aspx?docid=929, accessed July 7, 2007. Also, Thomas Piketty & Emmanuel Saez, Income Inequality in the United States: 1913–1998, *Quarterly Journal of Economics*, February 2003. The updated data series is available online at: http://elsa.berkeley.edu/~saez/ TabFig2005prel.xls, accessed May 10, 2008.

6. Forbes List of the 400 Richest Americans (2007). Online at: http://www.forbes. com/400richest/ accessed April 22, 2008.

7. Lynch and Ernst & Young , *World Wealth Report 2007.*

8. Quoted in the *Wall Street Journal* (2005). Don Weston, 1.

9. Todd Lewan, Gigayachts Lure the Mega-Rich. *Associated Press*, August 13, 2005. Better Boat Builder, South Florida CEO. Online at: http://www.southfloridaceo. com/article156.html, accessed July 7, 2007.

10. In contrast to Paul Allen, Bill Gates has donated a substantial part of the wealth acquired through building Microsoft to fight diseases in the third world. In fact, *Time* magazine named Bill and Melinda Gates the persons of the year for 2005, along with Bono.

11. Board of Governors of the Federal Reserve System, *Flow of Funds Accounts of the United States: Flows and Outstandings Third Quarter 2007.* See page 2.

"Household net worth—the difference between the value of assets and liabilities—was at an estimated level of $58.6 trillion at the end of the third quarter of 2007." Online at: http://www.federalreserve.gov/RELEASES/z1/Current/z1.pdf, accessed December 12, 2007. Also see Robert B. Avery, Gregory E. Elliehausen & Glenn B. Canner, Survey of consumer finances, 1983. *Federal Reserve Bulletin,* (1984 September): 679–682. Ana M. Aizcorbe, Arthur B. Kennickell, & Kevin B. Moore. Recent Changes in U.S. Family Finances: Evidence from the 1998 and 2001 Survey of Consumer Finances, *Federal Reserve Bulletin,* January, 2003, Board of Governors of the Federal Reserve System (U.S.), 1–32.

Avery, Elliehausen, & Canner, Survey of Consumer Finances, 1983: A Secondary Report. *Federal Reserve Bulletin,* (1984 December): 857–869.

12. Mark J. Perry, *U.S. Household Net Worth at Record High of 59 Trillion (RECORD: $528,000 Net Worth per Household).* Thursday, December 6, 2007. Online at: http://mjperry.blogspot.com/2007/12/us-household-net-worth-at-record-high.html, accessed December 12, 2007.

13. Brian K. Bucks, Arthur B. Kennickell, & Kevin B. Moore (2006). *Recent Changes in U.S. Family Finances: Evidence from the 2001 and 2004 Survey of Consumer Finances.* Federal Reserve Bulletin. Washington, DC: Board of Governors of the Federal Reserve System, table 3, Online at: http://www.federalreserve.gov/Pubs/Bulletin/2006/financesurvey.pdf, accessed May 9, 2008.

14. Bill Heyman (2005) 8.11.200 WSJ: US Household Net Worth Over $400K??? I'm mentioned in The Numbers Guy column in today's *Wall Street Journal.* Online at: http://techblurbs.com/2005/08/wsj-us-household-net-worth-over-400k, accessed March 2, 2006.

15. Note 13; Shawne Orzechowski & Peter Sepielli, *Net Worth and Asset Ownership of Households: 1998 and 2000.* Current Population Reports, P70–88. Data have been updated with estimates based on latest available data: Number of households in 2004 of 107 million and privately held wealth of 51 trillion dollars.

16. Sylvia Ann Hewlett (1991). *When the Bough Breaks: The Cost of Neglecting Our Children.* New York: Basic Books, 271.

17. John Meynard Keynes (1964). *The General Theory of Employment, Interest and Money.* New York: Harcourt, Brace and World.

18. Stuart Bruchey (1990). *Enterprise: The Dynamic Economy of a Free People.* Harvard University Press; Kevin Phillips (2002). *Wealth and Democracy.* New York: Broadway Books.

19. Isaac Shapiro (2005). *New IRS Data Show Income Inequality Is Again On The Rise. Center on Budget Priority.* Online at: http://www.cbpp.org/10-17-05inc. htm, accessed March 4, 2008; Myers, Samuel L., Jr. & William A. Darity, Jr., Changes in Black–White Income Inequality, 1968–1978: A Decade of Progress? *The Review of Black Political Economy* 10, no. 4 (1980): 355–379; Myers, Samuel L., Jr. & William A. Darity, Jr. (1998). *Persistent Disparity: Race and Economic Inequality in the United States Since 1945.* Northampton, MA: Edward Elgar.

20. David Cay Johnston, Richest Are Leaving Even the Rich Far Behind, *New York Times,* Series on Income in America, June 5, 2005.

21. Internal Revenue Service, "Table 2—Individual Income and Tax Data, by State and Size of Adjusted Gross Income, Tax Year 2005," from the Internal Revenue Service. Online at: http://www.irs.gov/pub/irs-soi/05in53us.xls, accessed October 22, 2007.

22. Maxwell King, *Philadelphia Inquiry.* Online at: http://www.nieman.harvard.edu/reports/98-3NRfall98/Kirkhorn_Widening.html, accessed July 7, 2007.

23. Lynch and Ernst & Young, *World Wealth Report 2007.*

24. Valerie Polakow (1993). *Lives on the Edge: Single Mothers and their Children in the Other America.* Chicago, IL: University of Chicago Press.

25. Koen Vleminckx & Timothy M. Smeeding (Eds.) 2001. *Child Well-Being, Child Poverty and Child Policy in Modern Nations: What do We Know?* Bristol, UK: The Policy Press, 1.

26. Jonathan Kozol (1992). *Savage Inequalities: Children in America's Schools.* New York: HarperCollins.

27. Polakow, 1993, p. 47; Joel F. Handler & Yeheskel Hasenfeld (1991). *The Moral Construction of Poverty: Welfare Reform in America.* Thousand Oaks, CA: Sage Publications.

28. Marian Wright Edelman (2002). *The Shame of Child Poverty in the Richest Land on Earth.* Washington, DC: The Children's Defense Fund.

29. Mary Riddell, Cradle to the Ballot Box: Baby Bonds are Welcome, but they'll Do Little to Remove the Root Causes of Poverty and Inequality. *The Guardian*, April 29, 2001. Online at: http://www.guardian.co.uk/society/2001/apr/29/1, accessed May 8, 2008.

30. Thomas Paine (originally published in 1795/1987). *Agrarian Justice.* New York: Penguin.

31. James Tobin (1968). Raising the Incomes of the Poor. In K. Gordon, ed., *Agenda for the Nation: Papers on Diplomatic and Foreign Policy Issues,* 77–116. Washington, DC: The Brookings Institution.

32. Ibid., p. 92.

33. Lester Thurow (1992). *Head to Head: The Coming Economic Battle Among Japan, Europe, and America.* San Francisco: William Morrow and Company.

34. Duncan Lindsey (1994). *The Welfare of Children.* New York: Oxford University Press, 301–320. In July 1998, I proposed an experimental test of the child savings account to the Eisner Family Foundation at their retreat in Colorado that would have involved 1000 children randomly assigned equally to an experimental and control group. Ten years later the universal progressive child savings account is being tested with a large scale experiment. See Michael Sherraden & Margaret Clancey (2007). *SEED for Oklahoma Kids: Summary of Project, Research and Policy Implications.* St. Louis, MO: Center for Social Development. Online at: http://gwbweb.wustl.edu/csd/SEED/Summary.pdf, accessed May 10, 2008; Michael Sherraden & Margaret Clancey (2005). *SEED Universal Policy Model and Research.* St. Louis, MO: Center for Social Development. Online at: http://gwbweb.wustl.edu/csd/SEEDUMsearch/brief.pdf, accessed May 10, 2008.

35. The proposal for a child future savings account included an experimental design that would provide 500 children randomly selected from birth records in

California and 500 in the control children. The proposal suggested an 18-year study that would have provided children in the experimental group US$1,000 at birth and US$500 in each subsequent year until they turned 18. The program was presented and considered. However, the family had just provided substantial funding for the Foundation and was not prepared to embark on this idea. One decade later, the universal child savings account will be tested using a rigorous experimental design in Oklahoma. See Michael Sherraden & Margaret Clancy (2007). *SEED for Oklahoma Kids.* George Warren Brown School of Social Work, Washington University. SEED for Oklahoma will provide about 1500 randomly selected treatment participants with a US$1000 Oklahoma College Savings Plan accounts. There will also be a randomly selected control group. The interest is to follow these children over the years to study the impact child savings account on the children and their families.

36. Robert Haveman (1988). *Starting Even: An Equal Opportunity Program to Combat the Nation's New Poverty.* New York: Simon and Schuster.
37. Ray Boshara, The $6000 Solution. *Atlantic Monthly.* December 1, 2002.
38. Bruce Ackerman & Anne Alstott (1999). *The Stake Holder Society.* New Haven, CT: Yale University Press, 191.
39. Henry David Thoreau (1910). *Walden.* New York: Merrill. Online at: http://xroads. virginia.edu/~HYPER/WALDEN/header.html, accessed July 7, 2007.
40. Jennifer Brooks, Kevin Keeley, Will Lambe, Carl Rist, & Barbara Rosen (2006). *Children's Savings Accounts: A State Policy Sourcebook.* Washington, DC: CFED.
41. Edward F. Denison (1985). *Trends in American Economic Growth, 1929–1982.* Washington, DC: The Brookings Institution.
42. George Will (1991). Society Challenged to Break Poverty Cycle that Traps Kids. *Register Guard* (Eugene, Oregon), B2.
43. Erik Erikson (1959). *Identity and the Life Cycle.* New York: International University Press.
44. Corporation for Enterprise Development. Online at: http://www.cfed.org
45. Children's Defense Fund (1986). *Preventing Adolescent Pregnancy: What Schools Can Do.* Washington, DC: Author; Lawrence L. Wu & Brian C. Martinson. Family Structure and the Risk of Premarital Birth. *American Sociological Review* 59 (1993): 210–232; Francine D. Blau, Lawrence M. Kahn, & Jane Waldfogel, Understanding Young Women's Marriage Decisions: The Role of Labor and Marriage Market Conditions (January 2000). NBER Working Paper No. W7510. Online at: http://ssrn.com/abstract=217917, accessed May 11, 2008.
46. Frank F. Furstenberg, Jr., As the Pendulum Swings: Teenage Childbearing and Social Concern. *Family Relations* 40 (1991): 127–138.
47. Pamela Burdman (October, 2005). *The Student Debt Dilemma: Debt Aversion as a Barrier to College Access.* Center for Studies in Higher Education, Research & Occasional Paper Series: CSHE.13.05. Berkeley, CA: University of California, Berkeley. Online at: http://cshe.berkeley.edu/publications/docs/ROP. Burdman.13.05.pdf, accessed May 10, 2008.
48. Ackerman & Alstott, *The Stake Holder Society.*

49. Edward F. Denison (1974). *Accounting for United States Economic Growth, 1929–1969.* Washington DC: Brookings Institution.

50. Margaret Clancy, Reid Cramer, & Leslie Parish (February, 2005). *Section 529 Savings Plans, Access to Post-Secondary Education, and Universal Asset Building. Issue Brief.* Washington, DC: New America Foundation.

51. James Lange (2005). *The Economic Growth and Tax Relief Reconciliation Act of 2001 Summary.* Online at: http://www.faculty-advisor.com/economicgrowth. htm, accessed July 7, 2007.

52. U.S. General Accounting Office (1995). *College Savings: Information on State Tuition Prepayment Programs.* Washington, DC: General Accounting Office.

53. An easy way to augment the 529 College Savings Plan is to sign up with Upromise (www.upromise.com) and let selected companies contribute to your child's account. Companies such as AT&T, America Online, Mobil, Exxon, JCPenney.com, and many more will contribute to your child's 529 account based upon a percentage of your purchases. Grocery stores and pharmacies also will contribute a percentage of your bill. Also, various manufacturers will contribute when you buy their products. These include Huggies diapers, Minute Maid, Kellogg's, Tylenol, and many more.

54. Limits are set by individual states. In 2002, the amount ranged from US$100,000 to US$305,000.

55. Marc E. Lackritz (June, 2004). *Investing for the Future: State Tuition Savings Plans.* Statement of the President of Securities Industry Association before the House Financial Services Subcommittee on Capital Markets, Insurance, and Government Sponsored Enterprises; Carl Rist, Jennifer Brooks & Kevin Keeley (2006). *Children's Savings Accounts and Financial Aid: An Examination of the Consequences of Children's Savings Account Ownership on Financial Aid Eligibility.* Washington, DC: CFED.

56. K. Kristof 529s Ease Burden of College Costs. *Los Angeles Times*, December 15, 2002.

57. NIA Group. Section 529 Plans. Online at: http://www.niagroup.com/529plan.cfm, accessed February 14, 2006.

58. Ibid.

59. Ibid.

60. Michael Sherraden (1991). *Assets and the Poor: A New American Welfare Policy.* New York: M. E. Sharpe; Michael Sherraden (Ed.) (2005). *Inclusion in the American Dream: Assets, Poverty, and Public Policy.* New York: Oxford University Press; Boshara, The $6000 Solution; Robert E. Friedman (1988). *The Safety Net as Ladder: Transfer Payments and Economic Development.* Council of State Planning Agencies; Robert E. Friedman (1995). *Building Assets: Self Employment for Welfare Recipients: Overview of the Findings From the Self Employment Investment Demonstration (SEID).* San Francisco: Corporation for Enterprise Development.

61. Sherraden, Ibid.

62. The purpose of the Child Future Savings account is to provide young people with the resources needed for effective transition to adulthood. The funds are not for

consumer needs and would not be made available for consumer items, but only for purposes that represent an investment in the young person's future.

63. Ruth Kelly (2003). *Strengthening the Saving Habits of Future Generations.* London: Inland Revenue.

64. David A. Nissan & Julian Le Grand (2000). *Capital Idea: Start-Up Grants for Young People.* Fabian Society; Julian Le Grand (2003). From Pawn to Queen: An Economics Perspective. In A. Oliver, ed., *International Perspectives on Equity and Health.* Nuffield Trust, 25–32; Tony Blair. The Saving Grace of the Baby Bond. *The Guardian,* April 10, 2003.

65. Gavin Kelly & Ravin Lissauer (2000). *Ownership for All.* London: Institute for Public Policy Research. Several videos available on YouTube.com provide an informative look at the success of the Child Trust Fund. Online at: http://www. youtube.com/watch?v=s4WLjRMjQdY, accessed May 10, 2008.

66. Fred Goldberg, cited in Michael Sherraden, (2002). *Asset-Based Policy and the Child Trust Fund.* St Louis: Center for Social Development, Washington University.

67. Ibid.

68. Mark Schreiner & Michael Sherraden (2005). *Can the Poor Save? Savings and Asset Building in Individual Development Accounts.* Piscataway, NJ: Aldine Transaction; R. Boshara, Individual Development Accounts: Policies to Build Savings and Assets for the Poor, *Brookings Institution Policy Brief, Welfare Reform & Beyond,* No. 32 (March, 2005).

69. Rakesh Kochhar (2004). *The Wealth of Hispanic Households 1996 to 2002.* Washington, DC: Pew Hispanic Center; See Melvin Oliver & T. M. Shapiro (1995). *Black Wealth and White Wealth: A New Perspective on Racial Inequality.* New York: Routledge.

70. Corporation for Enterprise Development (2004). *Hidden in Plain Sight: A Look at the $335 Billion Federal Asset-Building Budget.* Washington, DC: CFED. Online at: http://www.cfed.org/publications/Final%20HIPS%20%20Version.pdf, accessed May 11, 2008.

71. Bureau of Economic Analysis (2008). *Personal Savings Rate.* Washington, DC: U.S. Department of Commerce. Online at: http://www.bea.gov/briefrm/saving. htm, accessed May 10, 2008; Economajic.com (2008). Personal Savings Rate. Data set available online at: http://www.economagic.com/em-cgi/data.exe/ scratch/66-249-70-117!nipa_t2t1134q, accessed May 10, 2008.

72. Associated Press (February 1, 2007). Personal Savings Drop to a 73-year Low. Online at: http://www.msnbc.msn.com/id/16922582/, accessed May 10, 2008.

73. Quoted in Lisa A. Keister, note 5, p. 10.

74. We spend more than US$8000 a year for education of each child in the public school system. Making the small investment in a child savings account recommended in this proposal before these children enter school could fundamentally alter their approach and embrace of the opportunities education provides.

75. Lingxin Hao (2007). *Color Lines, Country Lines: Race, Immigration, and Wealth Stratification in America.* New York: Russell Sage Foundation.

Name Index

Subject Index